Vegetarian for Dinner

60 Comforting & Nourishing Meatless Meals for Every Occasion

Copyright © 2023 by Cozy Peach Kitchen LLC
Photographs copyright © 2023 by Cassidy Reeser

All rights reserved.
Published and printed in the United States of America. No part of this book may be used or reproduced in an manner whatsoever without written permission except in the case of brief quotations embodied in articles and reviews.

For more information, please contact
cozypeachkitchen@gmail.com
ISBN 979-8-9890195-1-9

Dedicated to my mom, who not only nurtured my love of cooking, but who is also the reason I hear *"mise en place"* every time I start cooking.

Table of Contents

Introduction — 7
    About this Book — 7
    Ingredient Swaps — 9
    Ingredient Notes — 11
    Kitchen Tools — 12
    Shopping List — 12

Balanced Bowls for Dinner — 15
    Quinoa Bowls with Zesty Mustard Sauce — 17
    Grown-Up Walking Tacos — 19
    Pearl Couscous Bowls with Marinated Artichoke Salad — 21
    Lemon Pepper Tofu Bowls with Garlicky Green Beans — 23
    Pan-Fried Polenta with Mushrooms & Asparagus — 25
    Miso Butter Bean Bowls — 27
    Grits, Greens, and Beans — 29
    Upside Down Lentil Shepherd's Pie — 31
    Roasted Sweet Potato Bowls with Marinated Tofu — 33
    Mac and Cheese with BBQ Tofu & Brussels Slaw — 35
    Smoky Loaded Baked Sweet Potatoes — 37

Skillets & Bakes for Dinner — 39
    BBQ Jackfruit Nachos with White Queso — 41
    Corn Fritters with Spicy Cherry Tomato Sauce — 43
    Crispy Baked Tacos with Tofu "Chorizo" — 45
    Red Lentil Curry with Spiced Cauliflower — 47
    "Chicken" Pot Pie with Drop Biscuits — 49
    Chili Cornbread Skillet — 51
    Quinoa Pizza Bake — 53
    Vegan Tater Tot Green Bean Casserole — 55
    Tofu Steak Dinner — 57
    Broccoli Farro Casserole — 59
    Spicy "Sausage" Pizza with Arugula & Hot Honey — 61
    Mediterranean-Inspired One Pot Rice & Beans — 63
    Summer Cherry Tomato and Corn Galette — 65

Pasta for Dinner — 67
    Tortellini with Cashew Pesto Cream Sauce — 69
    One Skillet Tomato Orzo with Honey Halloumi — 71
    Honey Garlic Noodles with Stir-Fried Green Veggies — 73
    Amish-Style Chicken & Noodles — 75
    Green Curry Noodle Bowls — 77
    Ricotta Gnocchi Primavera — 79
    Tahini Noodles with Roasted Vegetables — 81

Caramelized Shallot Pasta with Herby Breaded Tofu ... 83
Big Veggie & Lentil Lasagna ... 85

Handhelds & Sandwiches for Dinner ... 87

Buffalo Chickpea Wraps with Broccoli Slaw ... 89
Loaded Fries with Peanut Sauce and Fried Tempeh ... 91
Tempeh & Red Cabbage Reuben ... 93
Mushroom & Black Bean Burritos ... 95
Puff Pastry Broccoli & Chickpea Rollovers ... 97
Roasted Vegetable & Chickpea Wraps ... 99
Fried Tofu Sandwich ... 101
Tofu Patty Melt ... 103
Pizza Bread ... 105

Soup & Salad for Dinner ... 107

Chopped Pizza Salad ... 109
Spring Pasta Salad with Lemon Vinaigrette ... 111
Roasted Sweet Potato Salad with Jalapeño Dressing ... 113
Wild Rice Salad with Apple Cider Vinaigrette ... 115
Year-Round Pantry Tomato Soup with Herby Crackers ... 117
White "Chicken" Chili ... 119
Not-Chicken Miso Noodle Soup ... 121
Mushroom & Potato Soup ... 123
Lemony Lentil Soup ... 125

Breakfast for Dinner ... 127

Chocolate Peanut Butter Bites ... 129
All-Purpose Tofu & Vegetable Stir Fry ... 131
Georgia Peach Pancakes ... 133
Spinach & Quinoa Egg Muffins ... 135
Blueberry Oatmeal Bars with Almond Butter Drizzle ... 137
Savory Dutch Baby Pancake with Lemon Ricotta ... 139
Potato & Pepper Frittata ... 141
Sheet Pan Breakfast Potatoes & Peppers ... 143
Sweet Potato Biscuits & Mushroom Gravy ... 145

Index ... 146

Acknowledgments ... 149

Introduction

Hi! I'm Cassidy Reeser, the registered dietitian and recipe developer behind Cozy Peach Kitchen. I started Cozy Peach Kitchen in January 2018, and it's the only New Year's resolution that's ever stuck. My goal is to help make plant-based cooking easier for everyone, without sacrificing comfort or flavor.

I chose to become a registered dietitian because it was a practical way to pursue my love of food and nutrition, but I have always needed to express my creativity in day-to-day life, and the most exciting (and practical) way for me to pursue that creativity was actually through Cozy Peach Kitchen. After a few years of working as a registered dietitian in the more traditional sense, I took the blog full-time in 2021. I love it, and am so thankful that it has given me the opportunity to write this cookbook.

About this Book

I decided to write a cookbook about vegetarian dinners because this is the meal that most inspires excitement and dread in people. This book answers the question of "What in the world am I going to cook for dinner?".

Some of the recipes in this cookbook are all about getting a tasty and balanced meal on the table (Honey Garlic Noodles with Stir-Fried Green Vegetables, p. 73, and Quinoa Pizza Bake, p. 53), while others teach a new skill (Ricotta Gnocchi, p. 79) or require downtime and planning (Cabbage Reuben, p. 93).

Although these are dinner recipes, they are also great as leftovers for lunch. And the "Breakfast for Dinner" section is certainly just as delicious as "Breakfast for Breakfast." There are no hard and fast rules about how to use this cookbook, though, of course, some recipes might not turn out if you don't follow the instructions.

With this cookbook in hand, now you can confidently say "Let's do vegetarian for dinner."

About This Book (Cont'd)

COMPLETE MEALS

Every recipe in this cookbook is a complete meal (except for one or two, because I just can't seem to follow my own rules). A complete meal, at least in this cookbook, contains a protein source, a carbohydrate, vegetables or fruit, and often healthy fats. This is not the often vilified vegetarian "rabbit food," but meals that are designed to fill you up and fuel you through the day.

Even though each recipe is a complete meal, many include components that work well as standalone recipes. From roasted jalapeño dressing (p. 113) to mac and cheese (p. 35), parts of certain recipes in this cookbook can work for any occasion.

VEGETARIAN OR NOT

This book is meatless, but it's written for more than just vegetarians. It is written for the spouse who is trying to eat less meat without sacrificing comfort (Tater Tot Green Bean Casserole, p. 55), or the mother-in-law who wants a vegetable salad to go with her salmon dinner (Pasta Salad, p. 111), and maybe even the grandpa whose doctor told him to include more vegetables in his diet (Tofu Stir Fry, p. 131).

If you are here because you are trying to eat more vegetables and less meat, welcome! Let me show you how easy it is to cook delicious meatless meals. If you are here because you are a long-time vegetarian or vegan and want new recipe ideas, welcome! I can't wait to show you some of my favorite recipes.

I don't seek to vilify any single food or ingredient because it's seen as "less healthy." I believe that everyone's favorite foods and ingredients can be included in meals in a balanced way. In reality, those "less healthy" foods are often the ones that help encourage you to eat more vegetables and whole grains.

COMFORT ABOVE ALL

This originally started out as a vegetarian comfort food cookbook—in a way, it still is all about my personal flavor of comfort food. The problem with calling something comfort food is that the definition of comfort is different for everyone. It depends on your personal preferences, history, and desires.

This cookbook is an invitation into my definition of comfort food: cooking tater tot green bean casserole in my grandma's Illinois kitchen, pan-frying breaded tofu in a cast iron skillet in the heat of a Georgia summer with my partner, and always, always preparing breakfast casserole on Christmas Eve with my mom.

It's also the comfort of knowing that you've prepared a nourishing meal to enjoy with friends or to pack in your lunch for the week. It's the comfort of feeling just a little bit more confident that you can incorporate more meatless meals in your repertoire. And, of course, it's the comfort that all of your old favorites can be made vegetarian.

Ingredient Swaps

One of the reasons that I prefer cooking meals and savory recipes to baking is that it is endlessly flexible. While I write recipes so that they are "perfect" as-is, I understand that my taste in salt, sweet, and acidity is likely not 100% equivalent to yours. That is the beauty of cooking: here are the tools, the recipes, and the instructions for those who prefer a straightforward path, but for those who don't, I encourage you to fiddle with the recipes to make them your own.

That being said, all of the ingredients in this book are used with a purpose, so I do recommend cooking a recipe before omitting or adjusting the main ingredients. Salt, on the other hand, can be adjusted to your taste. I tend to lean on the less-salty side.

A vegetarian diet as used in this book is a lacto-ovo vegetarian, or a meatless diet that includes both dairy and eggs. While this book is all about vegetarian meals, it's easy to adapt many, if not most, of the recipes to either an egg-free or dairy-free diet.

There are several recipes that would likely need multiple rounds of testing to veganize, like Ricotta Gnocchi Primavera (p. 79), Potato & Pepper Frittata (p. 141), and Big Veggie & Lentil Lasagna (p. 85). Others only require simple swaps of equivalent dairy- or egg-free ingredients. When it comes to veganizing recipes, you'll likely have success if you use common cooking sense. When in doubt, shoot me an email!

Ingredient Swaps (Cont'd)

- **Milk**: I personally prefer soy milk to cow's milk, and that's what I use at home. However, to keep things versatile, I did test all recipes with both types of milk. Although I did not test them, oat milk and almond usually work as direct substitutions. When using non-dairy milk, be sure to choose unflavored.

- **Cheese, cream cheese, and butter**: Use your favorite brand of vegan cheese slices or shreds in place of the dairy option in a recipe. For example, Chao cheese is great on a Tofu Patty Melt (p. 103) and the Quinoa Pizza Bake (p. 53) works well with Violife shredded mozzarella.

- **Eggs**: In most cases, eggs cannot be omitted without multiple rounds of testing. The good news is that there aren't a ton of egg recipes in this book. In baked goods, I start with a "flax egg" in place of a large egg, which is 1 tablespoon of ground flaxseed mixed with 3 tablespoons of water. In frittatas, I recommend a product like Just Egg, which emulates the consistency and texture of whisked eggs.

- **Mayonnaise**: Any kind of vegan mayonnaise works just fine in place of regular mayonnaise.

- **Yogurt**: Both Greek and plain yogurts exist in non-dairy forms, and both options are a good place to start in making a recipe dairy-free. Note that plain yogurt can also be used in place of mayonnaise in most of my sauce recipes.

- **Gluten**: Use tamari in place of soy sauce for a gluten-free option. In most cases, a gluten-free all-purpose flour blend can be used in place of regular all-purpose flour, though there might be a slight difference in texture due to gluten-free flour consistencies. I don't recommend using almond or coconut flour in place of all-purpose flour in most recipes, as it will not yield the same results.

Ingredient Notes

- **Beans**: I personally prefer cooking beans from dry in my Instant Pot. I realize that is not always practical or realistic, so the recipes in this book are written for canned beans. One 15-ounce can of beans usually yields about 1 ½ cups of cooked beans.
- **Cheese**: I prefer to shred my own cheese in most recipes, but pre-shredded is a time-saver, and I have no qualms about using it when the need arises. That said, I recommend grating your own cheese for mac and cheese because pre-shredded cheese is more likely to clump up in the sauce.
- **Citrus juice and zest**: I use whole lemons and limes in my recipes because I often use the zest from the lemon/lime as well. Do not skip citrus in recipes, as just a small amount of acid can take a recipe from good to great.
- **Cooking oils**: Extra virgin olive oil and canola oil are my go-to cooking oils. I use olive oil when I want the flavor to come through, such as with sautéing or in vinaigrettes. In most cases, other oils like avocado or peanut oil can be used in place of olive oil or canola oil.
- **Freshly ground black pepper**: While I prefer measuring this ingredient with my heart, I have included measurements in some recipes for the sake of standardization.
- **Herbs**: Fresh cilantro and parsley are used frequently throughout this book. I recommend sticking to fresh for those herbs. For rosemary, sage, and thyme, either fresh or dry can be used. One tablespoon of fresh-chopped herbs is equal to one teaspoon of dried herbs.
- **Parmesan**: Parmesan, by the European definition, is not vegetarian because it uses rennet from animal sources. In the United States, the name Parmesan can be used for cheeses not sourced from rennet. More often than not, Parmesan is not technically vegetarian unless noted on the package. If this matters to you, seek out vegetarian Parmesan or just use a block of vegan Parmesan.
- **Pasta water**: In several recipes the water leftover from boiling pasta is reserved and added to the sauce. The starches in the water add silkiness and saltiness to sauces, and also help the sauce cling to the pasta.
- **Salt**: This cookbook uses both table salt and kosher salt. When referring to kosher, I exclusively use Diamond Crystal Kosher Salt. Teaspoon by teaspoon, it is less salty than table salt, so I highly recommend using Diamond Crystal, or other kosher salts, in recipes that call for it. For more information on salt in cooking, I highly recommend Samin Nosrat's book *Salt, Fat, Acid, Heat*.
- **Soy sauce**: I use both regular Kikkoman soy sauce and reduced-sodium soy sauce in my daily cooking. Use tamari in place of soy sauce for a gluten-free option.
- **Tofu**: In most recipes, unless otherwise noted, firm and extra-firm tofu are interchangeable with super-firm tofu. Firmness indicates the amount of water pressed out of a block of tofu, with super firm containing the least amount of water. Pressing tofu removes water, which allows the tofu to more readily absorb marinade and flavor.
- **Tomato paste**: This is one of my favorite ingredients—just a small amount increases the umami, savory flavors of a recipe significantly. Leftover tomato paste freezes well.
- **Vegetable bouillon**: Nine times out of ten I use Better Than Bouillon vegetable bouillon to make vegetable broth. All of the recipes in this cookbook were tested with Better Than Bouillon. It is much more flavorful than most canned vegetable broths and costs less per ounce. Use the ratio of bouillon to water suggested on the bouillon jar.

Kitchen Tools

- **Box grater**: This is used throughout the cookbook to grate vegetables and cheese. I most frequently use the large shredding holes, but the fine holes come in handy if you don't have a microplane. That being said, I highly recommend investing in a microplane to use to zest citrus and grate ginger and garlic into a paste.
- **Braiser or other oven-safe skillet**: Braising pans are usually enamel-coated cast iron pans with taller walls than standard skillets. They are great for recipes that require both sautéing and oven baking, like frittatas (p. 141). If you don't have a braising pan, a cast iron skillet will get the job done in most cases. If you have neither, just transfer skillet contents to an 11x11 inch or similarly sized baking dish.
- **Cast iron skillet**: I use my 12-inch Lodge cast iron skillet for the majority of recipes that call for a skillet, especially those that benefit from char (Tofu Stir Fry, p. 131, and Tofu Steak Dinner, p. 57).
- **Citrus juicer**: I use this for lemon and limes almost daily. I prefer a classic rim juicer, but any kind of juicing contraption works as long as it removes juice from citrus.
- **Garlic press**: It just makes life easier. Less time chopping, more time enjoying garlic.
- **Mason jars**: I use pint- and quart-sized mason jars to whisk up sauces and store small portions of soup. These can be found in thrift stores or at most grocery stores. I purchase plastic lids because the metal ones tend to rust.
- **Tofu press**: I promise that this is a worthwhile investment if you plan to cook tofu even once a week.

Shopping List

I am a huge proponent of spending a little time at home making a shopping list before heading to the store. It not only saves money at the store—it also saves you from the frustration of forgetting ingredients.

I prefer making grocery lists with pen and paper, but you can use whatever app or electronic device works best for you.

Here is how I recommend making a shopping list for this book:
- Scan the recipe and instructions.
- Divide all ingredients, even the ones that you think you already have, between three columns: produce, dry ingredients, and cold ingredients. Feel free to add additional columns.
- Shop your pantry. Cross off ingredients that you already have enough of at home. I actually take a photo of the list as soon as I complete it, just in case I forget it at home.
- Take your list to the store. Shop and cross off ingredients as you go.

DICE SIZES
When I mention dicing, slicing, or chopping styles in the cookbook, the above image shows what I am referring to. There is no need to be so precise that you whip out a measuring tape. Instead, use the above image as a general reference.

TOFU PRESSING
While I recommend just purchasing a tofu press, you can make your own DIY press at home. Drain the block of tofu and wrap it in a clean dish towel or paper towels. Place the wrapped tofu on a plate. On top the of the tofu, place a sheet pan or another plate. Weigh that down with a bag of beans, can of vegetables, books, anything that causes the tofu to compress slightly and leak water over time.

LEFTOVERS
The U.S. Department of Agriculture (USDA) states that "Leftovers can be kept in the refrigerator for 3 to 4 days or frozen for 3 to 4 months. Although safe indefinitely, frozen leftovers can lose moisture and flavor when stored for longer times in the freezer." That is also my recommendation.

Chapter 1: Balanced Bowls for Dinner

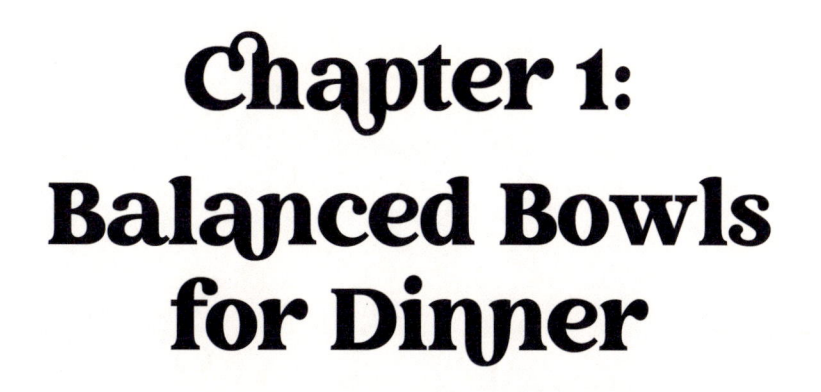

This recipe section includes many of the quickest meals in the cookbook, so most of these recipes are great for weeknights and are equally delicious as leftovers. Bowls are the perfect visualization of a balanced plate because they clearly show protein, carbohydrate, and vegetable components.

Cassidy's Favorite: Grits, Beans, and Greens Bowl (p. 29)

Quinoa Bowls with Zesty Mustard Sauce

30 MINUTES • 4 SERVINGS

Sometimes a simple meal is the best kind of meal. This bowl is easy to customize and make your own. Just don't skip the jammy tomatoes, because they are heavenly! The zesty sauce is inspired by the mustard sauce at the Whole Bowl in Portland, Oregon. It's tangy, acidic, and definitely tastes like mustard! Not a mustard fan? Try with Jalapeño Lime Dressing (p. 113).

BOWLS

¾ cup dry quinoa
1 ½ cups vegetable broth
½ teaspoon kosher salt, divided
1 tablespoon extra virgin olive oil
1 (15-ounce) can chickpeas, drained and rinsed
3 cloves garlic, minced
1 teaspoon dried parsley
4 cups chopped curly kale
1 pint grape tomatoes, sliced in half
¼ cup roasted salted sunflower seeds

ZESTY MUSTARD SAUCE

2 tablespoons lemon juice (about one small lemon)
2 tablespoons nutritional yeast
1 tablespoon canola oil
1 ½ teaspoons Dijon mustard
¼ teaspoon kosher salt
¼ teaspoon ground turmeric
1 to 3 tablespoons water, as needed

1. In a medium pot, combine the quinoa, vegetable broth, and ¼ teaspoon salt. Bring to a rapid simmer over medium-high heat, then reduce to a gentle simmer over medium-low heat. Cover and simmer until the liquid is completely absorbed and the quinoa is cooked through, about 15 minutes. Fluff with a fork before serving.

2. While the quinoa cooks, heat a large skillet over medium heat. Drizzle with olive oil. Once hot, add the chickpeas, garlic, parsley, and remaining ¼ teaspoon salt. Sauté for 5 minutes, stirring occasionally, until the chickpeas and garlic are golden.

3. Stir in the chopped kale and sliced grape tomatoes. Reduce heat to medium-low and cover with a lid to wilt the kale, about 2 to 3 minutes.

4. Remove the lid and stir in the sunflower seeds. Turn the heat up to medium. Continue cooking until the grape tomatoes are broken down and jammy, about 5 minutes.

5. **To make the sauce:** To a small bowl, add the lemon juice, nutritional yeast, canola oil, Dijon mustard, salt, and turmeric. Whisk until smooth. Add water as needed, 1 tablespoon at a time, to reach a thin, pourable consistency. Taste for seasonings and adjust as needed. The sauce should be acidic and tangy.

6. Divide the quinoa, chickpeas, and vegetables between 3 to 4 servings. Serve drizzled with the mustard sauce, to taste.

Grown-Up Walking Tacos

30 MINUTES • 4 SERVINGS

The first time I ever tried walking tacos was at a fair in Indiana with my extended family. If the concept of walking tacos is new to you, the explanation is in the name: taco fillings served in a corn chip bag, which gives you the ability to walk around while eating (at a fair, perhaps). Feel free to keep things classic by serving walking tacos the old school way, bag and all.

LENTILS

1 tablespoon canola oil
8 ounces white mushrooms, roughly chopped
1 teaspoon each chili powder, onion powder, dried oregano
½ teaspoon each ground cumin, garlic powder, paprika
¼ teaspoon kosher salt
1 (8-ounce) can tomato sauce
1 (15-ounce) can brown lentils, drained and rinsed
1 (15-ounce) can pinto beans, drained and rinsed

SALSA

2 Roma tomatoes, cored and diced
½ cup finely diced red onion (about ½ small onion)
2 tablespoons fresh chopped cilantro
1 tablespoon lime juice
½ teaspoon Tajín (optional)
¼ teaspoon kosher salt

AVOCADO CREAM

1 large ripe avocado
1 (5.3-ounce) container plain Greek yogurt
2 tablespoons lime juice
1 clove garlic, grated
¼ teaspoon table salt
Black pepper, to taste

ASSEMBLY

4 cups finely shredded romaine lettuce
4 ounces corn chips (I use Fritos)
Hot sauce (optional; I use Cholula)

1. Heat a large skillet over medium heat. Drizzle with oil. Once hot, add chopped mushrooms. Cook until the mushrooms are turning golden, about 6 to 8 minutes.

2. Season with chili powder, onion powder, oregano, cumin, garlic powder, paprika, and salt. Cook an additional 30 seconds to toast the spices, stirring continuously.

3. Stir in the tomato sauce, lentils, and pinto beans. Reduce heat to a gentle simmer over medium-low heat. Cover and simmer for at least 10 minutes.

4. **For the salsa:** In a medium bowl, combine the tomatoes, red onion, cilantro, lime juice, optional Tajín, and salt. Taste for seasonings.

5. **For the avocado cream:** Remove the skin and seed from the avocado. In another medium bowl, mash the avocado until smooth. Stir in the Greek yogurt, lime juice, garlic, salt, and black pepper, to taste. For a smoother sauce, blend all ingredients in a blender until completely smooth. The sauce should be scoopable, like a very thick dressing. Add water 1 tablespoon at a time to thin, if needed.

6. Assemble the walking tacos between four bowls. First add the shredded lettuce, then the corn chips, lentils, and salsa. Top with a scoop of avocado cream and optional hot sauce.

Pearl Couscous Bowls with Marinated Artichoke Salad

30 MINUTES (PLUS 1 HOUR CHILL TIME) • 4 SERVINGS

This is a chilled grain bowl that's just perfect for hot summer days. Marinated artichoke hearts are sold already marinated and quartered, so they're both delicious as-is and require no prep. Pearl couscous is larger than couscous and has a similar texture to pasta.

TAHINI COUSCOUS

1 ½ cups water
½ teaspoon kosher salt, divided
1 cup dry pearl couscous
1 (15-ounce) can cannellini beans
¼ cup tahini, plus more for serving
2 tablespoons lemon juice (about one small lemon)
Zest from the lemon

ARTICHOKE SALAD

1 (12-ounce) jar quartered, marinated artichoke hearts
1 cup thinly sliced sweet yellow onion (about ½ medium onion)
2 Roma tomatoes, cored and diced
1 medium English cucumber, diced
¼ cup fresh chopped parsley
1 clove garlic, grated
2 tablespoons extra virgin olive oil
¼ teaspoon kosher salt
⅛ teaspoon black pepper
Lemon wedges, for serving

1. In a medium pot, bring the water and ¼ teaspoon salt to boil. Add the pearl couscous. Reduce to a gentle simmer over medium-low heat. Cover and cook until tender, about 8 minutes. Drain the couscous, if needed.

2. Transfer the couscous to a medium bowl. Stir in the beans, tahini, lemon juice, lemon zest, and the remaining ¼ teaspoon salt. Taste for salt. Cover and chill in the fridge for at least an hour.

3. Drain the jar of artichoke hearts. Transfer the artichoke hearts to another bowl along with the onion, tomato, cucumber, and parsley.

4. In a small bowl, whisk together the grated garlic, olive oil, salt, and pepper. Drizzle on the artichoke salad.

5. Cover and chill the salad for at least an hour. Assemble each serving with a portion of chilled couscous and salad. Garnish with a lemon wedge and an additional drizzle of tahini.

Lemon Pepper Tofu Bowls with Garlicky Green Beans

30 MINUTES • 4 SERVINGS

Taking inspiration from lemon pepper wings, this tofu is a burst of acidic, sweet, and salty flavor. Tearing tofu instead of slicing it allows for intentionally uneven cooking, resulting in a variety of textures. Once you start tearing tofu instead of slicing it, you might find it hard to stop!

GREEN BEANS

12 ounces whole green beans, ends trimmed
2 teaspoons extra virgin olive oil
¼ teaspoon kosher salt
4 cloves garlic, roughly chopped
1 teaspoon lemon zest (about one small lemon)
Freshly ground black pepper, to taste

LEMON PEPPER TOFU

1 (14-ounce) block extra-firm tofu
2 tablespoons canola oil, divided
1 ½ tablespoons lemon pepper seasoning
2 teaspoons cornstarch
¼ teaspoon kosher salt
2 tablespoons lemon juice (about 1 small lemon)
1 tablespoon honey or maple syrup
Cooked basmati rice and butter, for serving
1 teaspoon lemon zest (about 1 small lemon)
Freshly ground black pepper, to taste

> **Note:** I like the salt-free lemon pepper seasoning from Dash. If using lemon pepper seasoning that contains salt, I recommend adding salt to taste.

For the green beans

1. Preheat the oven to 400°F. Add the green beans to a sheet pan. Drizzle with olive oil, tossing with a spatula to coat. Sprinkle with salt. Roast for 12 to 14 minutes, or until the green beans are starting to turn golden.

2. Remove from the oven and add the roughly chopped garlic, stirring to combine in the oil on the pan. Return to the oven for 5 to 7 minutes, or until the garlic is golden and the green beans are tender. Garnish with lemon zest and black pepper, to taste.

For the tofu and assembly

3. Press the tofu for at least 10 minutes. Using your hands, tear tofu into bite-sized pieces. In a medium bowl, toss tofu with 1 tablespoon canola oil, lemon pepper seasoning, cornstarch, and salt.

4. Heat a medium skillet over medium heat. Drizzle in the remaining 1 tablespoon of oil. Once hot, add the tofu. Cook until golden and crisp throughout, stirring occasionally, about 8 to 10 minutes.

5. In a small bowl, whisk together the lemon juice and honey. Decrease the skillet heat to medium-low, then pour the lemon sauce into the skillet with the tofu. Continue cooking until the tofu starts to blacken, about 5 minutes.

6. **To assemble:** Stir butter into the hot basmati rice. I recommend 1 tablespoon of butter per 1 cup of cooked rice. Assemble the bowls with buttered basmati rice, garlic green beans, and tofu. Season with lemon zest and freshly ground black pepper, to taste.

Pan-Fried Polenta with Mushrooms & Asparagus

40 MINUTES • 4 SERVINGS

Not to be confused with grits (p. 29), which are basically the same thing as polenta, save for the corn-kernel color and standard serving methods, the polenta used in this recipe is sold ready-to-eat in a sliceable tube. I won't bore you with the specifics of grits vs. polenta, but I will let you know that this recipe is so, so tasty. Just look at it: buttery pan-fried polenta, marinated balsamic portobello mushrooms, and roasted asparagus. This is a relatively quick meal but also works for special occasions!

VEGETABLES

2 tablespoons balsamic vinegar
1 tablespoon + 1 teaspoon extra virgin olive oil, divided
1 teaspoon Italian seasoning
1 teaspoon soy sauce
½ teaspoon Dijon mustard
4 large portobello caps, sliced into ½-inch strips
1 bunch asparagus, woody stems snapped off
¼ teaspoon kosher salt

POLENTA AND ASSEMBLY

1 (18-ounce) tube polenta
2 tablespoons unsalted butter
3 cloves garlic, roughly chopped
¼ cup (¼ ounce) grated Parmesan, plus more for serving
1 small lemon, sliced into wedges
Freshly ground black pepper

1. Preheat the oven to 425°F. In a medium bowl, whisk together the balsamic vinegar, 1 tablespoon olive oil, Italian seasoning, soy sauce, and Dijon mustard. Add the sliced portobellos, tossing to coat. Marinate until the oven is preheated, or for at least 10 minutes.

2. While the mushrooms marinate, line a large sheet pan with parchment paper. Add the asparagus to the pan, and toss with 1 teaspoon olive oil and ¼ teaspoon salt. Remove the portobellos from the marinade and add them to the pan. Roast at 425°F for 20 to 25 minutes, or until the asparagus and mushrooms are both shriveled and golden.

3. While the vegetables cook, prepare the polenta. Slice polenta into 10 rounds, each about ½-inch thick.

4. Heat a large skillet over medium heat. Add the butter. Once melted, add the polenta. Flip when golden and crisp, about 4 to 5 minutes. Add the garlic and continue cooking until both the polenta and garlic are golden, another 4 to 5 minutes.

5. Remove the pan from the heat. Sprinkle each piece of polenta with Parmesan cheese.

6. Assemble each serving with the roasted vegetables, polenta, a lemon wedge, and freshly ground black pepper and grated Parmesan, to taste.

> **Note:** I don't remove the gills on portobello mushrooms, but you can remove them if you prefer. For additional protein, serve with a fried egg or tofu.

Miso Butter Bean Bowls

40 MINUTES • 4 SERVINGS

These bowls are comforting without being heavy, thanks to a spicy kick from pan-seared red cabbage. While unassuming at first, the almost-blackened cabbage is a staple in our house. It becomes sweeter and more tender when charred, and when paired with savory beans and a big bowl of rice, it feels like so much more than just cabbage. For a variation on this meal, we often serve pan-fried cabbage with rice, a fried egg, and shelled edamame for a quick but satisfying dinner.

1 small red cabbage (about 1 ½ pounds)
2 tablespoons canola oil, divided
4 cloves garlic, minced
1 inch ginger, grated
1 bunch green onions, thinly sliced, with green and white sections separated
1 tablespoon yellow miso
1 tablespoon water
1 tablespoon rice vinegar
1 tablespoon soy sauce
¼ teaspoon kosher salt
2 (16-ounce) cans butter beans, drained and rinsed
1 cup vegetable broth
¼ cup garlic chili sauce
2 cups cooked long-grain white rice, for serving
Fresh chopped cilantro, lime wedges, and freshly ground black pepper, for serving

1. To prepare the cabbage, first cut it in half from core to top. Cut each half into 8 wedges about 1 inch thick, cutting through the core to leave each wedge intact.

2. Heat a medium pot over medium heat. Drizzle with 1 tablespoon of oil. Once hot, add the garlic, ginger, and the white parts of the green onions. Cook until aromatic and golden, about 2 to 3 minutes.

3. In a small bowl, whisk together the miso and water. This thins miso and makes it easier to distribute into the sauce. To the pot, add the thinned miso, rice vinegar, soy sauce, and salt. Stir to combine.

4. Add the butter beans and broth. Bring to a rapid simmer over medium-high heat, then reduce to a very gentle simmer over low heat. Simmer uncovered for at least 10 minutes.

5. To cook the cabbage, heat a large skillet over medium-high heat. Drizzle with the remaining oil. Once hot, add 6 to 8 cabbage wedges, working in batches as needed. Sear until the side touching the pan is golden and almost blackened, about 6 to 8 minutes.

6. Brush the uncooked side of the cabbage with enough garlic chili sauce to coat. Flip the cabbage wedge so that the side with the chili sauce is touching the pan. Cook until almost blackened, about 4 to 6 minutes. When ready, the cabbage will be softened but still have a bit of crunch to it. If the cabbage is burning but still too firm, reduce the heat to medium.

7. Assemble the bowls by dividing the butter beans with broth, rice, and cabbage between four servings. Garnish with the green parts of the green onions, chopped cilantro, a lime wedge, and black pepper.

Grits, Greens, and Beans

45 MINUTES • 4 SERVINGS

Because much of the classic Southern food found in restaurants near me is decidedly not vegetarian, one of my favorite meals to make at home is a big pot of greens and beans. The addition of cheesy grits makes this a meal that's fit for breakfast or dinner. This method works just as well with collard greens, though I recommend simmering them for at least 30 minutes. When I have extra time, I like to serve this with a drop biscuit (p. 49) or meatless sausage patties.

CHEESY GRITS

- 4 cups water
- 1 cup old-fashioned grits
- ½ teaspoon table salt
- 3 tablespoons unsalted butter
- ¾ cup to 1 cup (3 to 4 ounces) shredded Vermont extra-sharp white cheddar cheese

BEANS & GREENS

- 1 tablespoon extra virgin olive oil
- 2 cups diced sweet yellow onion (about 1 medium onion)
- 2 tomatoes on the vine, diced and vine removed
- ¼ teaspoon kosher salt
- 1 bunch lacinato kale, leaves sliced into thin strips and stems roughly chopped
- 4 cloves garlic, minced
- 1 (15-ounce) can cannellini beans, drained and rinsed
- 1 cup vegetable broth
- 1 teaspoon light brown sugar
- 1 teaspoon red pepper flakes
- 1 teaspoon apple cider vinegar
- 1 teaspoon soy sauce
- ¼ teaspoon smoked paprika
- 4 large eggs, for frying
- Roasted salted pumpkin seeds, for serving

1. To make the grits, bring the water to a boil in a medium pot over high heat. Stir in the grits and salt. Reduce heat to a gentle simmer over medium-low heat. Cover and simmer until the grits are fully cooked, stirring occasionally, about 20 minutes. When the grits are fully cooked, remove the lid and stir in butter and shredded cheddar cheese. Adjust salt and cheese to taste.

2. While the grits cook, heat a large skillet over medium heat. Drizzle in olive oil. Once hot, add the diced onion, tomatoes, and salt. Sauté until the tomatoes are reduced and the onion is softened, about 6 to 8 minutes.

3. Add in the sliced kale and garlic. Sauté an additional 3 to 4 minutes, until the kale is wilted. Add the beans, vegetable broth, brown sugar, red pepper flakes, apple cider vinegar, soy sauce, and smoked paprika. Reduce to a gentle simmer over medium-low heat. Simmer uncovered for at least 10 minutes to marry the flavors.

4. Meanwhile, in a separate skillet, fry an egg for each serving. When the eggs are ready, assemble the bowls by dividing the grits, beans & greens, and eggs between each bowl. Serve topped with roasted pumpkin seeds.

> **Note:** Feel free to use instant grits or quick-cooking grits instead of old-fashioned. Just cook according to package instructions but use the same amount of butter and cheese.
>
> Lacinato kale is also called "dinosaur" or "Italian" kale. Curly kale works as a direct substitution.

Upside Down Lentil Shepherd's Pie

50 MINUTES • 4-6 SERVINGS

Shepherd's pie is a comfort food classic! It is traditionally served with the mashed potatoes on top, but the "meaty" lentil and mushroom base in this upside-down version has an almost gravy-like sauce that melts perfectly into the mashed potatoes. The mashed potatoes also work well as a standalone recipe.

MASHED POTATOES

- 2 ½ pounds russet potatoes
- ¾ teaspoon table salt, divided
- 3 tablespoons unsalted butter
- 3 ounces Neufchâtel (low-fat) cream cheese
- ¾ to 1 cup whole milk

LENTILS

- 1 tablespoon extra virgin olive oil
- 1 cup diced sweet yellow onion (about ½ medium onion)
- 8 ounces baby bella mushrooms, chopped
- ¼ teaspoon kosher salt
- 4 cloves garlic, minced
- 2 tablespoons tomato paste
- 1 teaspoon dried thyme
- ¼ cup dry red wine (such as Cabernet or Pinot Noir)
- 2 tablespoons nutritional yeast
- 1 tablespoon soy sauce
- ¾ cup vegetable broth
- ½ cup starchy potato water
- 2 (15-ounce) cans brown lentils, drained and rinsed

Note: Choose wine that you would enjoy drinking with the meal, not one that's been sitting on the counter for a week. For an alcohol-free option, add 1 tablespoon of balsamic vinegar just before serving and increase total broth to 1 cup.

For the mashed potatoes

1. Peel and dice potatoes into 1-inch cubes. Add potatoes to a large pot. Add enough cold water to cover the potatoes by 1 inch. Stir in ½ teaspoon salt. Bring to a boil. Boil until the potatoes are easy to pierce with a fork, about 10 to 12 minutes. **Reserve at least ½ cup of the water before draining the potatoes.** Set the drained potatoes aside.

2. Return the now empty pot to medium heat. Add the butter. Once melted, return potatoes to the pot along with the cream cheese and remaining salt. Use a potato masher to mash the potatoes until mostly smooth. Stir in milk, starting with ¾ cup and using an extra ¼ cup as needed to reach a silky smooth consistency. Cover with a lid and leave over low heat until the lentils are ready.

For the lentils

3. While the potatoes are boiling, heat a large pan over medium heat. Drizzle with olive oil. Once hot, add the onions and mushrooms. Cook until golden, about 8 to 10 minutes.

4. Stir in the salt, minced garlic, tomato paste, and thyme. Stir frequently, cooking until the garlic is golden and aromatic, about 2 minutes. Deglaze the pan with the wine, then stir in the nutritional yeast, soy sauce, vegetable broth, reserved starch water, and lentils.

5. Bring to a gentle simmer over medium-low heat. Simmer uncovered for at least 10 minutes to marry the flavors.

6. To serve, add a portion of mashed potatoes to each bowl and top with a scoop of lentils.

Roasted Sweet Potato Bowls with Marinated Tofu

50 MINUTES • 4 SERVINGS

This is my go-to way to make marinated tofu. A few tips: always press tofu before marinating so that the marinade actually has a chance to soak into the tofu; the longer the tofu marinates, the more flavorful it becomes; and the longer tofu bakes, the firmer it becomes.

MARINATED TOFU

1 (14-ounce) block extra-firm tofu
¼ cup vegetable broth
3 tablespoons soy sauce
2 tablespoons nutritional yeast
1 tablespoon apple cider vinegar
1 teaspoon maple syrup
½ teaspoon garlic powder
½ teaspoon onion powder
¼ teaspoon freshly ground black pepper

SWEET POTATOES

1 ½ pounds sweet potato
1 tablespoon canola oil
½ teaspoon garlic powder
½ teaspoon kosher salt
½ teaspoon onion powder
½ teaspoon smoked paprika

BRUSSELS SPROUTS

1 pound Brussels sprouts, stems removed and sprouts sliced in half
1 tablespoon canola oil
¼ teaspoon kosher salt
⅛ teaspoon black pepper
2 tablespoons lemon juice (about one small lemon)
1 tablespoon honey
½ teaspoon red pepper flakes

SAUCE

¼ cup mayonnaise
1 ½ tablespoons vinegar-based hot sauce, such as Cholula
1 tablespoon honey
¼ teaspoon salt
1 clove garlic, grated

1. Press the tofu for at least 10 minutes. Meanwhile, whisk together the marinade in a medium bowl: vegetable broth, soy sauce, nutritional yeast, apple cider vinegar, maple syrup, garlic powder, onion powder, and black pepper. Slice the pressed tofu into 1-inch cubes and add to the marinade. Marinate for at least 10 minutes and up to overnight.

2. Preheat the oven to 425°F. Dice the sweet potato into roughly ½-inch pieces. In a large bowl, toss the sweet potatoes with canola oil, garlic powder, salt, onion powder, and smoked paprika. Transfer to a large baking sheet with the marinated tofu. Roast for just 10 minutes on the middle oven rack.

3. In the same large bowl, toss the Brussels with oil, salt, and pepper. After the potatoes and tofu have roasted for 10 minutes, remove from the oven and add the Brussels sprouts to the pan. Return to the oven for 20 minutes.

4. Whisk together the lemon juice, honey, and red pepper flakes in a small bowl. Drizzle onto the Brussels sprouts after they have baked for 20 minutes, then return to the oven for 5 more minutes, or until the Brussels sprouts are golden and the sweet potatoes are tender.

5. In a small bowl, whisk together the mayonnaise, hot sauce, honey, salt, and grated garlic. Assemble servings by dividing the vegetables and tofu between bowls. Serve topped with a drizzle of the sauce.

> **Note:** If the Brussels sprouts are very large, I recommend quartering them instead of just slicing them in half.

Mac and Cheese with BBQ Tofu & Brussels Slaw

55 MINUTES • 4 SERVINGS

I think of this recipe as a cookout in a bowl because it has smoky barbecued protein, crunchy slaw, and saucy mac and cheese. Shredded tofu becomes chewy and firm when baked, giving it a surprisingly meaty texture. Stick to super-firm tofu for this recipe, as extra-firm and firm crumble too much when grated, even if pressed for an extended period of time.

VINEGAR BRUSSELS SLAW

8 ounces Brussels sprouts
1 cup matchstick carrots
¼ cup apple cider vinegar
1 tablespoon Dijon mustard
1 teaspoon honey
¼ teaspoon kosher salt
⅛ teaspoon black pepper

SHREDDED TOFU

1 (16-ounce) block super-firm tofu
1 tablespoon extra virgin olive oil
¼ teaspoon kosher salt
⅓ cup sweet barbecue sauce
1 teaspoon chili powder
½ teaspoon smoked paprika

MAC AND CHEESE

8 ounces elbow pasta
2 tablespoons unsalted butter
2 tablespoons all-purpose flour
1 ¼ cup whole milk
6 ounce block sharp cheddar cheese, grated
½ teaspoon Old Bay seasoning
⅛ teaspoon table salt
Freshly ground black pepper, to taste

1. Remove stems from the Brussels sprouts. Slice each sprout in half from stem to top, then slice each half into thin strips. In a mixing bowl, toss together the Brussels sprouts and matchstick carrots.

2. In a small bowl, whisk together the apple cider vinegar, Dijon mustard, honey, salt, and pepper. Toss the Brussels sprouts and carrots with the vinaigrette. Cover and chill until the other components are ready.

3. Preheat the oven to 375°F. Using the large holes on a box grater, grate the tofu into shreds. In a bowl, toss the tofu with olive oil and salt. Spread in an even layer on a large sheet pan lined with parchment paper.

4. Cook the tofu at 375°F for 12 to 15 minutes, until golden and starting to crisp around the edges. Remove from the oven and stir in the BBQ sauce, chili powder, and smoked paprika. Toss with a spatula to coat. Return to the oven for 6 to 8 minutes, or until the tofu is firm and deepened in color.

5. While the tofu cooks, boil the elbow pasta in a pot of well-salted water until al dente. Drain and set aside.

6. Meanwhile, heat a large skillet over medium heat. Add the butter. Once melted, sprinkle in the flour. Toast, stirring frequently, until the flour is golden, about 2 minutes. Slowly whisk in the milk, stirring constantly. Stir in the grated cheddar, Old Bay seasoning, salt, and pepper.

7. Simmer over medium-low to medium heat until the sauce thickens enough to coat the back of a spoon without sliding off. Just a few bubbles should be popping at a time. Stir in the cooked pasta.

8. To serve, divide the mac and cheese, shredded tofu, and Brussels slaw between bowls. Serve with freshly ground black pepper, to taste.

Smoky Loaded Baked Sweet Potatoes

1 HOUR • 4 SERVINGS

This is not quite your traditional baked potato, but it is delicious nonetheless. These potatoes are made with a vegan "queso"-style sauce that works well on more than just potatoes. Use the queso to veganize Jackfruit Nachos (p. 41) or pair it with shredded tofu (p. 35) in a flour tortilla to make a delicious quesadilla. For a faster meal, cook the sweet potato in advance and refrigerate until ready to use. Pop in the microwave for a couple of minutes to reheat.

ASSEMBLY

4 medium sweet potatoes
1 medium head broccoli, sliced into small florets
Salt & pepper, to taste
Salsa verde, fresh chopped cilantro, and ½ bunch thinly sliced green onions, for serving

BEANS

¼ cup adobo sauce from a can of chipotle peppers in adobo sauce
¼ cup water
2 teaspoons apple cider vinegar
2 teaspoons maple syrup
1 teaspoon smoked paprika
1 to 2 teaspoons canola oil
1 cup diced sweet yellow onion (about ½ medium onion)
¼ teaspoon kosher salt
1 (15-ounce) can pinto beans, drained and rinsed
½ cup fresh chopped cilantro

VEGAN "QUESO"

1 cup raw unsalted cashews
1 cup very hot water, heated in a kettle or in a pot on the stove
¼ cup nutritional yeast
2 tablespoons lime juice (about one small lime)
½ teaspoon kosher salt

1. Preheat the oven to 400°F. Poke the sweet potatoes a few times with a fork. Place on a sheet pan and bake at 400°F for 45 minutes to an hour, or until completely soft on the inside and easy to mash with a fork.

2. In a small bowl, whisk together the adobo sauce, water, apple cider vinegar, maple syrup, and smoked paprika. Set aside.

3. Heat a medium skillet over medium heat. Drizzle with a small coating of canola oil. Once hot, add the diced onion and salt. Sauté for 6 to 8 minutes, or until the onion is softened and starting to turn golden.

4. Add the pinto beans, bowl of seasonings from above, and cilantro. Bring to a gentle simmer over medium-low heat. Cover and simmer until all other components are ready, or for at least 10 minutes.

5. Place broccoli florets in a steamer basket over simmering water. Cover and steam until vivid green and tender enough to pierce with a fork, about 10 to 12 minutes. Season with salt and pepper to taste.

6. To make the queso, add the cashews, hot water, nutritional yeast, lime juice, and salt to a blender. Blend on high speed until completely smooth. Add additional water as needed to create a thick but pourable sauce.

7. To assemble the sweet potatoes, first slice the potatoes in half. Mash with a fork and season with salt and pepper, to taste. Divide the beans between each sweet potato. Top with steamed broccoli, queso, a scoop of salsa verde, cilantro, and green onions.

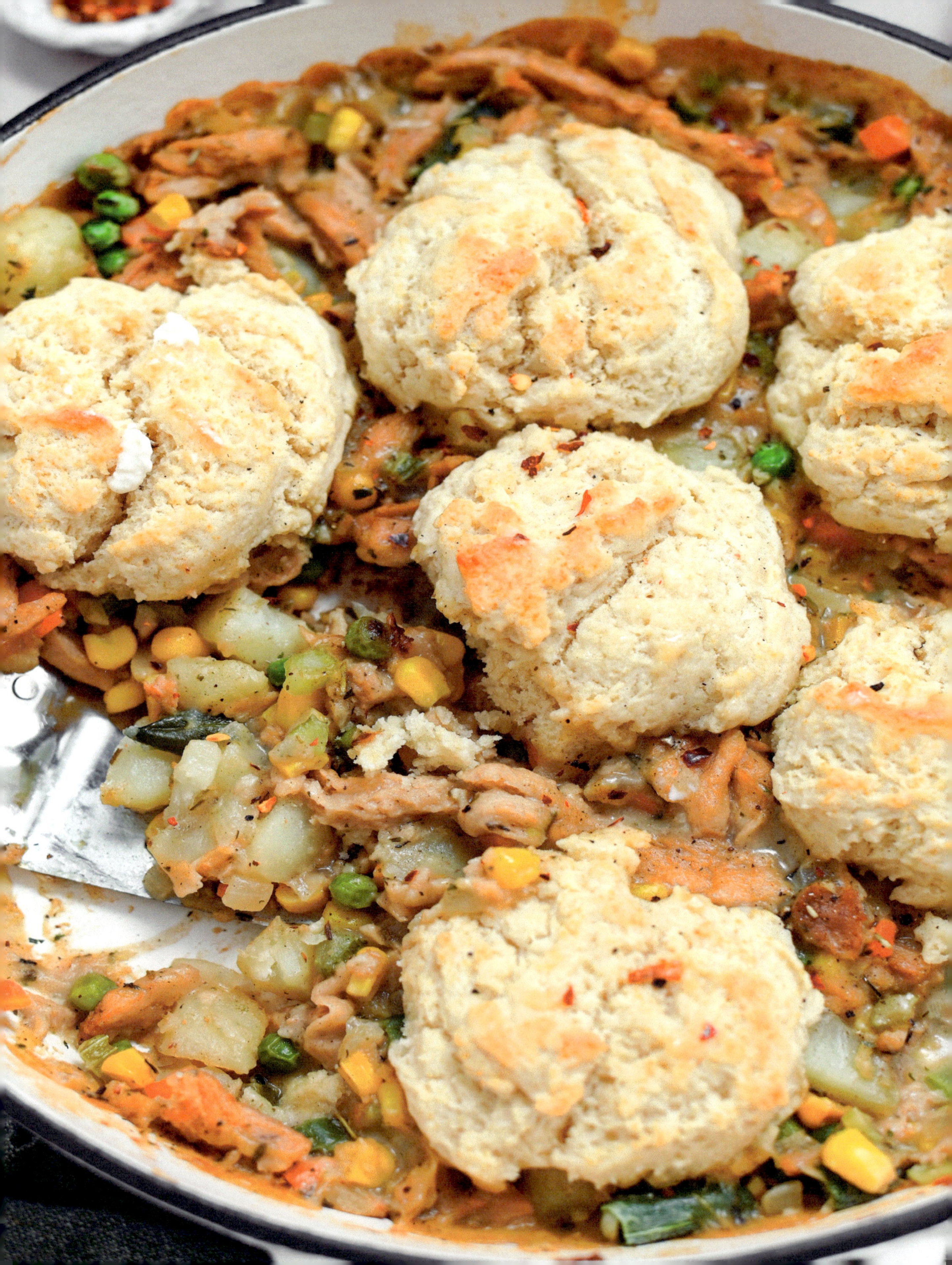

Chapter 2: Skillets & Bakes for Dinner

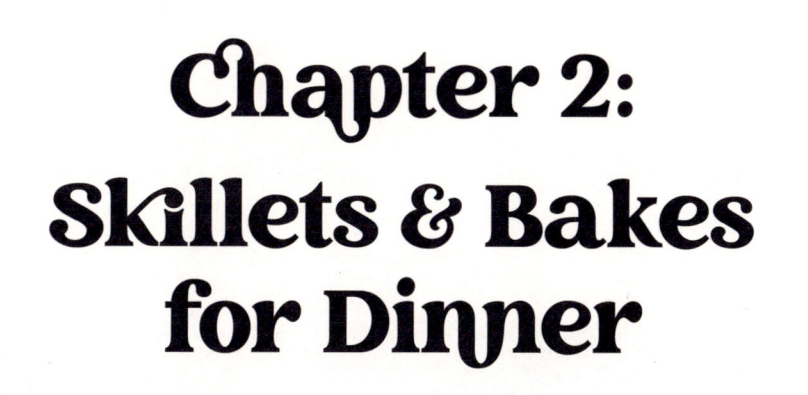

Also known as Cassidy's Comfort Food chapter, these skillets and bakes feature stove top, stove-to-oven, and baked meals. This section includes year-round recipes, but it really shines with seasonal favorites like Broccoli Farro Casserole (p. 59) in the winter and Cherry Tomato Galette (p. 65) in the summer.

Cassidy's Favorite: "Chicken" Pot Pie with Drop Biscuits (p. 49)

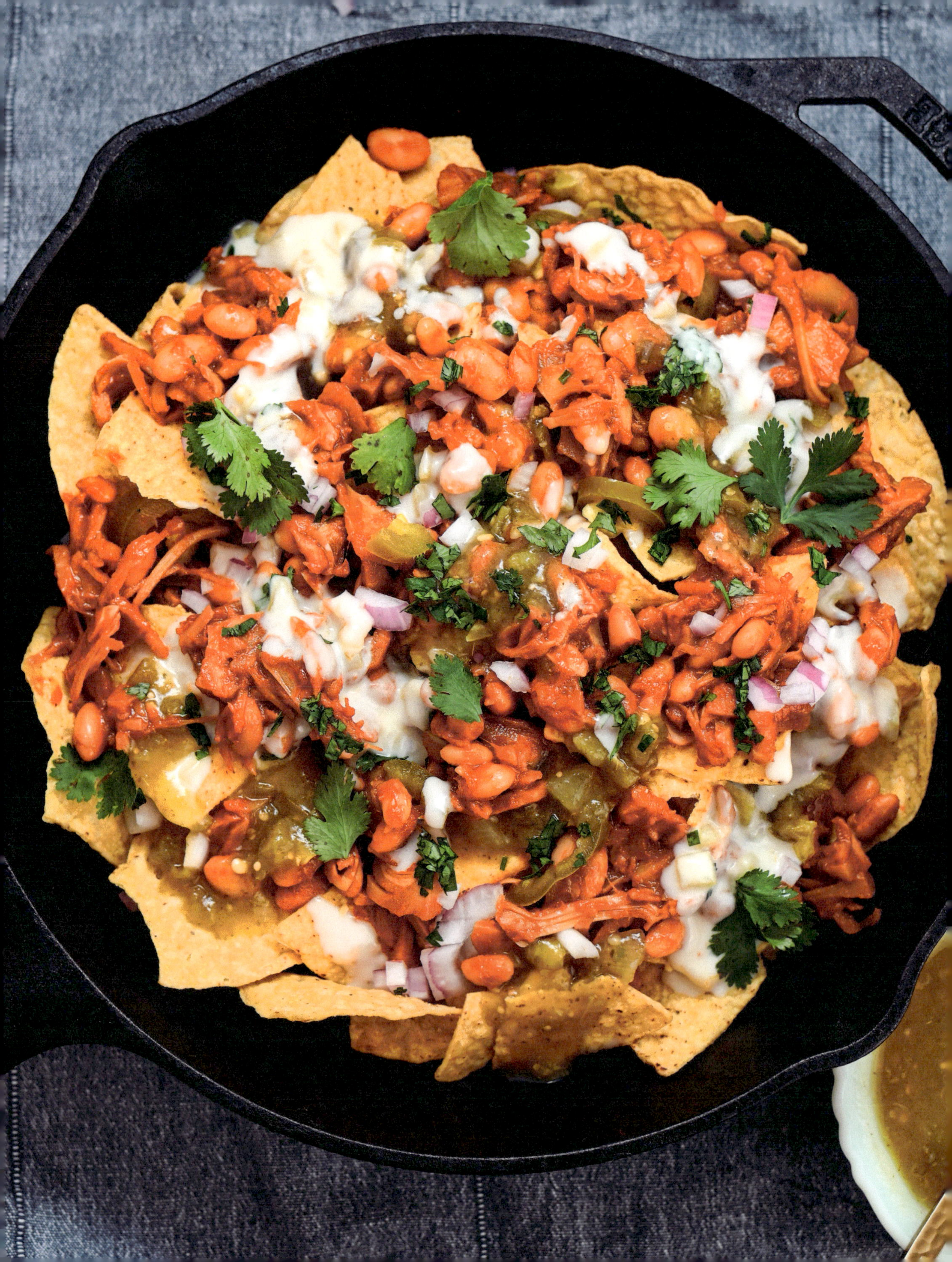

BBQ Jackfruit Nachos with White Queso

30 MINUTES • 4 SERVINGS

Nachos are my favorite food. The crunch, the variety of flavors, the melty cheese. These have a BBQ twist, where the sweetness from the BBQ-simmered beans and jackfruit balance out the zesty salsa verde, crisp red onion, and gently spicy pickled jalapeño. Make it dairy-free with Vegan Queso (p. 37). The jackfruit/bean filling is fantastic in quesadillas with the vegan queso!

BBQ PULLED JACKFRUIT

1 (20-ounce) can of jackfruit
1 (8-ounce) can tomato sauce
½ cup vegetable broth
3 tablespoons light brown sugar
2 tablespoons apple cider vinegar
2 tablespoons molasses
2 teaspoons Dijon mustard
2 teaspoons soy sauce
¼ teaspoon garlic powder
¼ teaspoon onion powder
1 (15-ounce) can great northern beans, drained and rinsed

WHITE QUESO

2 tablespoons unsalted butter
2 tablespoons all-purpose flour
¾ to 1 cup whole milk
8 ounce round of quesadilla melting cheese, shredded
1 (4-ounce) can diced green chile peppers, drained
¼ teaspoon table salt

ASSEMBLY

8 ounces tortilla chips
1 cup salsa verde
1 cup diced red onion (about ½ medium onion)
½ cup fresh chopped cilantro
½ cup pickled jalapeños

1. Drain the can of jackfruit. Slice the jackfruit into thin strips so that it resembles pulled pork or chicken.

2. Heat a medium skillet over medium heat. Add the tomato sauce, vegetable broth, light brown sugar, apple cider vinegar, molasses, mustard, soy sauce, garlic powder, and onion powder. Whisk to combine, then add the sliced jackfruit and beans.

3. Bring to a rapid simmer over medium-high heat, then reduce to a gentle simmer over medium-low heat. Simmer uncovered for 8 to 10 minutes to thicken the sauce and infuse the beans and jackfruit with flavor.

4. Meanwhile, make the queso. Heat a small pot over medium heat. Add the butter. Once melted, sprinkle in the flour. Cook, stirring frequently, until the flour is golden and toasted, 2 to 3 minutes. Reduce heat to medium-low. Whisk in ¾ cup of milk. Whisk in the cheese a handful at a time, waiting for it to melt before adding more. Add the green chiles and salt. Heat over medium-low, stirring frequently, until the sauce is thickened like queso cheese, 2 to 3 minutes. If needed, add the remaining ¼ cup of milk to thin the sauce.

5. Heat a large skillet over medium heat. Working in batches, add enough tortilla chips to fill the pan. Toast for just 1 to 2 minutes to warm the chips.

6. **Assemble the nachos:** Top each serving of chips with BBQ jackfruit and beans and a drizzle of queso. Top with a scoop of salsa verde and a sprinkle of red onion, cilantro, and pickled jalapeños, to taste.

> Note: Choose melting cheese, not queso fresco. This can usually be found by salsa and other Mexican cheeses.

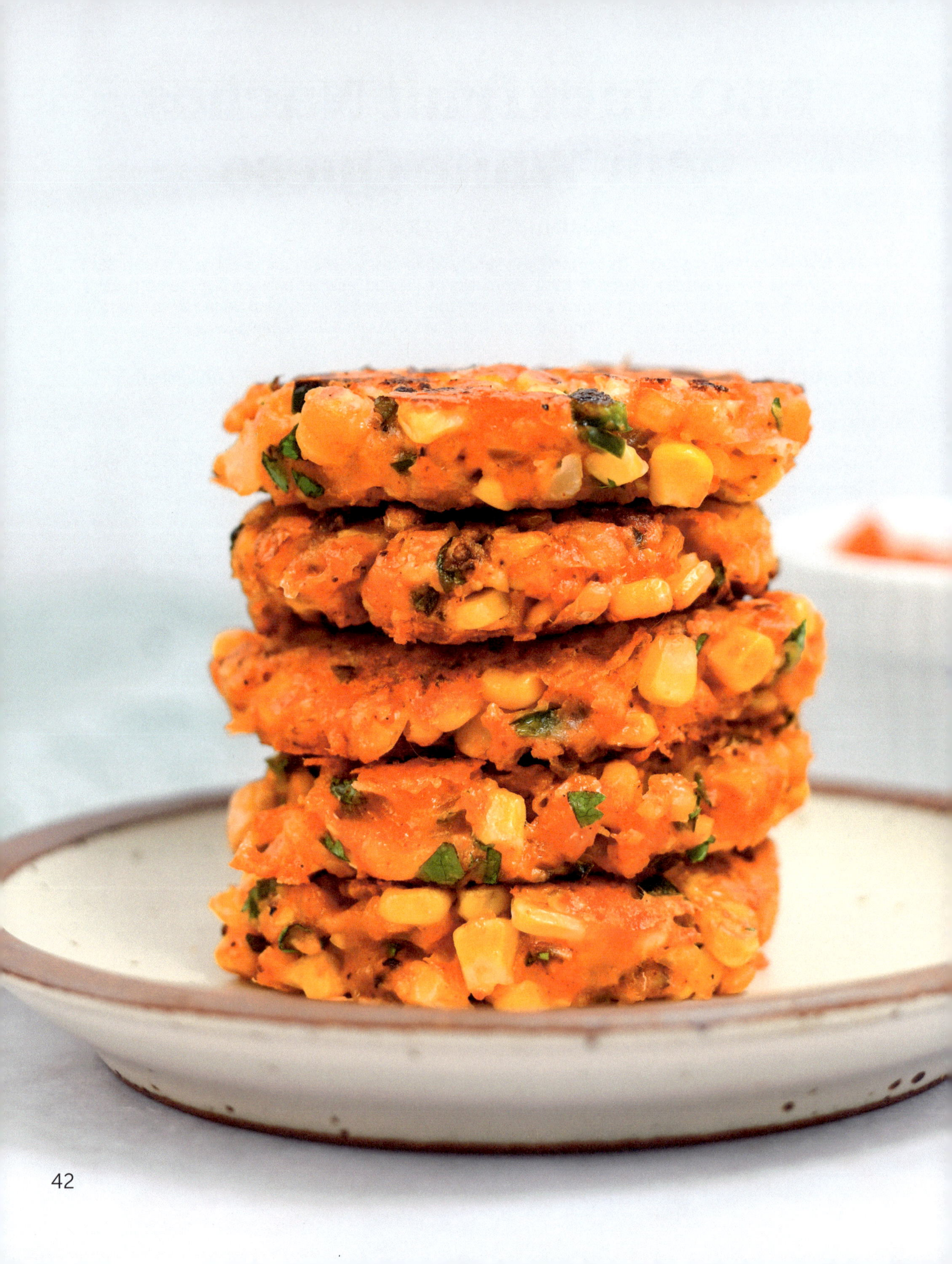

Corn Fritters with Spicy Cherry Tomato Sauce

35 MINUTES • 8-10 FRITTERS

These fritters are great as a light meal or appetizer/party food. The tomato sauce is gently spicy, but the red pepper flakes can be omitted for a spice-free option. Cherry tomatoes or grape tomatoes work in the tomato sauce. Fresh sweet corn from the cob is a great swap when it's in season.

CORN FRITTERS

2 tablespoons canola oil, divided
½ cup diced yellow onion (about ½ small onion)
½ cup diced poblano pepper (about 1 medium pepper)
2 cloves garlic, minced
1 (15-ounce) can chickpeas, drained and rinsed
1 (15-ounce) can sweet yellow corn, drained and rinsed
1 large egg, whisked
½ cup all-purpose flour
¼ cup chopped fresh cilantro
1 teaspoon paprika
¾ teaspoon kosher salt
½ teaspoon each chili powder, garlic powder, smoked paprika
¼ teaspoon black pepper
¼ teaspoon cayenne pepper
1 cup (4 ounces) shredded sharp cheddar cheese

SPICY TOMATO SAUCE

2 teaspoons extra virgin olive oil
10 ounces cherry tomatoes, quartered
1 teaspoon light brown sugar
½ teaspoon chili powder
½ teaspoon red pepper flakes
¼ teaspoon kosher salt
1 teaspoon lemon juice

1. Heat a large skillet over medium heat. Drizzle in 1 tablespoon canola oil. Once hot, add the diced onion and poblano pepper. Sauté until golden, about 6 to 8 minutes. Add the minced garlic. Continue cooking until golden and aromatic, about 2 minutes.

2. While the peppers cook, add the chickpeas to a medium mixing bowl. Using a fork or potato masher, mash until mostly broken down. Stir in the sweet corn, whisked egg, flour, cilantro, paprika, salt, chili powder, garlic powder, smoked paprika, black pepper, and cayenne pepper. Fold in shredded cheese and cooked peppers and onions. The batter should be relatively wet.

3. Heat a large skillet over medium heat. Drizzle with remainder of canola oil to coat the pan, about 1 tablespoon. Once hot, use a ¼ cup measuring cup to scoop fritters into the hot oil. Gently press with the back of the scoop or a spatula to flatten the fritters. Pan-fry until golden, about 3 minutes. Flip and continue cooking until golden on both sides. You may need to work in batches to avoid overcrowding the pan.

4. Meanwhile, make the tomato sauce. Heat 2 teaspoons of olive oil in a small pot over medium heat. Once hot, add the cherry tomatoes. Sauté for about 6 to 8 minutes, stirring occasionally, until the cherry tomatoes start to break down. Reduce heat to low and stir in the brown sugar, chili powder, red pepper flakes, and salt. Simmer for 5 minutes to marry the flavors, then remove from heat and stir in the lemon juice.

5. Serve fritters with tomato sauce on the side. The fritters are best enjoyed immediately, but leftover batter can be refrigerated for 3 to 4 days.

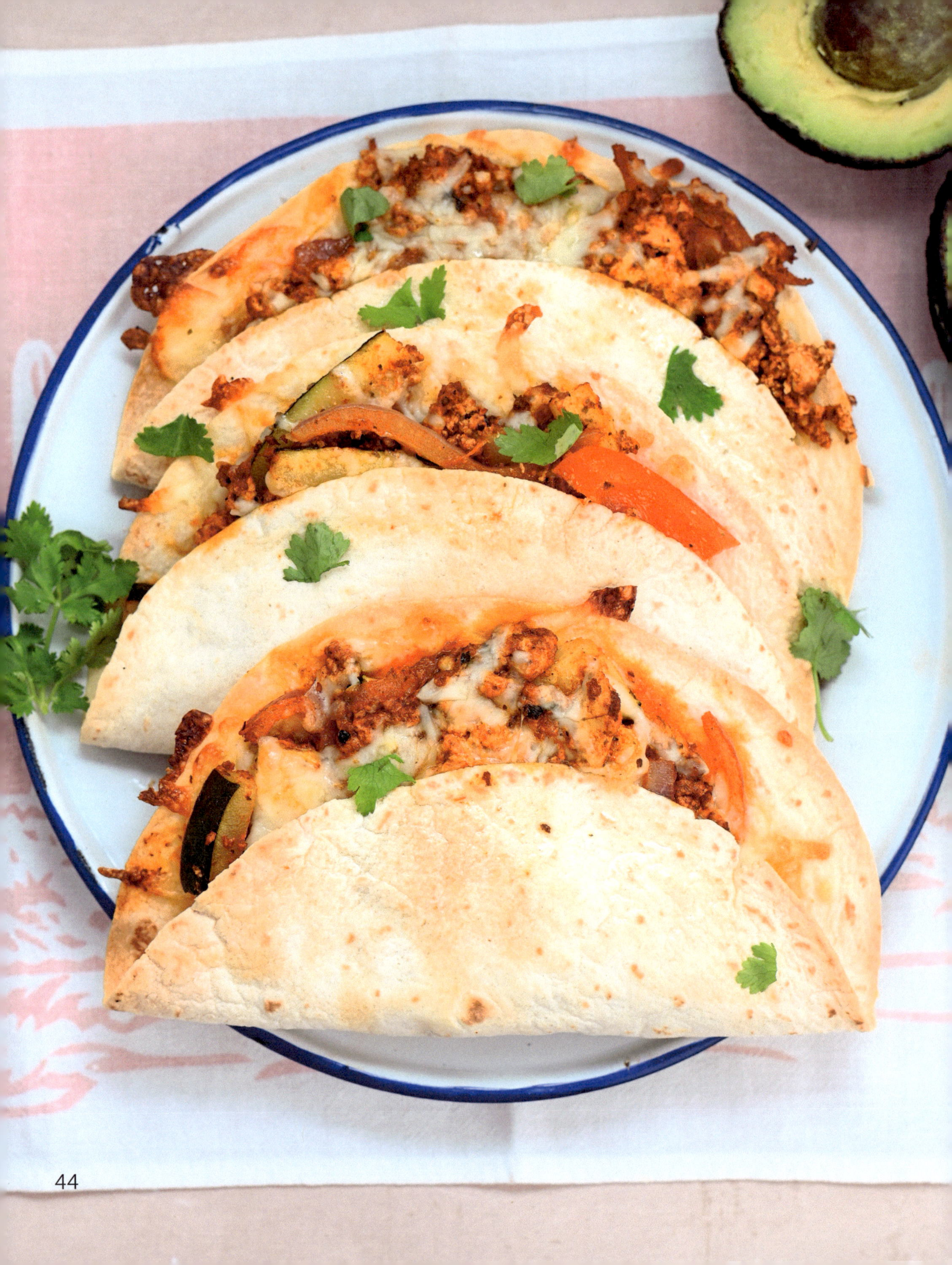

Crispy Baked Tacos with Tofu "Chorizo"

40 MINUTES • 8 TACOS OR 4 SERVINGS

My tofu "chorizo" is inspired by the Trader Joe's soyrizo, which is inspired by Mexican chorizo. I often make this recipe with Trader Joe's brand soyrizo when I don't feel like the extra step of marinating tofu. I like baked tacos because they require less hands-on time, but this recipe makes delicious pan-fried tacos as well. Just heat a skillet over medium heat, drizzle with oil, and cook on each side until crisp.

TOFU "CHORIZO"

1 (14-ounce) block extra-firm tofu
2 tablespoons apple cider vinegar
2 tablespoons vegetable broth
1 tablespoon canola oil
1 tablespoon tomato paste
1 ½ tablespoons ancho chili powder (regular chili powder works as well)
1 tablespoon dried oregano
1 ½ teaspoons paprika
1 teaspoon ground cumin
¾ teaspoon kosher salt
½ teaspoon each garlic powder, granulated sugar, ground coriander
¼ teaspoon ground cinnamon
Pinch ground cloves (optional)

ASSEMBLY

1 tablespoon canola oil
1 medium zucchini, sliced into 2-inch strips
1 medium red bell pepper, sliced into thin strips
½ medium red onion, sliced into thin strips
½ cup fresh chopped cilantro
8 (9-inch) flour tortillas
1 cup (4 ounces) shredded mozzarella cheese
Salsa, for serving

1. Press the tofu for at least 10 minutes. Meanwhile, whisk together the tofu marinade in a medium bowl: apple cider vinegar, vegetable broth, oil, tomato paste, ancho chili powder, oregano, paprika, cumin, salt, garlic powder, sugar, coriander, cinnamon, and cloves. Use your hands to crumble the pressed tofu into the marinade. Toss to coat. Marinate while the vegetables cook and up to overnight.

2. Heat a large skillet over medium heat. Drizzle with 1 tablespoon of canola oil. Once hot, add the zucchini, bell pepper, and onion. Sauté for 5 to 7 minutes, or until golden and fragrant.

3. Preheat the oven to 375°F. Line a large sheet pan with parchment paper or foil. Set aside.

4. Add the tofu, marinade, and cilantro to the pan with the vegetables. Sauté for 8 to 10 minutes, or until the tofu is starting to brown and most of the sauce is reduced.

5. To assemble tacos, add a heaping ⅓ cup of the tofu and vegetable filling to one side of a tortilla. Sprinkle with 2 tablespoons (about two big pinches) shredded mozzarella.

6. Close the tortillas and arrange on the baking sheet so that the tacos don't overlap. Bake at 375°F for 12 minutes. Flip and bake an additional 4 to 6 minutes, or until the taco shells are crisp and golden. Remove from the oven and serve with salsa.

> **Note:** For crispier tacos, brush each tortilla with oil before baking. This filling is also delicious in burritos or regular tacos.

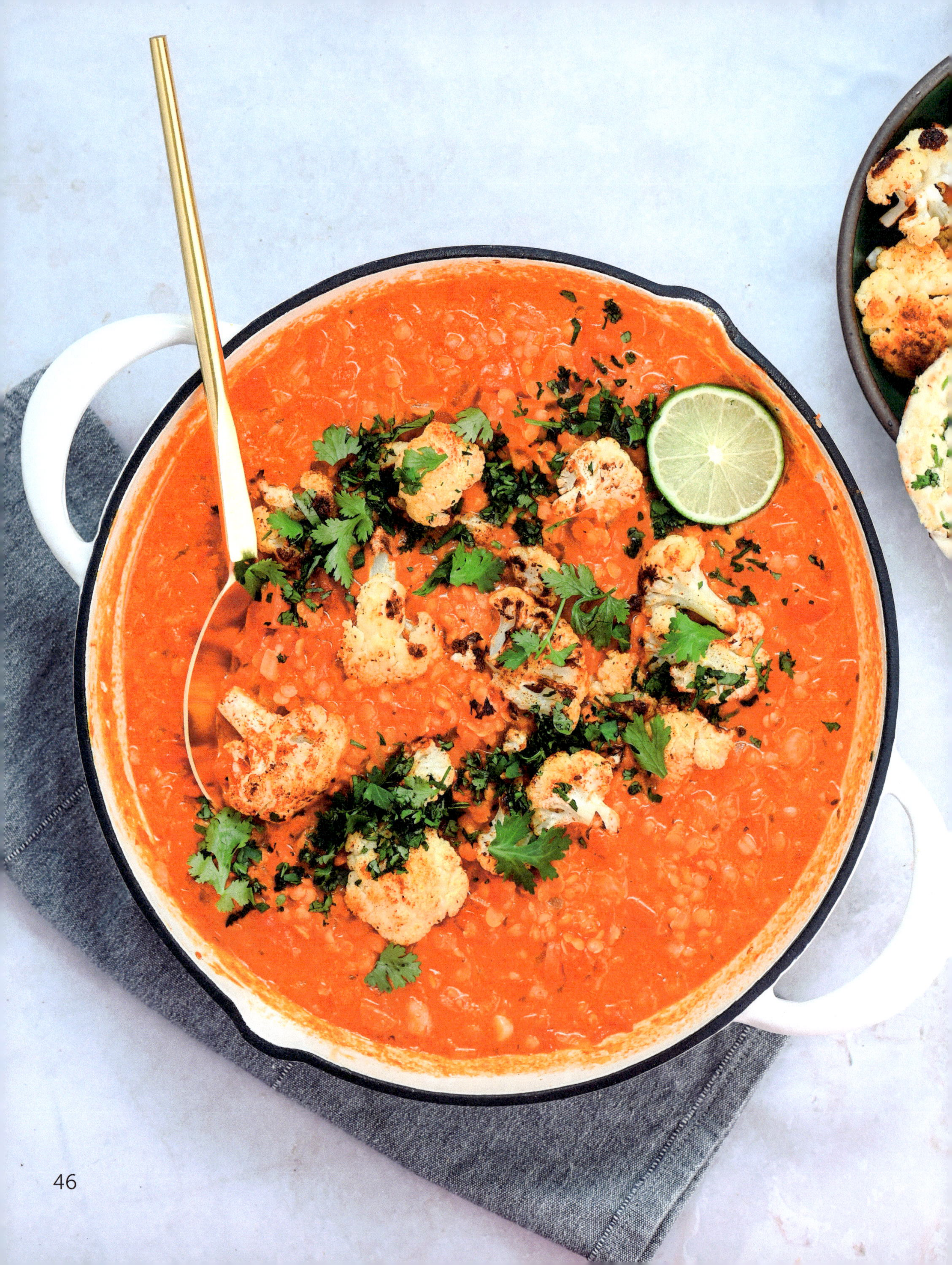

Red Lentil Curry with Spiced Cauliflower

45 MINUTES • 4-6 SERVINGS

This lentil curry is a warming, nourishing fusion of flavors. It's gently spicy from gochujang, which is a fermented Korean red pepper paste. If needed, sambal oelek or sriracha can be used in place of gochujang, while ½ teaspoon ground cumin can be used in place of cumin seeds and added at step 4 (though I recommend sticking to cumin seeds, as they are incredibly flavorful). I use my 12-inch braising pan for this recipe, but any large, tall-walled skillet works.

SPICED CAULIFLOWER

- 1 medium head (about 1 ½ pounds) cauliflower, cut into florets
- 1 tablespoon canola oil
- ½ teaspoon garam masala
- ¼ teaspoon ground cumin
- ¼ teaspoon kosher salt

LENTIL CURRY

- 2 tablespoons canola oil
- 2 cups diced Roma tomatoes (about 5 tomatoes)
- 2 cups diced sweet yellow onion (about 1 medium onion)
- ½ cup diced carrot (2 large carrots)
- 1 tablespoon minced garlic (4 to 5 cloves)
- 2 teaspoons grated ginger (about 1 inch of ginger)
- 2 teaspoons whole cumin seeds
- ½ teaspoon kosher salt
- 2 tablespoons tomato paste
- 1 tablespoon gochujang
- 2 teaspoons garam masala
- ¼ teaspoon ground turmeric
- 1 (13.5-ounce) can coconut milk
- 1 ½ cups vegetable broth
- 1 cup dry red lentils, rinsed
- ¼ cup fresh chopped cilantro
- 2 tablespoons lime juice (about one small lime)
- Cooked basmati rice, naan or flatbread, and lime wedges, for serving

For the cauliflower

1. Preheat the oven to 425°F. In a large bowl, toss the cauliflower florets with the oil, garam masala, ground cumin, and salt. Transfer to a half sheet pan.

2. Roast at 425°F for 25 to 30 minutes, or until the florets are golden and tender.

For the curry

3. While the cauliflower roasts, heat a large, deep skillet over medium heat. Add the oil. Once hot, add the tomatoes, onion, carrots, garlic, ginger, whole cumin seeds, and salt.

4. Sauté until the onions are golden and the carrots are softened, about 8 to 10 minutes. Stir in the tomato paste, gochujang, garam masala, and turmeric. Cook an additional minute to toast the tomato paste, stirring frequently.

5. Transfer contents of the skillet to a blender along with the coconut milk and vegetable broth. Pulse until mostly broken down but with some texture retained. Transfer back to the hot skillet.

6. Bring to a simmer over medium-high heat. Stir in the lentils. Reduce to a gentle simmer over medium-low heat. Cover and simmer until the lentils are completely tender, about 8 to 10 minutes. Remove the lid and continue cooking on low until the cauliflower is ready.

7. Just before serving, stir in the cilantro and lime juice and top with the roasted cauliflower. Serve with basmati rice, naan, and lime wedges.

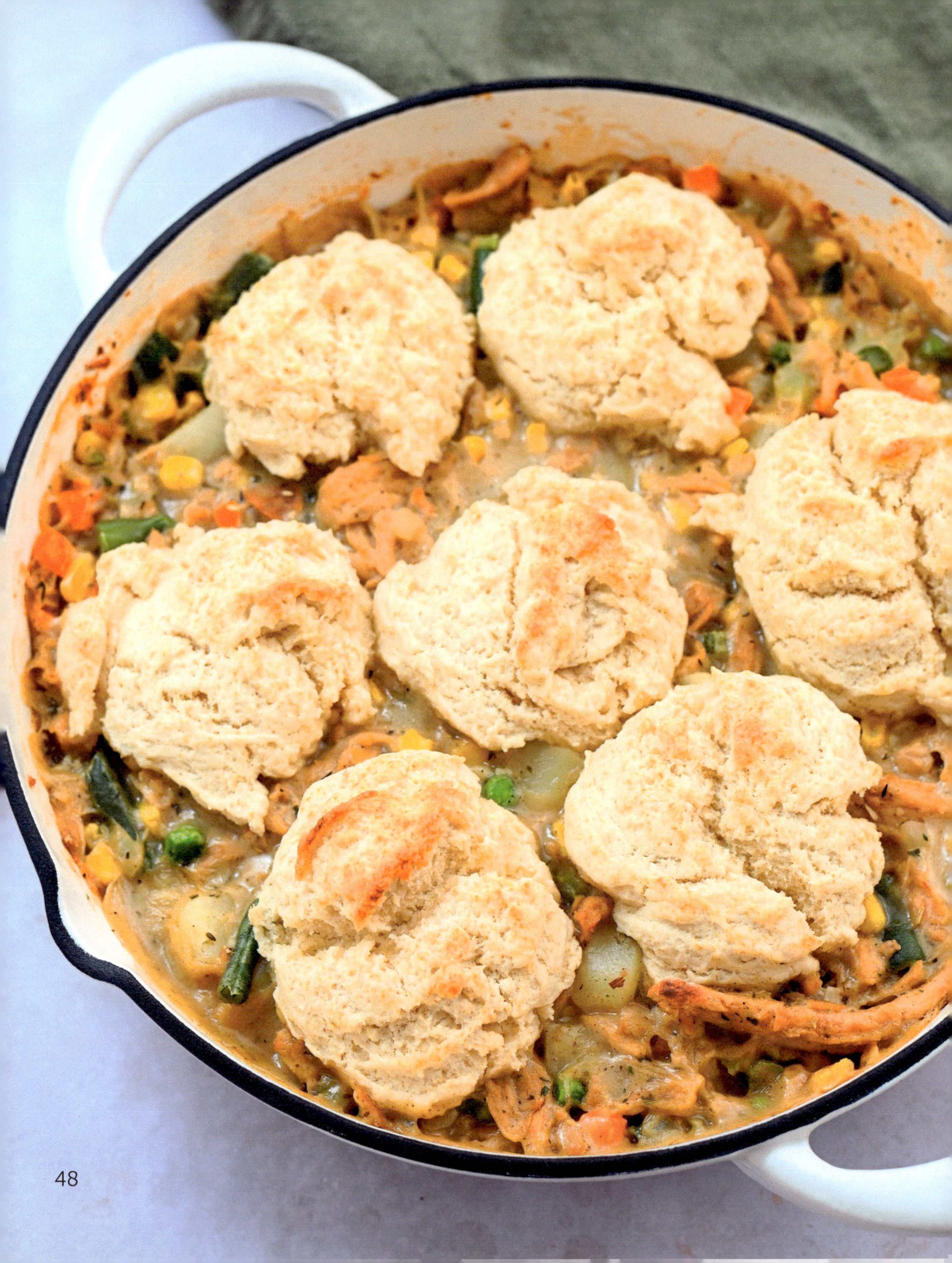

"Chicken" Pot Pie with Drop Biscuits

50 MINUTES • 4-6 SERVINGS

This recipe combines two dishes that I started making long before I started my food blog: pot pie and drop biscuits. If you find pie crust intimidating but still want to try your hand at making a pot pie, this is the meal for you. The biscuits are great as a standalone recipe; simply bake them at 425°F for 14 to 16 minutes.

POT PIE FILLING

1 large russet potato, peeled and diced into ½-inch cubes
1 teaspoon table salt, divided
3 cups vegetable broth, divided
1 ½ cups soy curls
1 (10-ounce) bag frozen mixed vegetables
2 tablespoons unsalted butter
1 medium sweet yellow onion, diced
2 ribs celery, diced
4 cloves garlic, minced
3 tablespoons all-purpose flour
1 cup 2% milk or milk of choice
2 tablespoons nutritional yeast
1 teaspoon each dried parsley, rosemary, thyme, and poultry seasoning
¼ teaspoon black pepper

BISCUITS

2 cups all-purpose flour
1 tablespoon baking powder
1 tablespoon granulated sugar
¼ teaspoon table salt
½ cup unsalted butter, melted
¾ cup whole milk

> **Note:** No oven-safe skillet? No problem! After cooking, transfer the filling to a baking dish, then top with the drop biscuit batter.
>
> See Amish-Style Chicken & Noodles (p. 75) for more information on soy curls.

For the filling

1. In a medium pot, cover the cubed potatoes with an inch of cold water. Add ½ teaspoon salt. Bring to a boil over high heat. Boil until tender, about 10 to 12 minutes. Drain and set aside.

2. Meanwhile, add 2 cups vegetable broth to a small pot. Bring to a boil. Once boiling, remove from the stove and stir in the soy curls. Let sit 5 minutes, then drain the soy curls and set aside.

3. Cook the mixed vegetables according to package instructions. Season with salt and pepper, to taste.

4. Heat a 12-inch oven-safe skillet over medium heat. Add the butter. Once melted, add diced onion, celery, and remaining ½ teaspoon salt. Sauté until the onions are softened, about 6 to 8 minutes. Stir in the soy curls and garlic. Continue cooking until the soy curls begin to brown, about 3 minutes.

5. Sprinkle in the flour. Toast for 2 minutes, stirring frequently. Using a whisk, slowly stir in the milk. Stir in the remaining 1 cup of vegetable broth, along with the nutritional yeast, parsley, rosemary, thyme, poultry seasoning, and black pepper. Stir in the cooked mixed vegetables and cooked potato.

6. Reduce heat to a gentle simmer over low heat. Simmer until thickened into a thin, gravy-like consistency, about 3 to 4 minutes. Cover and set aside.

Biscuits and Assembly

7. Preheat the oven to 425°F. In a large bowl, whisk together the flour, baking powder, sugar, and salt. Pour in the melted butter and milk. Stir until just combined. The batter should be thick but scoopable. Remove the lid from the pot pie filling. Drop 7 large mounds of batter (roughly ¼ cup each) onto the filling.

8. Bake at 425°F on the middle oven rack for 15 to 18 minutes, or until the filling is bubbling and the biscuit tops are golden. Let rest for 5 minutes before serving.

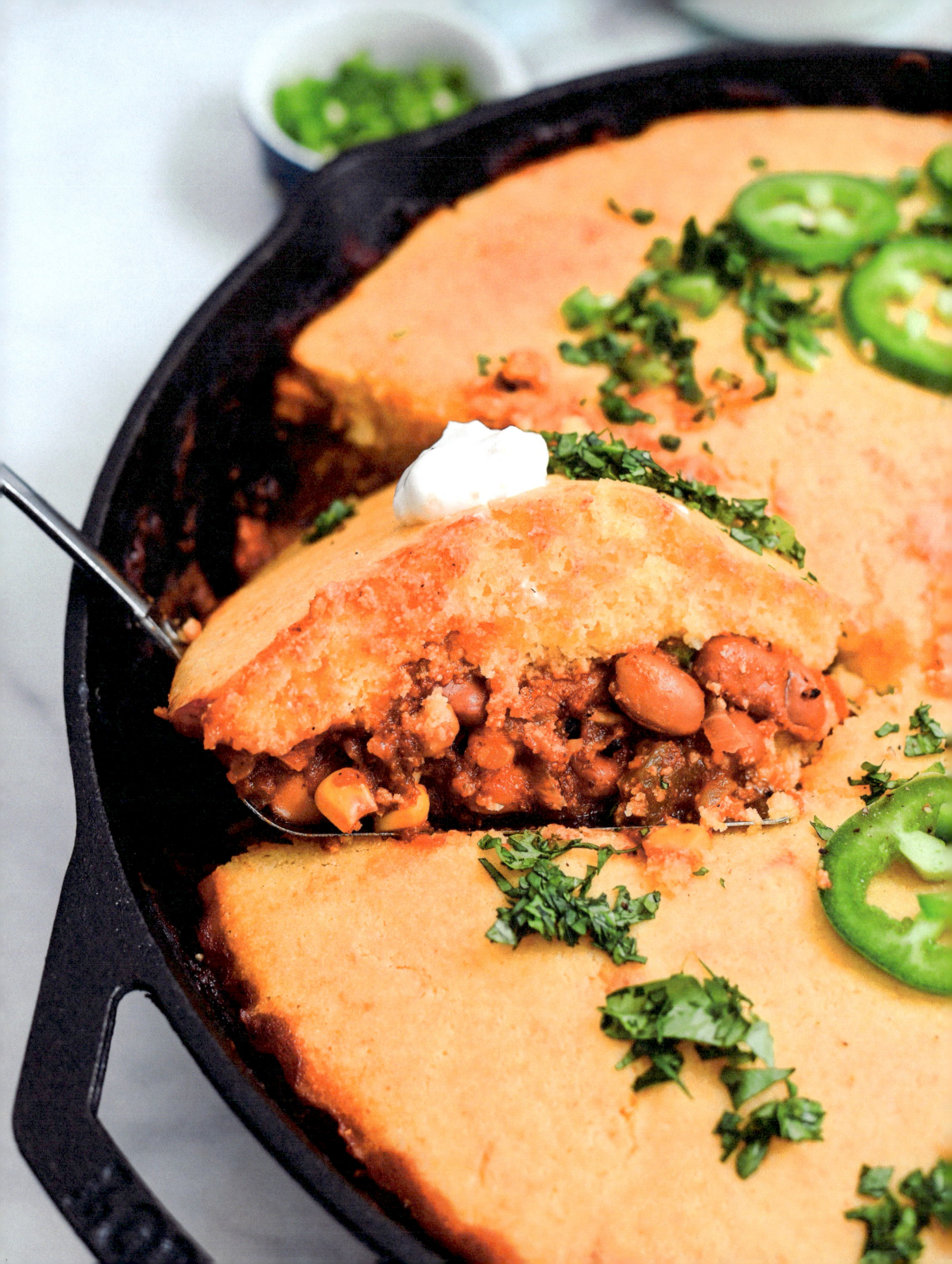

Chili Cornbread Skillet

50 MINUTES • 6 SERVINGS

Chili is incomplete without cornbread, so why not just serve the two together? This is basically like a chili recipe without all of the broth, which results in concentrated chili flavor. The cornbread is fantastic as a standalone recipe; simply bake it in a cast iron skillet or similarly sized baking dish at 400°F for 18 to 20 minutes.

CHILI
1 tablespoon canola oil
1 medium red onion, diced
1 medium green bell pepper, diced
½ teaspoon kosher salt
2 tablespoons tomato paste
3 cloves garlic, minced
2 teaspoons chili powder
1 teaspoon ground cumin
½ teaspoon dried oregano
½ teaspoon smoked paprika
1 (28-ounce) can crushed fire-roasted tomatoes
1 (15-ounce) can pinto beans, drained and rinsed
1 (15-ounce) can light red kidney beans, drained and rinsed
1 (15-ounce) sweet golden corn kernels, drained and rinsed

CORNBREAD
1 cup 2% milk
1 tablespoon apple cider vinegar
1 large egg
½ cup canola oil
1 cup fine cornmeal
1 cup all-purpose flour
¼ cup granulated sugar
2 teaspoons baking powder
½ teaspoon baking soda
½ teaspoon table salt
¾ to 1 cup (3 to 4 ounces) shredded sharp cheddar cheese
Fresh chopped cilantro, Jalapeño, and sour cream, for serving

1. In a 12-inch cast iron skillet or other oven-safe skillet, heat canola oil over medium heat. Once hot, add onions, bell peppers, and salt. Sauté until softened and golden, 6 to 8 minutes. Add the tomato paste and garlic. Sauté another 2 to 3 minutes or until the garlic is aromatic, stirring frequently to avoid burning.

2. Add in the chili powder, cumin, oregano, and smoked paprika. Sauté for 30 seconds, stirring continuously.

3. Add the crushed tomatoes, drained pinto and kidney beans, and corn. Reduce heat to low and let simmer while assembling the cornbread.

4. Preheat the oven to 400°F. To make the cornbread, mix together the milk and vinegar in a medium bowl. Leave for 10 minutes, or until thickened. Whisk in the egg and canola oil.

5. In a medium mixing bowl, whisk together the cornmeal, flour, sugar, baking powder, baking soda, and salt. Pour in the wet ingredients, folding with a spatula until just combined. Fold in the cheese.

6. Flatten the chili mixture in the skillet. Pour the cornbread batter on top. Bake at 400°F for 18 to 20 minutes, or until the cornbread is golden-brown and crackled on top. If browning too quickly, cover with foil. Remove from the oven and garnish with chopped cilantro, jalapeño, and dollops of sour cream.

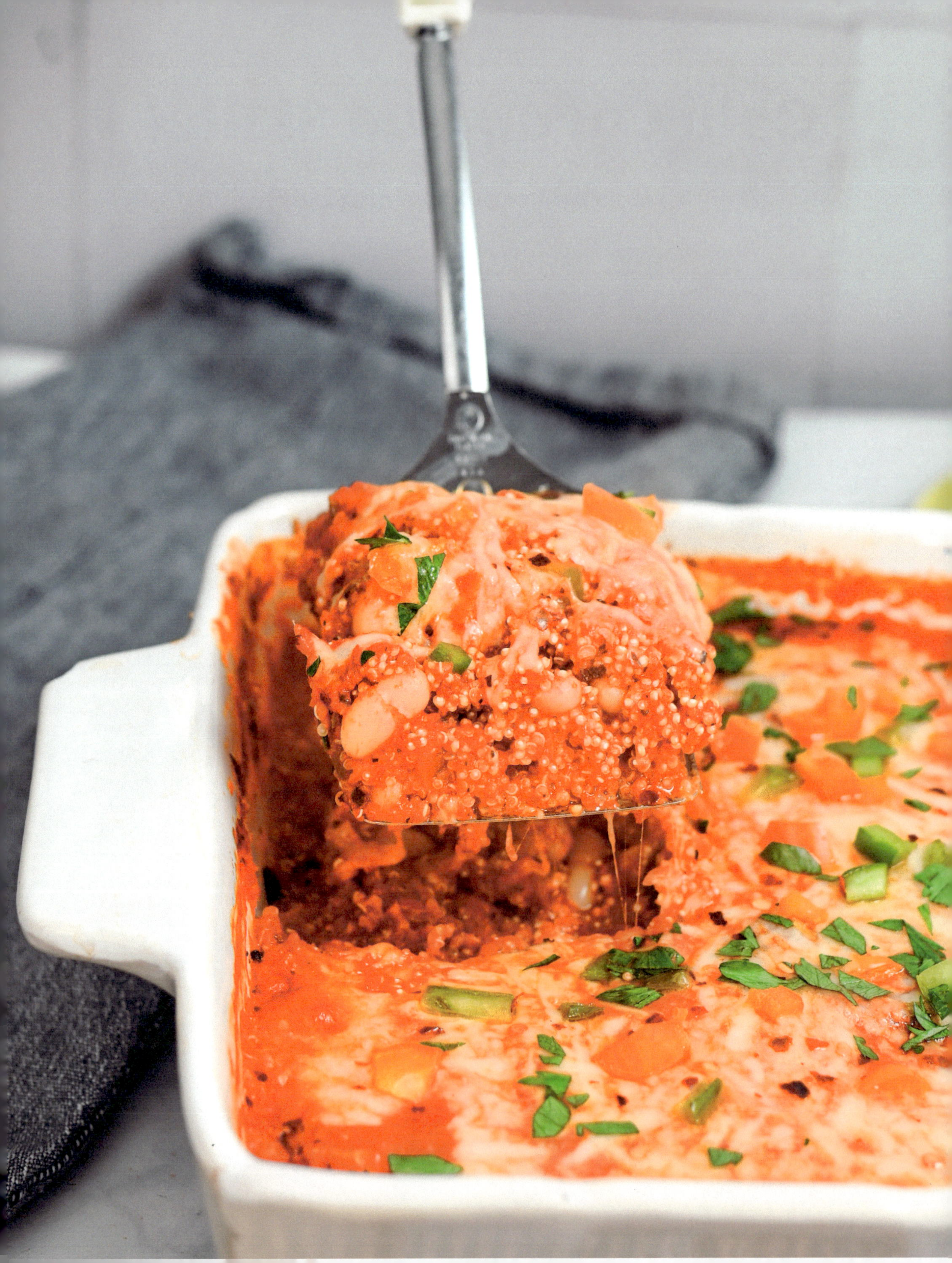

Quinoa Pizza Bake

1 HOUR • 4 SERVINGS

If five years of running a vegetarian food blog has taught me anything, it's that people like easy meals with minimal prep. That's basically the definition of a "dump and bake" casserole. I'm sure that someone bought this cookbook just with the hope that I would share a new dump and bake recipe. Well, here you go! This is like if pizza and quinoa had a baby that turned into a casserole.

1 (15-ounce) can great northern beans, drained and rinsed
1 (24-ounce) jar marinara sauce
1 cup vegetable broth
1 teaspoon dried basil
1 teaspoon dried oregano
½ teaspoon each garlic powder, onion powder, kosher salt, red pepper flakes (optional)
¼ teaspoon black pepper
1 medium green bell pepper
1 large red bell pepper
1 cup dry quinoa
1 ½ cups (6 ounces) shredded mozzarella
Fresh basil, for topping

1. Preheat the oven to 375°F. In a medium pot, stir together the beans, marinara sauce, vegetable broth, basil, oregano, garlic powder, onion powder, salt, optional red pepper flakes, and black pepper. Bring to a rapid simmer over medium-high heat.

2. While waiting for the sauce to simmer, dice the peppers. Rinse the quinoa in a fine mesh sieve. Add the quinoa and peppers to an 8x8 inch or similarly sized baking dish. Pour in the simmering sauce, stirring to combine with the quinoa.

3. Cover tightly with foil or an upside down baking sheet. Bake at 375°F for 25 minutes. Remove from the oven and stir the quinoa. If the quinoa is not mostly cooked through, cover with foil and cook for an additional 5 minutes. Otherwise, top with the shredded cheese. Return to the oven for 15 to 20 minutes, or until the cheese is melted, bubbly, and golden.

4. Remove from the oven. Let cool for 5 minutes before slicing. Serve topped with fresh basil.

> **Note:** This recipe is just begging for you to get creative and push the definition of pizza to it's very limits! Add veggie sausage, black olives, veggie pepperoni, banana peppers, or whatever you want to make this recipe your own.

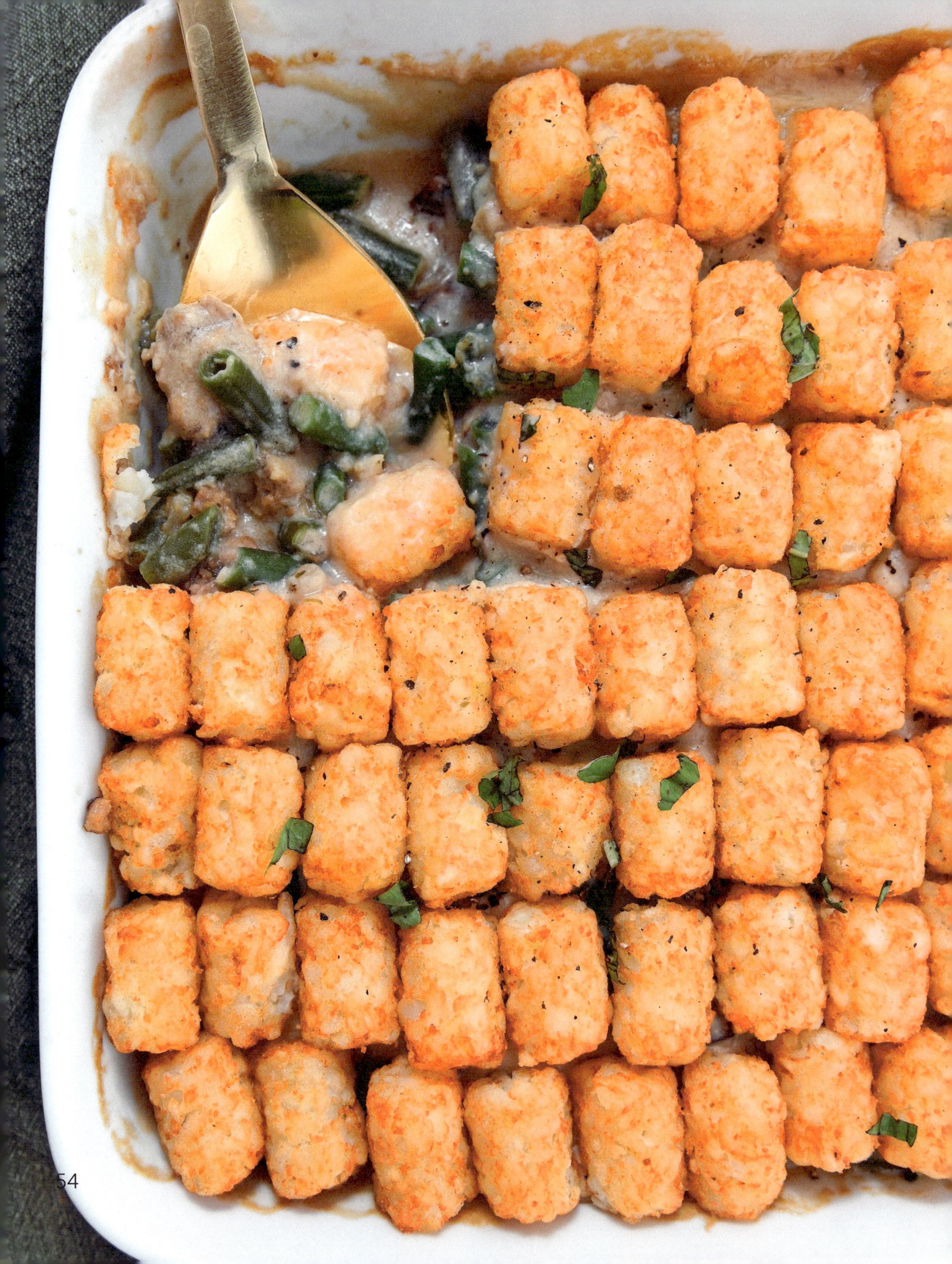

Vegan Tater Tot Green Bean Casserole

1 HOUR • 5 SERVINGS

I can't tell you how many times my mom served this recipe when I was a kid. It's about as Midwestern as it gets, with a creamy mushroom base, ground "beef," frozen green beans, and crispy-golden tater tots on top. These kinds of casseroles were created with convenience in mind. While my vegan version takes a bit more time than the version that I grew up eating, thanks to a homemade dairy-free sauce, it's just as comforting and possibly even more delicious than the original (sorry, mom).

1 tablespoon extra virgin olive oil
1 cup diced yellow onion (about ½ medium onion)
8 ounces baby bella mushrooms, roughly chopped
¼ teaspoon kosher salt
8 ounces thawed meatless ground beef, such as Impossible or Beyond brands
4 cloves garlic, minced
1 teaspoon dried thyme
¼ teaspoon black pepper
¼ cup vegan butter
¼ cup all-purpose flour
3 cups unsweetened non-dairy milk (soy or oat milk preferred)
1 tablespoon soy sauce
1 (12-ounce) bag frozen cut green beans
Salt and pepper, to taste
1 (24-ounce) bag frozen tater tots

Note: This recipe works with fresh green beans, but they should be steamed to al-dente before adding to the casserole. This recipe also works with dairy ingredients.

1. Preheat the oven 375°F. Coat an 8x8 inch or similarly sized casserole dish with non-stick cooking spray.

2. Heat a medium skillet over medium heat. Drizzle with olive oil. Once hot, add the diced onion, mushrooms, and salt. Sauté for 6 to 8 minutes, or until the onions are softened.

3. Add in the "meat," minced garlic, thyme, and black pepper. Use a spatula to break up the meat. Cook until browned, stirring as needed.

4. Remove the cooked mushrooms and meat from the pan and set aside. To the now empty pan (it does not need to be cleaned between steps), add ¼ cup vegan butter. Once melted, sprinkle in ¼ cup flour. Whisk the butter and flour together. Cook for 2 to 3 minutes, stirring frequently, until the flour is lightly golden.

5. Slowly whisk in the milk ½ cup at a time. Bring the sauce to a rapid simmer over medium-high heat, then reduce to a gentle simmer over medium-low heat. Stir in the soy sauce. Simmer until the sauce is thick enough to coat the back of a spoon without sliding off, about 6 to 8 minutes.

6. Add the mushroom mixture to the lightly oiled baking dish. Top with the frozen green beans. Season with salt and black pepper, to taste. Pour the sauce over the green beans. Cover with an even layer of frozen tater tots.

7. Bake uncovered on the middle oven rack for 30 minutes, or until the tater tots are golden brown and the casserole is bubbling. Remove from the oven and let sit for 10 minutes before serving.

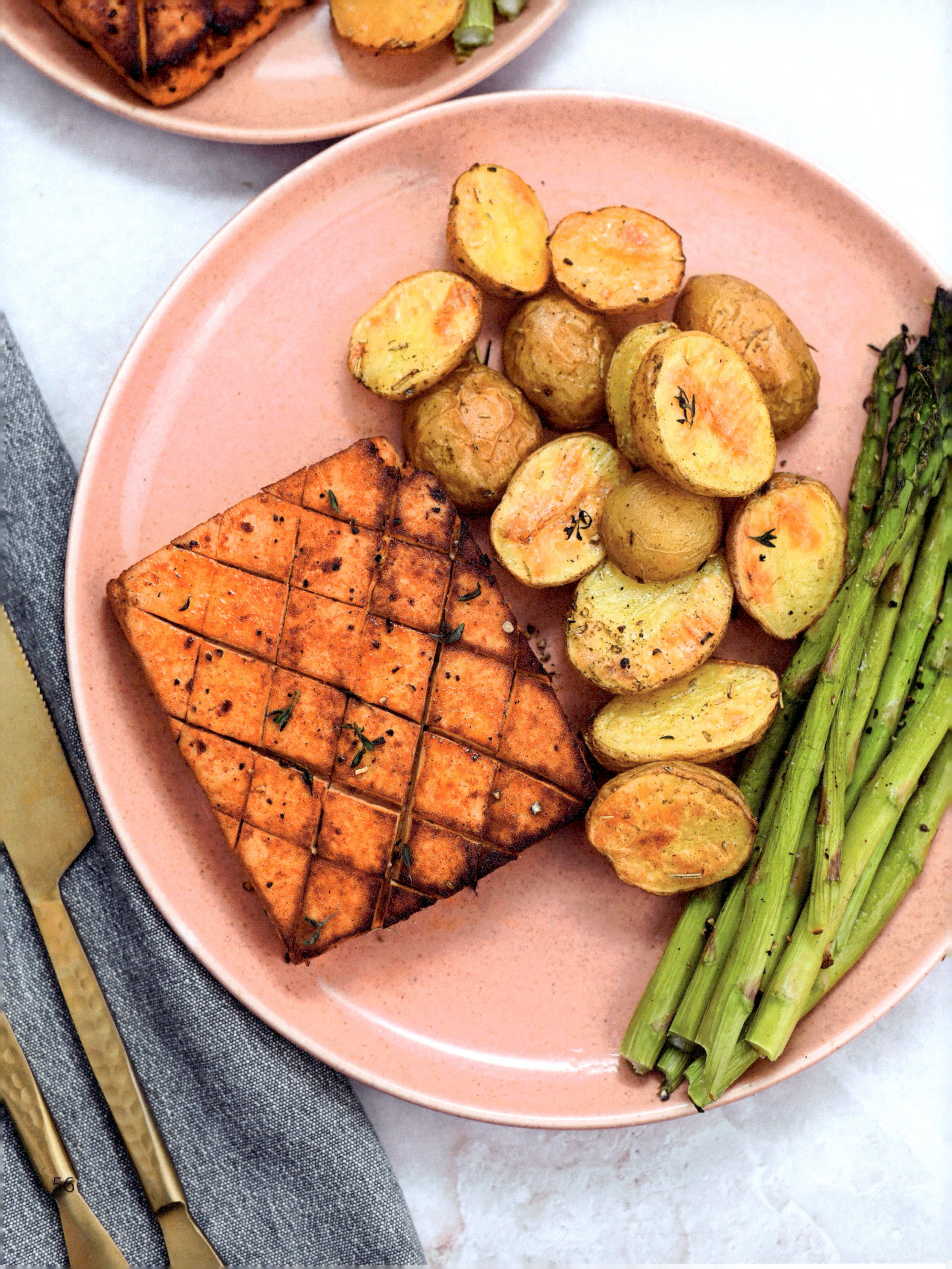

Tofu Steak Dinner

1 HOUR (PLUS 30 MINUTE MARINADE TIME) • 4 SERVINGS

Growing up, I loved having dinner at a friend's house where the meals frequently looked like the classic meat and potatoes supper. Of course, their "steak" was not tofu, but actual meat. I wanted to recreate the classic American meat and potatoes meal with my own vegetarianized rendition, featuring a savory, gently smoky, and beyond flavorful seared slab of tofu. It's paired with golden roasted baby potatoes and vegetables for a steakhouse feel.

TOFU

2 (14-ounce) blocks extra-firm tofu
¾ cup vegetable broth
¼ cup soy sauce
1 tablespoon tomato paste
2 teaspoons canola oil, plus more for sautéing
1 teaspoon smoked paprika
½ teaspoon each garlic powder, onion powder, black pepper, granulated sugar

POTATOES AND ASPARAGUS

1 ½ pounds baby potatoes
2 tablespoons canola oil, divided
½ teaspoon kosher salt, divided
½ teaspoon dried rosemary
½ teaspoon dried thyme
1 bunch asparagus, woody ends removed
1 medium lemon

> **Note:** For a foolproof tofu slicing method, place chopsticks on either side of the block of tofu. This will prevent the knife from accidentally slicing through the entire tofu block. The easiest way to slice the tofu without chopsticks is to gently rock the knife back and forth until it just presses into the tofu.

1. Press the blocks of tofu for at least 10 minutes. Transfer to a cutting board. Slice each block in half lengthways to make two thinner rectangles out of each block, four pieces total. Using a sharp knife, make a diagonal grid pattern on the tofu by gently pressing the knife just ¼ inch into the tofu. Do not slice all the way through.

2. In a shallow dish, whisk together the vegetable broth, soy sauce, tomato paste, canola oil, smoked paprika, garlic powder, onion powder, black pepper, and sugar. Gently transfer the scored tofu to the dish. Marinate at least 30 minutes and up to overnight. If the tofu isn't completely covered by the marinade, gently flip it halfway through marinating.

3. Preheat the oven to 400°F. Slice the baby potatoes in half. In a large bowl, toss the potatoes with 1 tablespoon oil, ¼ teaspoon salt, rosemary, and thyme. Arrange the potatoes cut-side down on a large baking sheet lined with parchment paper. Clear space for the four tofu pieces. Place the tofu scored-side up. Bake at 400°F for 25 minutes, then remove from the oven.

4. Meanwhile, toss the asparagus with 1 tablespoon oil and ¼ teaspoon salt. After the tofu and potatoes have cooked for 25 minutes, remove the tofu from the pan and replace it with the asparagus. Return to the oven for 20 more minutes, or until the potatoes are tender.

5. While the vegetables roast, heat a large skillet over medium heat. Coat with a thin layer of oil. Once hot, add the baked tofu scored-side down. Pan fry for 6 to 8 minutes, or until the scored side is golden brown. Carefully flip the tofu to sear the reverse side for 6 to 8 minutes.

6. The tofu, potatoes, and asparagus should all finish at about the same time. Squeeze the asparagus and potatoes with juice from the lemon just before serving.

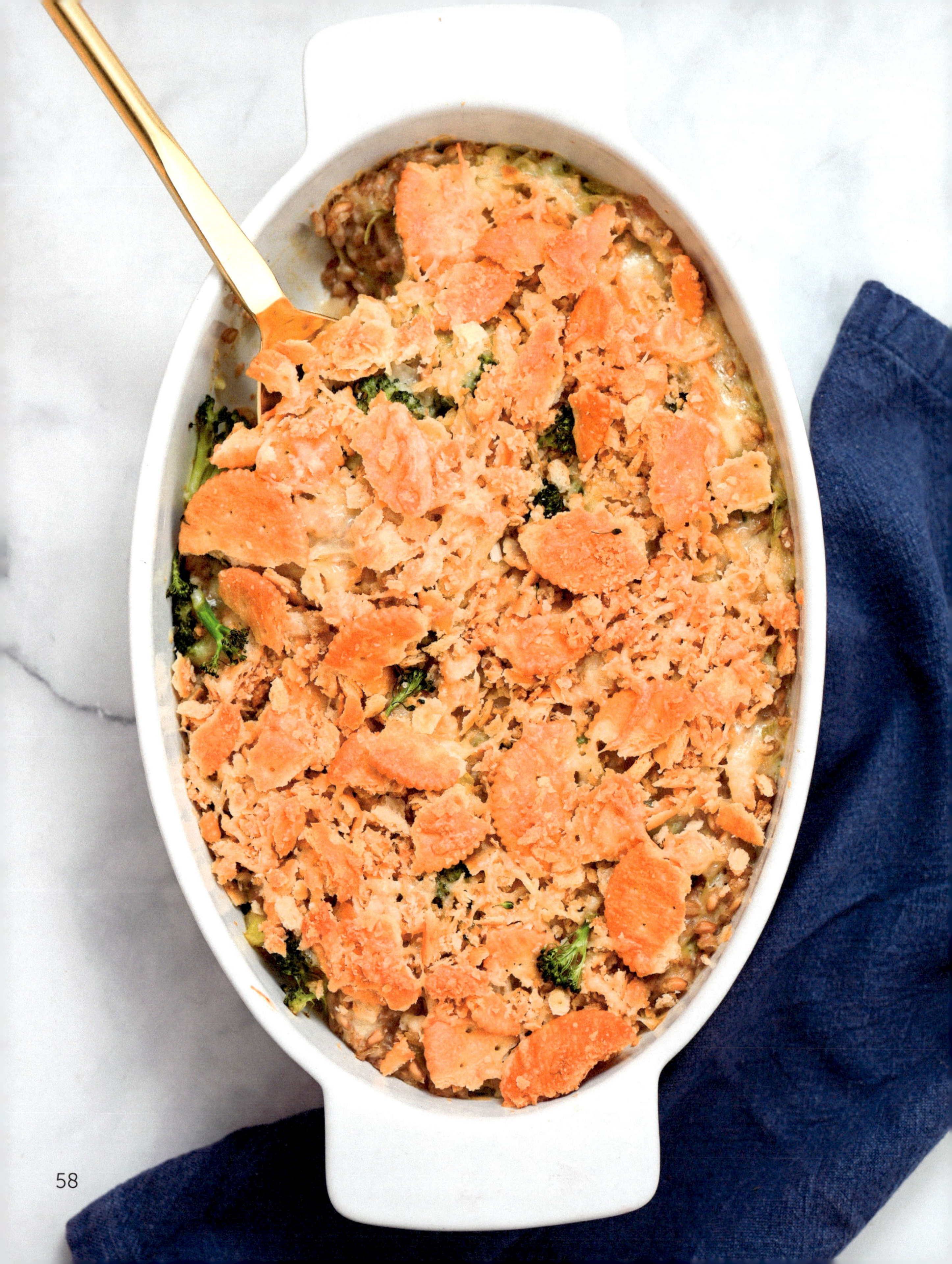

Broccoli Farro Casserole

1 HOUR • 4-6 SERVINGS

Inspired by broccoli and rice casserole, this is an old-fashioned-style casserole made new with chewy farro and cannellini beans. The creamy sauce is infused with two types of mustard, which adds a subtle complexity to an otherwise classic comfort food dish.

1 cup pearled farro
2 ½ cups vegetable broth
1 large head broccoli, cut into small florets
2 tablespoons unsalted butter
2 cups thinly sliced leeks (about 2 large leeks)
4 cloves garlic, minced
½ teaspoon kosher salt, divided
2 tablespoons all-purpose flour
1 ½ cups 2% milk
1 teaspoon Dijon mustard
¾ teaspoon dry ground mustard
½ teaspoon onion powder
¼ teaspoon garlic powder
⅛ teaspoon black pepper
⅛ teaspoon white pepper
1 (15-ounce) can cannellini beans, drained and rinsed
6 ounce block of sharp white cheddar, shredded
2 cups butter crackers (such as Ritz)
3 tablespoons melted unsalted butter

Note: Farro comes pearled and whole. Pearled farro cooks in 15 to 20 minutes, while whole farro takes upwards of 45 minutes. Trader Joe's has a 10 minute farro that I love.

1. Add the farro and vegetable broth to a medium pot. Bring to a boil over high heat, then reduce to a gentle simmer and cover. Cook until the farro is tender but still chewy, about 20 minutes. Drain any excess liquid.

2. Meanwhile, place broccoli florets in a steamer basket over simmering water. Sprinkle with salt, to taste. Cover and steam until tender and easy to pierce with a fork, about 10 to 12 minutes.

3. Preheat the oven to 350°F.

4. While the farro and broccoli cook, heat a large skillet over medium heat. Add the butter. Once melted, add sliced leeks, garlic, and ¼ teaspoon salt. Sauté until the leeks are softened and starting to turn golden, about 8 to 10 minutes.

5. Sprinkle in the flour. Toast, stirring frequently, for 2 minutes. Reduce heat to medium-low. Slowly whisk in the milk until it is all combined. Add the Dijon mustard, ground mustard, onion powder, garlic powder, black pepper, and white pepper. The sauce should be gently bubbling. Continue cooking until thickened into a thin gravy-like consistency.

6. Stir the farro, half of the broccoli, the beans, and 4 ounces of the shredded cheese into the sauce. Transfer to a lightly greased 8x11 inch or similarly sized baking dish. Top with the remaining broccoli.

7. Add crackers to a Ziploc bag or bowl. Crush with the palm of your hand until broken down into smaller pieces, but not crumbs. Toss the crackers with the melted butter and the remaining 2 ounces of shredded cheese in the bag or in a bowl. Sprinkle on top of the casserole.

8. Bake at 350°F for 15 to 20 minutes, or until the casserole is bubbling and the topping is golden. Let rest for 5 minutes before slicing and serving.

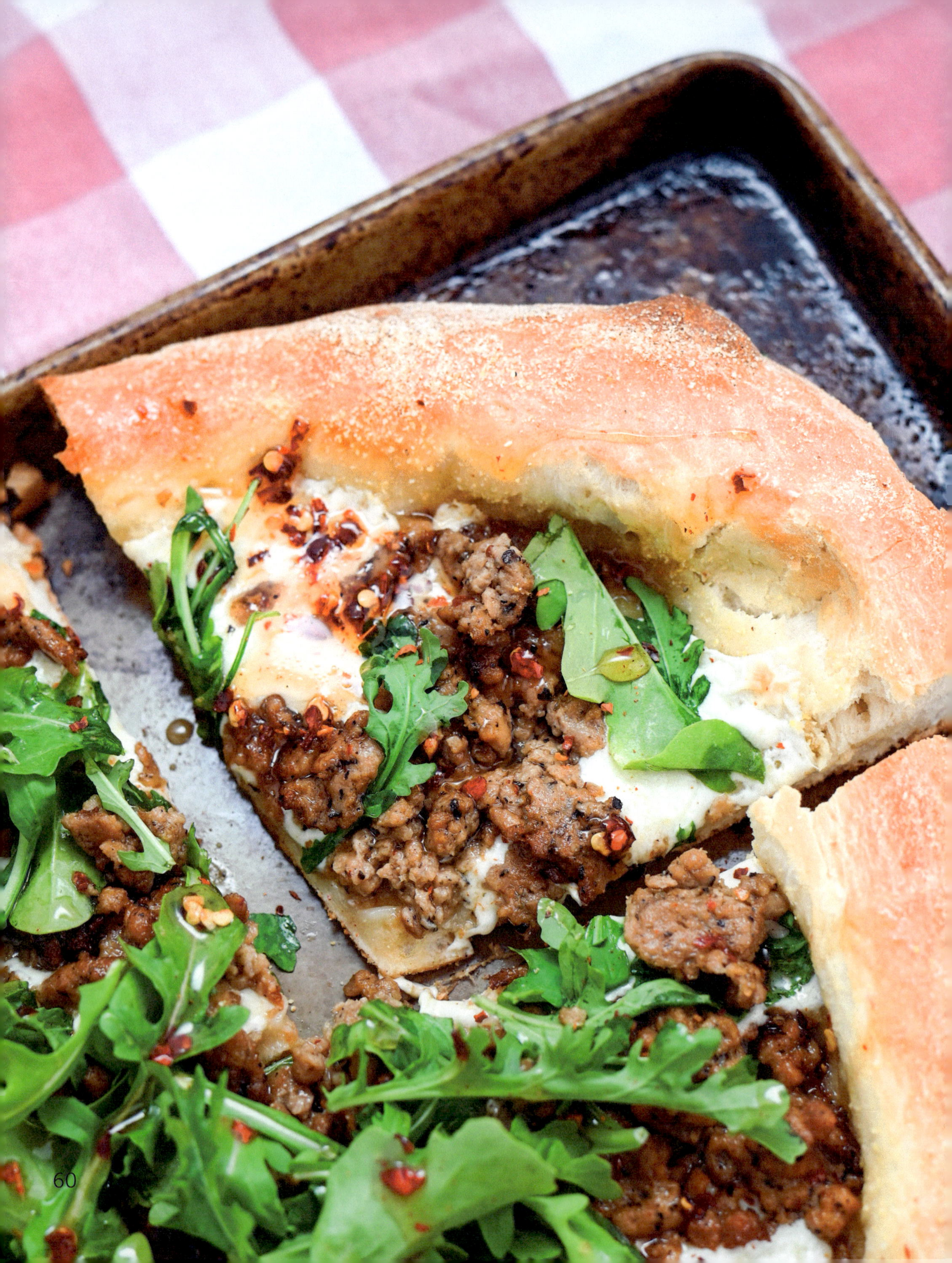

Spicy "Sausage" Pizza with Arugula & Hot Honey

1 HOUR • 4 SERVINGS

Store-bought pizza dough turns this into a surprisingly easy recipe, while sliced mozzarella makes a cheesy base in lieu of traditional pizza sauce. I recommend Impossible or Beyond brand for spicy "sausage." Double or even triple the hot honey recipe to keep extra on hand for more sweet and spicy creations.

- 1 pound store-bought pizza dough
- 1 (14-ounce) package thawed meatless spicy ground sausage (I recommend either Impossible or Beyond brand)
- ¼ cup honey
- 1 ½ teaspoons red pepper flakes
- 1 teaspoon hot sauce (optional; I prefer Cholula)
- 1 to 2 tablespoons all-purpose flour, as needed
- 2 teaspoons extra virgin olive oil, more as needed
- ¼ teaspoon garlic salt
- 8 ounces fresh mozzarella, thinly sliced
- 3 handfuls arugula

1. Remove pizza dough from the fridge and allow it to reach room temperature on the counter, about 30 minutes.

2. Meanwhile, in a medium skillet over medium heat, brown the sausage until cooked throughout, about 4 to 6 minutes. Remove from heat and set aside.

3. Make the hot honey by combining the honey and red pepper flakes in a small sauce pot over medium heat. Once bubbling at the edges, remove the pot from the heat. Let sit 5 minutes, then stir in the optional hot sauce. For less spice, run hot honey through a strainer to separate the red pepper flakes and honey.

4. Preheat oven to 450°F. If using a pizza stone, place it in the oven. Otherwise, line a baking sheet with parchment paper.

5. Sprinkle a large cutting board or a clean surface with a fine layer of flour, about 1 to 2 tablespoons. Roll out the pizza dough, leaving a lip at the edges for the crust. Transfer to a baking sheet lined with parchment paper, if using. Brush the entire pizza with a thin layer of olive oil. Season the crust with garlic salt. Using a fork, gently poke the dough throughout to keep the pizza from inflating in the oven.

6. Top with sliced mozzarella, then the crumbled sausage. If using a pizza stone, transfer the pizza to it now. Transfer pizza to the oven to bake at 450°F for 15 to 17 minutes, until the sliced mozzarella is bubbly and the pizza crust is golden.

7. Drizzle hot honey over the pizza, to taste. Top with arugula. Slice and serve.

Note: I recommend using a pre-heated pizza stone if you have one. For those that don't have a pizza stone, the instructions include a sheet pan option.

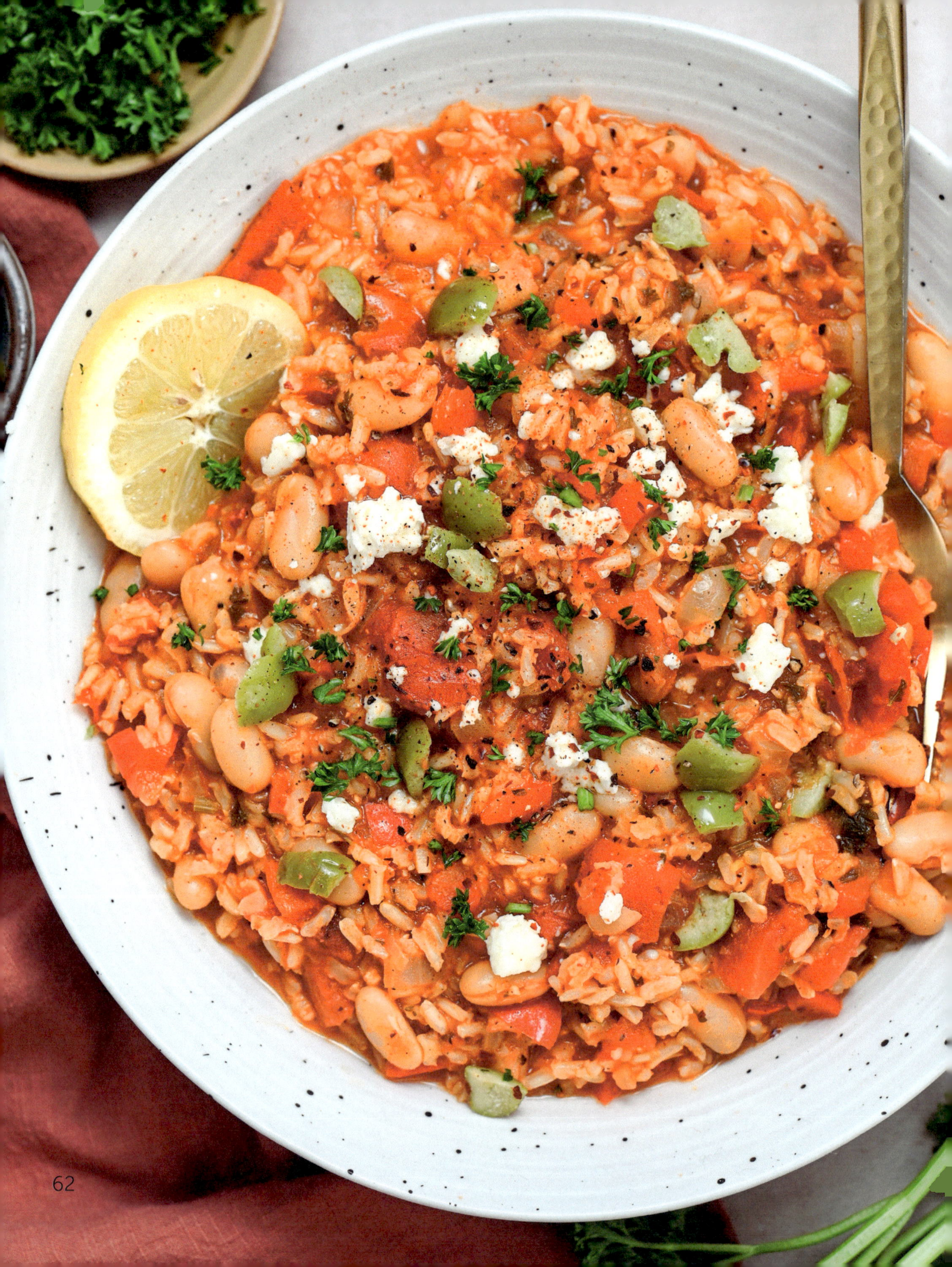

Mediterranean-Inspired One Pot Rice & Beans

1 HOUR 10 MINUTES • 4-6 SERVINGS

This is a big, nutritious pot of rice and beans tossed with salty feta and olives, gently spicy harissa, and a touch of warmth from cinnamon. One recipe tester served it with raisins, diced dried apricots, and yogurt, which I imagine takes the dish to a whole other level.

- 2 tablespoons extra virgin olive oil
- 2 cups diced sweet yellow onion (about 1 large onion)
- 1 medium red bell pepper, diced
- 1 teaspoon kosher salt
- 5 cloves garlic, minced
- 2 teaspoons grated ginger (about 1 inch of fresh ginger)
- 2 tablespoons harissa
- 2 tablespoons tomato paste
- 1 teaspoon ground cumin
- 1 teaspoon paprika
- 3 cups vegetable broth
- 1 (14.5-ounce) can diced fire-roasted tomatoes
- ¼ cup chopped fresh parsley, plus more for serving
- ½ teaspoon garlic powder
- ½ teaspoon onion powder
- ¼ teaspoon black pepper
- Pinch of cinnamon
- 1 ½ cups long-grain brown rice, rinsed well
- 1 (15-ounce) can cannellini beans, drained and rinsed
- ½ cup (2 ounces) crumbled feta cheese
- ½ cup chopped Castelvetrano olives (optional)
- 1 lemon, sliced into wedges

1. Heat a 4-quart Dutch oven or pot over medium heat. Drizzle with olive oil. Once hot, add the onion, bell pepper, and salt. Sauté until the onions are softened and golden, about 8 to 10 minutes.

2. Stir in the minced garlic, grated ginger, harissa, tomato paste, cumin, and paprika. Cook until the garlic is golden and aromatic, stirring frequently, about 2 to 3 minutes.

3. Deglaze the pot with a splash of vegetable broth, stirring to remove any stuck-on bits. Add in the remaining vegetable broth, fire-roasted tomatoes with juices, parsley, garlic powder, onion powder, black pepper, and pinch of cinnamon.

4. Bring to a rapid simmer over medium-high heat. Stir in the brown rice and beans. Reduce to a very gentle simmer over low heat. Cover tightly with a lid and simmer until the broth is completely absorbed, about 45 minutes.

5. Stir the rice and test for doneness. If it is still chewy, return the lid and cook an additional 5 minutes. Add additional broth as needed. When the rice is completely cooked through, stir in the feta cheese and olives. Serve garnished with parsley and lemon wedges.

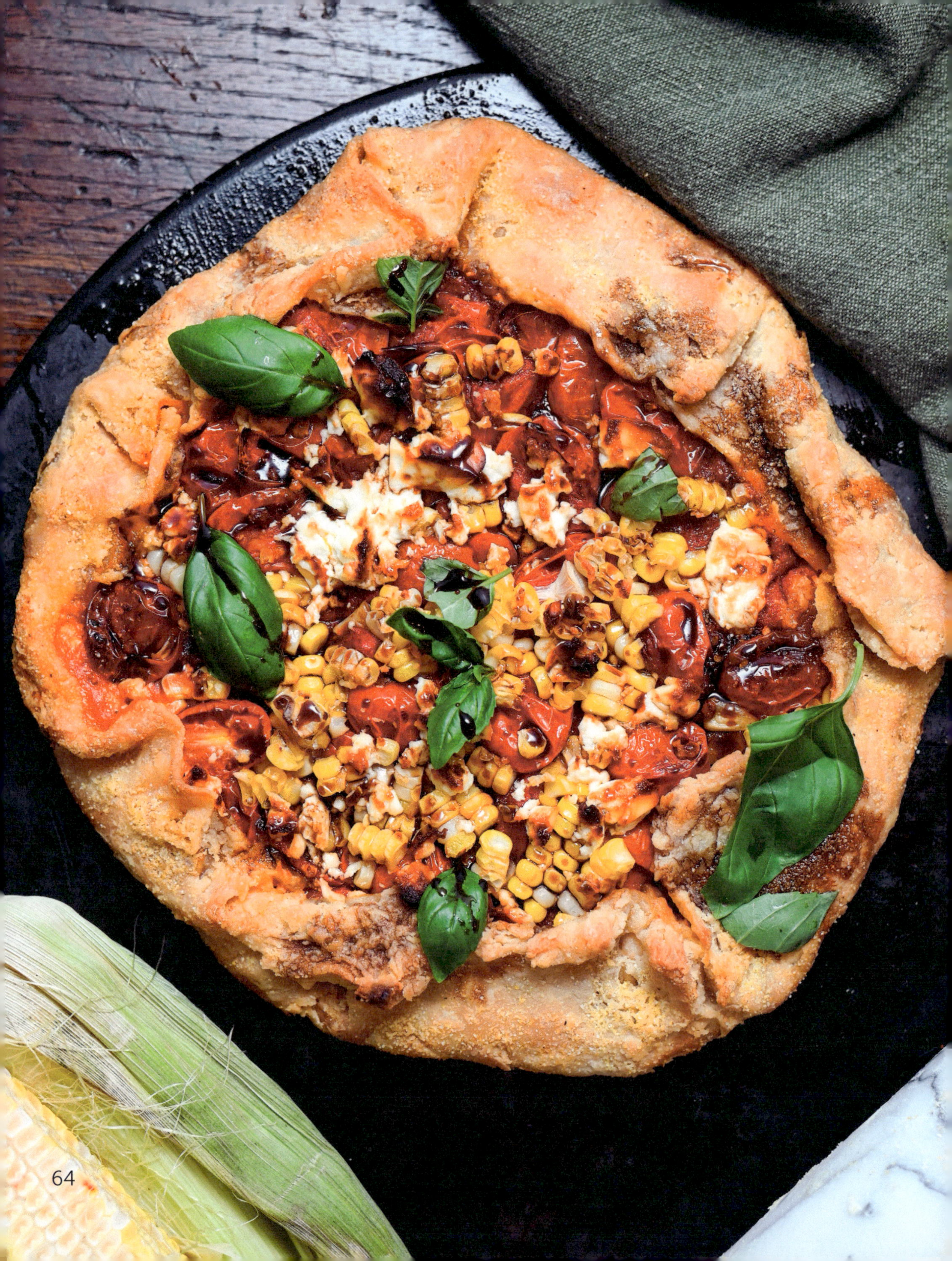

Summer Cherry Tomato and Corn Galette

1 HOUR 10 MINUTES • 2 TO 3 SERVINGS

This is summer all wrapped up in a flaky, buttery crust. Each bite is dappled with acidic tomatoes and sweet corn, which is balanced out by the sweet and tangy balsamic reduction. For a quicker option, store-bought balsamic reduction works just fine in place of homemade.

GALETTE CRUST

1 ½ cups all-purpose flour
½ teaspoon table salt
½ cup cold unsalted butter, diced into cubes
6 to 8 tablespoons ice cold water
4 tablespoons coarse cornmeal, divided

ASSEMBLY

2 tablespoons extra virgin olive oil
1 pound cherry tomatoes (grape tomatoes also work)
6 cloves garlic, quartered
½ cup + 1 tablespoon balsamic vinegar, divided
¼ teaspoon kosher salt
1 cup fresh corn kernels (about 2 large ears of sweet corn)
½ cup (2 ounces) crumbled feta
A few leaves of fresh basil, chiffonade (sliced thinly)

> **Notes:** Cornmeal is used to add crunch and texture, but if you don't have any on hand flour will work.
>
> The easiest way to make ice cold water is by measuring from a bowl filled with both ice cubes and water.
>
> Canned or frozen corn work if fresh corn isn't in season. Thaw frozen corn and drain fresh corn before using.

1. To make the galette crust, mix together the flour and salt in a medium mixing bowl. Using a pastry cutter or fork, mix the butter into the flour until crumbly. Add the ice cold water one tablespoon at a time, stirring with a spoon to make a ball of dough. It will be a little crumbly. Wrap in plastic wrap or foil and place in the fridge to chill for 30 minutes.

2. Heat a medium skillet over medium heat. Drizzle with olive oil. Once hot, add the cherry tomatoes, garlic, 1 tablespoon balsamic vinegar, and salt. Cook until the cherry tomatoes begin to shrivel, 6 to 8 minutes. Carefully press with a potato masher to fully burst the cherry tomatoes. Turn off the heat and set aside.

3. Preheat the oven to 425°F. Line a sheet pan with parchment paper. After 30 minutes of chilling, remove the dough from the fridge. Sprinkle a clean surface with 2 tablespoons of cornmeal. Use a rolling pin or jar to roll the dough out into a roughly 12-inch circle. Transfer to sheet pan.

4. Place the cherry tomato filling in the center of the dough, leaving about 2 inches around the edges. Fold the dough just over the edge of the filling. Pinch the edges to create a tight seal. Top with the sweet corn and feta. Sprinkle the galette crust with the remaining cornmeal. Bake at 425°F for 25 to 30 minutes, until the crust is golden and the filling is bubbling.

5. Make the balsamic reduction by adding ½ cup balsamic vinegar to a small pot. Bring to a rapid simmer over medium-high heat, then reduce to a gentle simmer over medium-low heat. Simmer, whisking occasionally, until it reaches the consistency of thin maple syrup, about 12 to 14 minutes.

6. Top the finished galette with a drizzle of the balsamic vinegar reduction. Serve garnished with basil.

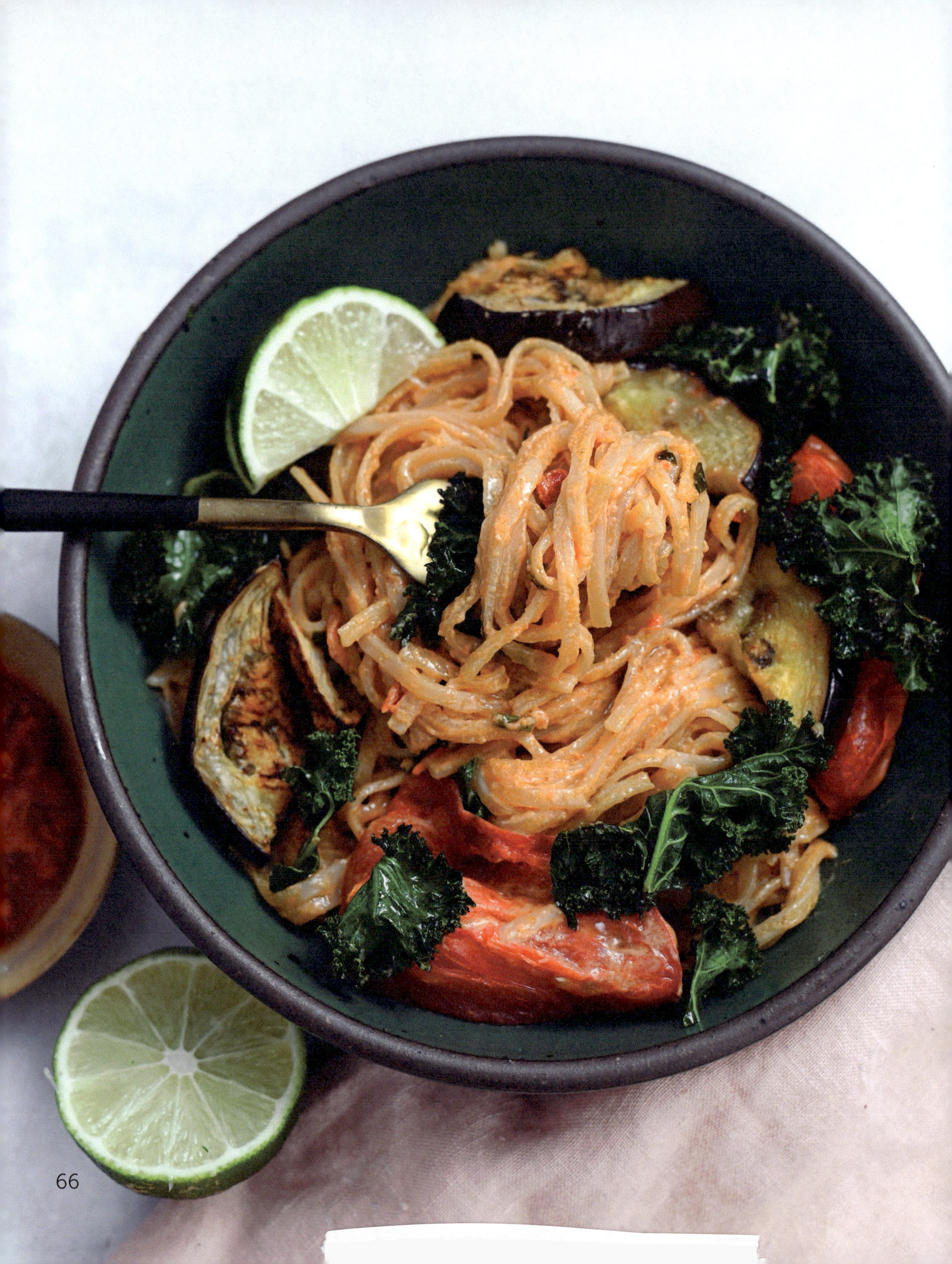

Chapter 3: Pasta for Dinner

Pasta made its way into these dinner recipes so often that it claimed its own cookbook section. Tortellini, lasagna, orzo, and even homemade gnocchi find a way to the dinner table alongside creamy vegan cashew pesto sauce, a variety of vegetables, and pan-fried halloumi.
Many of these pasta recipes can easily be made gluten-free by using your favorite gluten-free pasta. If you'd like to include more whole grains in your diet, use the whole wheat pasta equivalent.

Cassidy's Favorite: Spicy Tahini Soba Noodles with Roasted Summer Vegetables (p. 81)

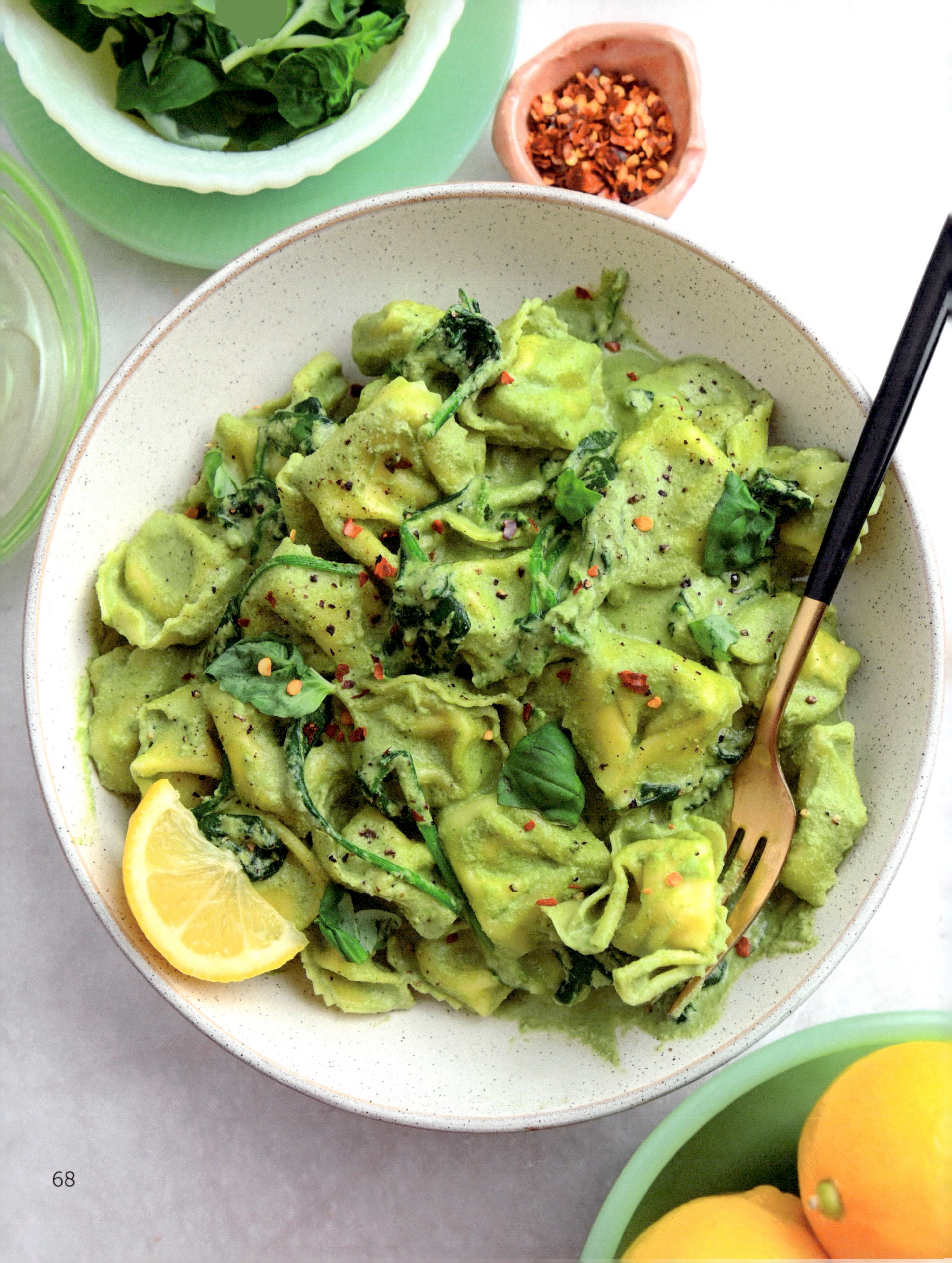

Tortellini with Cashew Pesto Cream Sauce

20 MINUTES • 4 SERVINGS

I'm a huge fan of cashews. Cover them in hot water, add in a few seasonings, and blend until ultra creamy to create a thick and rich dairy-free sauce. Tortellini and cashew cream combine to make a relatively hearty meal, but you can make it even more satisfying by adding additional sautéed vegetables or herby tofu (p. 83).

- 1 cup raw unsalted cashews
- 1 cup boiling water
- 20 ounces fresh cheese tortellini
- 1-2 teaspoons extra virgin olive oil
- 4 cups roughly torn spinach
- ¼ cup roughly chopped Parmesan cheese
- 1 clove garlic
- 2 ounces (about 2 cups) basil leaves, plus more for serving
- 3 tablespoons lemon juice (about 1 large lemon)
- 1 teaspoon lemon zest, plus more for serving
- ½ teaspoon kosher salt, adjust to taste
- ½ teaspoon red pepper flakes
- ¼ teaspoon freshly ground black pepper

1. In a heatproof bowl or sauce pot, combine the cashews and boiling water. Let sit for at least 10 minutes to soften the cashews.

2. While the cashews are soaking, bring a large pot of well-salted water to a boil. Add the tortellini and cook until just tender. Drain and set tortellini aside.

3. Lightly drizzle the now-empty pot with olive oil. Adjust to medium heat. Once hot, add the spinach. Sauté until wilted, just a few minutes.

4. Add the Parmesan and garlic to a blender. Pulse a few times to break down into small pieces. Add the cashews and soaking water, basil leaves, lemon juice, lemon zest, and salt. Blend until completely smooth. Time varies depending on blender strength, but it should take between 1 to 2 minutes.

5. Add the tortellini and cream sauce to the pot with the spinach. Toss to combine. Taste for salt and garnish with thinly sliced fresh basil, red pepper flakes, freshly ground black pepper, and lemon zest.

Note: I recommend using fresh refrigerated tortellini instead of shelf-stable. Cashews do not need to be soaked for very strong blenders. If you have a weak blender, I recommend soaking cashews overnight in cool water.

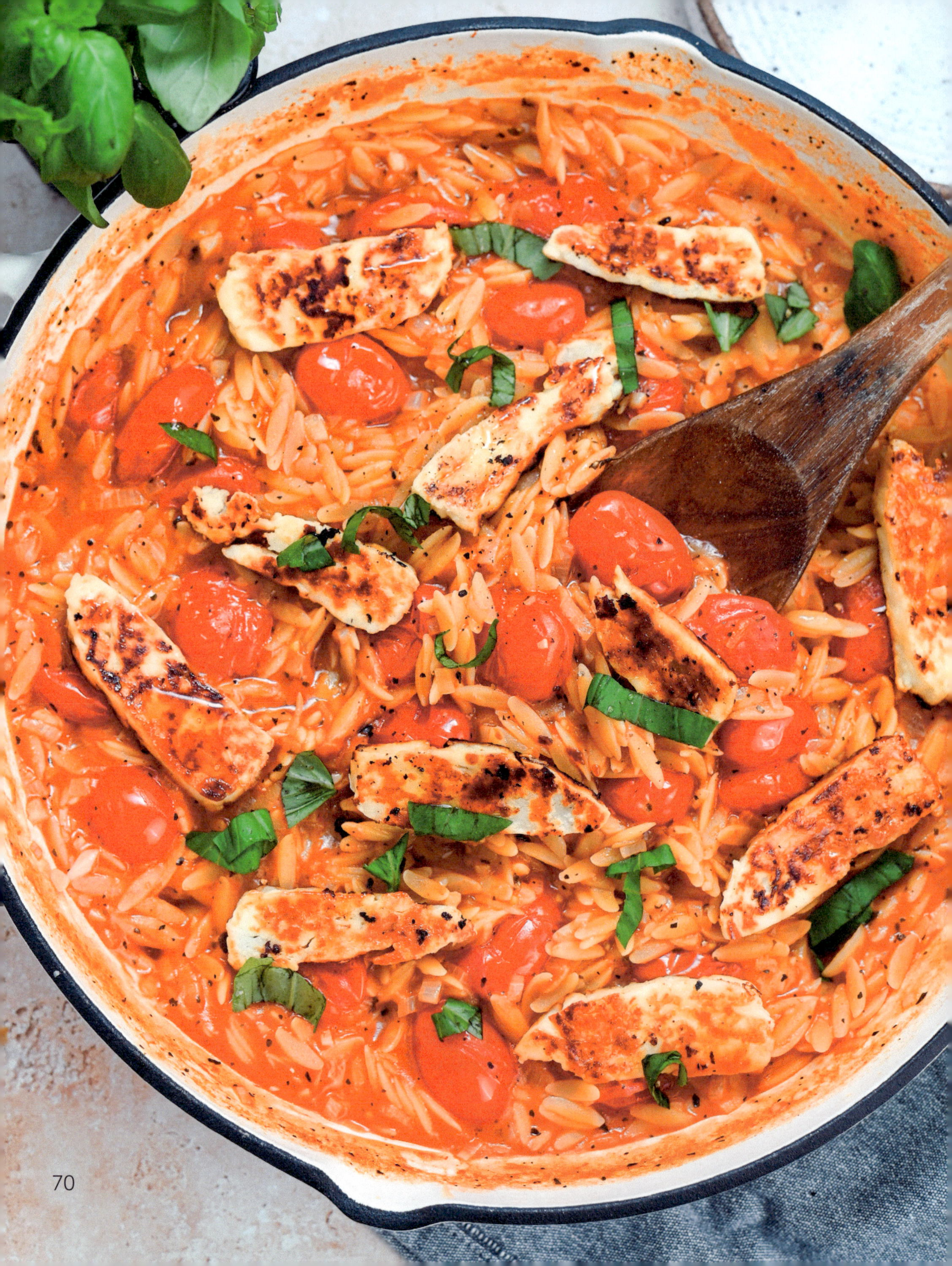

One Skillet Tomato Orzo with Honey Halloumi

30 MINUTES • 4 SERVINGS

This recipe was developed as a result of a very happy and overproductive cherry tomato plant and a love for one-pot pasta dishes. It's now one of my favorite orzo dishes to make! Halloumi is a very salty, squeaky cheese that is mellowed out by a honey drizzle and the natural sweetness from the tomatoes.

HONEY HALLOUMI

- 8 ounces halloumi, sliced lengthwise
- 2 teaspoons honey, more as needed

TOMATO ORZO

- 2 tablespoons unsalted butter
- 1 pint grape tomatoes
- 2 small shallots, diced
- 4 cloves garlic, minced
- 2 tablespoons tomato paste
- 3 cups vegetable broth
- 1 ½ cups orzo
- ¼ teaspoon kosher salt, adjust to taste
- ¼ cup fresh chopped basil leaves

Note: For a higher-protein meal, stir in a can of chickpeas or serve with a side of panko-breaded tofu (p. 83).

For the halloumi

1. I like to cook the halloumi while the orzo simmers, but for those who don't like multitasking, it can be prepared after cooking the orzo.

2. Heat a medium skillet over medium heat. Once hot, add the halloumi. Pan fry until golden on one side, about 4 to 5 minutes. Flip and reduce heat to medium-low. Drizzle with honey. Continue cooking until the halloumi is completely golden.

For the orzo

3. Heat a large skillet or 4-quart Dutch oven over medium heat. Add the butter. Once melted, add the tomatoes and diced shallot. Sauté for 3 to 4 minutes, or until the shallot is turning golden.

4. Add the minced garlic and tomato paste. Sauté for another 2 to 3 minutes, stirring frequently, until the garlic is aromatic and golden. Use a potato masher or spatula to carefully burst the tomatoes.

5. Pour in the vegetable broth and bring to a rapid simmer over medium-high heat. Once simmering, stir in the orzo and salt. Reduce heat to a very gentle simmer over low heat. There should be just one or two bubbles popping at a time. Cover tightly with a lid and cook for 10 to 12 minutes. Stir every 3 to 4 minutes to keep the orzo from sticking to the pan.

6. When the orzo is mostly cooked, remove the lid from the pot. Continue simmering until the orzo is completely cooked and the sauce is thickened, about 2 to 3 minutes.

7. Stir in the chopped basil. Taste for salt and pepper. Serve each portion topped with honey halloumi.

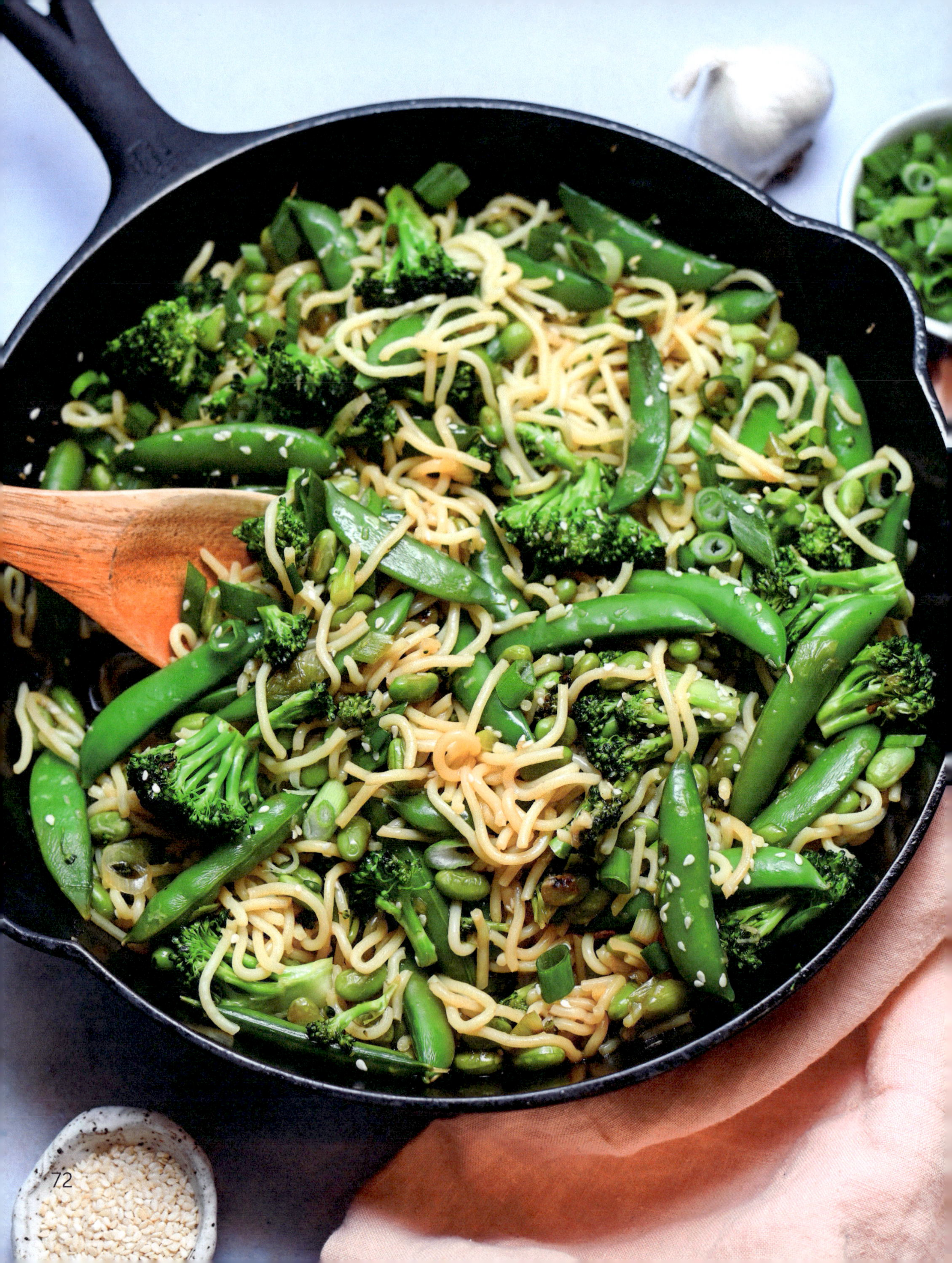

Honey Garlic Noodles with Stir-Fried Green Veggies

30 MINUTES • 4 SERVINGS

This recipe is all about convenience and versatility. I recommend a wok for stir fries, but you can get away with any large skillet. Hokkien stir-fry noodles come already cooked, which makes them great for a convenience meal, but feel free to cook your own udon, lo mein, or rice noodles. The theme is quite obviously green, green, green, but this recipe works just as well with sliced carrots, bell peppers, or other vegetables. Just cook any additional vegetables until they are tender yet still crisp.

HONEY GARLIC SAUCE

2 teaspoons cornstarch
2 teaspoons water
4 cloves garlic, grated
¼ cup honey
¼ cup soy sauce
¼ cup vegetable broth
1 tablespoon rice vinegar
1 teaspoon toasted sesame oil

STIR FRY INGREDIENTS

1 tablespoon canola oil
2 cups frozen mukimame (shelled edamame)
1 medium head broccoli, cut into small florets
8 ounces sugar snap peas
1 (14-ounce) package cooked Hokkien stir fry noodles (I use Ka-Me brand)
Sesame seeds and sliced green onions, for serving

1. In a small bowl, whisk together the cornstarch and water. Add the grated garlic, honey, soy sauce, vegetable broth, rice vinegar, and sesame oil. Whisk to combine, then set aside.

2. Heat a wok or a large non-stick skillet over medium-high heat. Drizzle with canola oil. Once hot, add in the frozen mukimame, broccoli florets, and snap peas. Stir fry for 6 to 8 minutes, until the vegetables are vivid green but starting to brown in places.

3. Add the cooked noodles and honey sauce. Reduce heat to medium. Cook until the sauce is thickened slightly, stirring occasionally, about 3 to 4 minutes.

4. Serve garnished with sesame seeds and sliced green onions.

> **Note:** For a higher-protein meal, serve with baked tofu (p. 33).

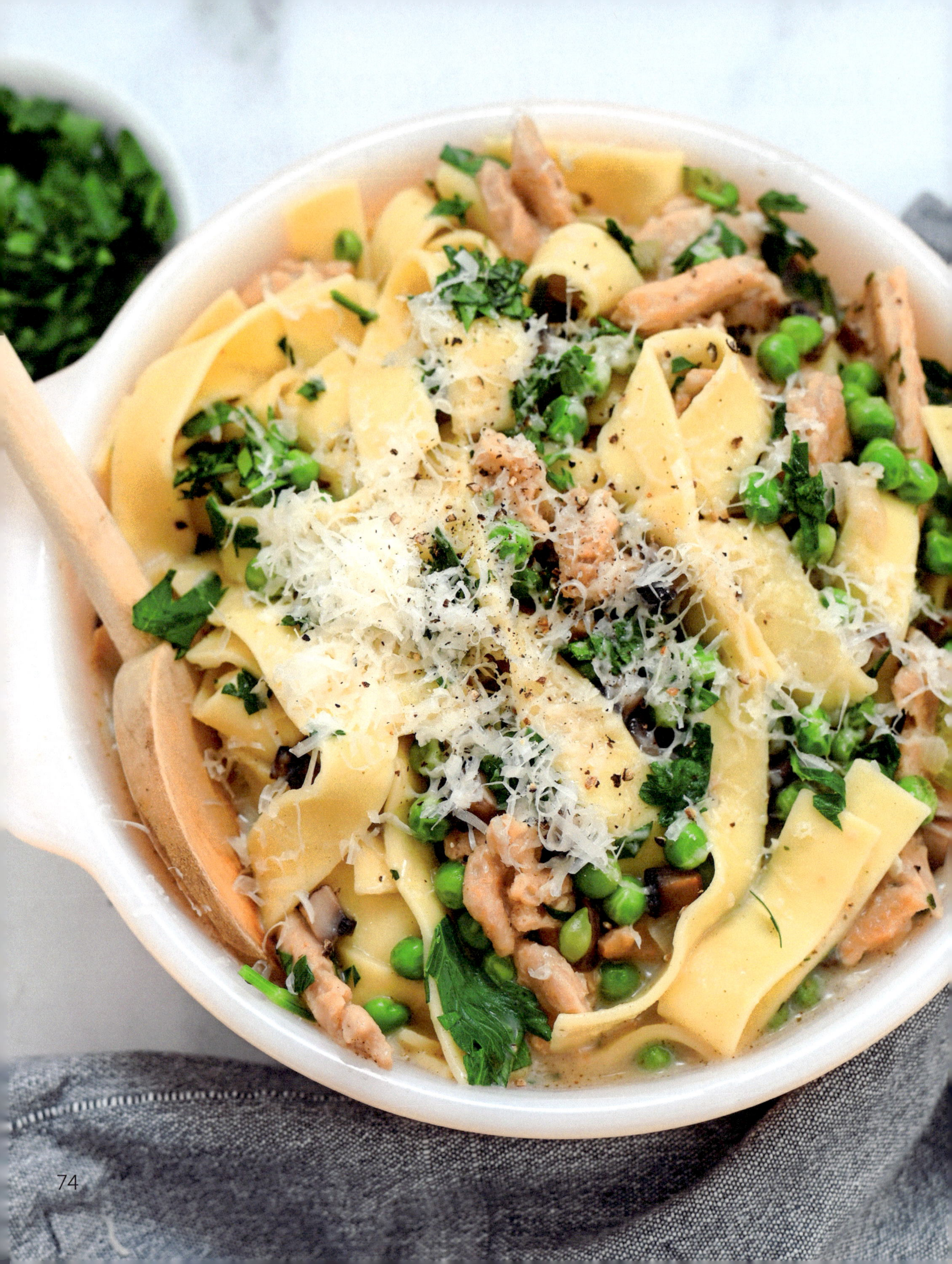

Amish-Style Chicken & Noodles

40 MINUTES • 4 SERVINGS

My parents served chicken and noodle casserole at their wedding reception, and in eating the same dish and hearing the story many times as a child, I often confused it with Amish-style chicken and noodles. My great-grandpa left the Amish when he was in his teens, but it seems that much of that food remained intertwined in his life, as it made its way to my mom's cooking and my own. My take on the casserole/noodle dish that I grew up eating is just as cozy, though I can say with near 100% certainty that my great-grandfather never ate it with Parmesan cheese or soy curls.

8 ounces extra-wide egg noodles
2 cups vegetable broth
1 ½ cups soy curls
2 tablespoons unsalted butter
1 cup diced yellow onion (about ½ medium onion)
4 ounces baby bella mushrooms, chopped
1 cup diced celery (about 2 ribs)
1 teaspoon kosher salt, divided
4 cloves garlic, minced
2 tablespoons all-purpose flour
1 cup 2% milk
1 ½ cups reserved pasta water
1 cup frozen peas, thawed
½ cup (½ ounce) grated Parmesan, plus more for serving
¼ cup fresh chopped parsley, plus more for serving
2 tablespoons nutritional yeast
1 teaspoon dried parsley
¾ teaspoon poultry seasoning
½ teaspoon onion powder
¼ teaspoon black pepper
Additional freshly grated Parmesan, black pepper, and fresh parsley, for serving

1. Cook noodles in well-salted boiling water until al dente. **Reserve 1 ½ cups pasta water before draining.**

2. Meanwhile, add the vegetable broth to a small pot. Bring to a boil. Once boiling, add the soy curls and remove from the stove. Let sit for 5 minutes, then drain the soy curls and set aside.

3. While the noodles cook, heat a large Dutch oven or pot over medium heat. Add butter. Once melted, add onion, mushrooms, celery, and ½ teaspoon salt. Sauté until the onions are softened and golden, about 8 to 10 minutes.

4. Add in the rehydrated soy curls and garlic. Cook until the soy curls are starting to brown and the garlic is softened, about 3 minutes.

5. Sprinkle in the flour, stirring frequently for 2 minutes to toast. Slowly stir in the milk to form a thick sauce. Whisk in the reserved pasta water, thawed frozen peas, Parmesan, fresh parsley, nutritional yeast, dried parsley, poultry seasoning, remaining ½ teaspoon salt, onion powder, and black pepper.

6. Simmer gently over medium-low heat to form a thin sauce, about 4 to 6 minutes. Stir in the cooked egg noodles. Garnish with additional freshly grated Parmesan, freshly ground black pepper, and parsley.

Note: I buy Butler brand soy curls online, but some health food stores carry them in bulk. You can also use meatless "chicken," such as Gardein brand, or even chickpeas. Omit the 2 cups of vegetable broth if not using soy curls.

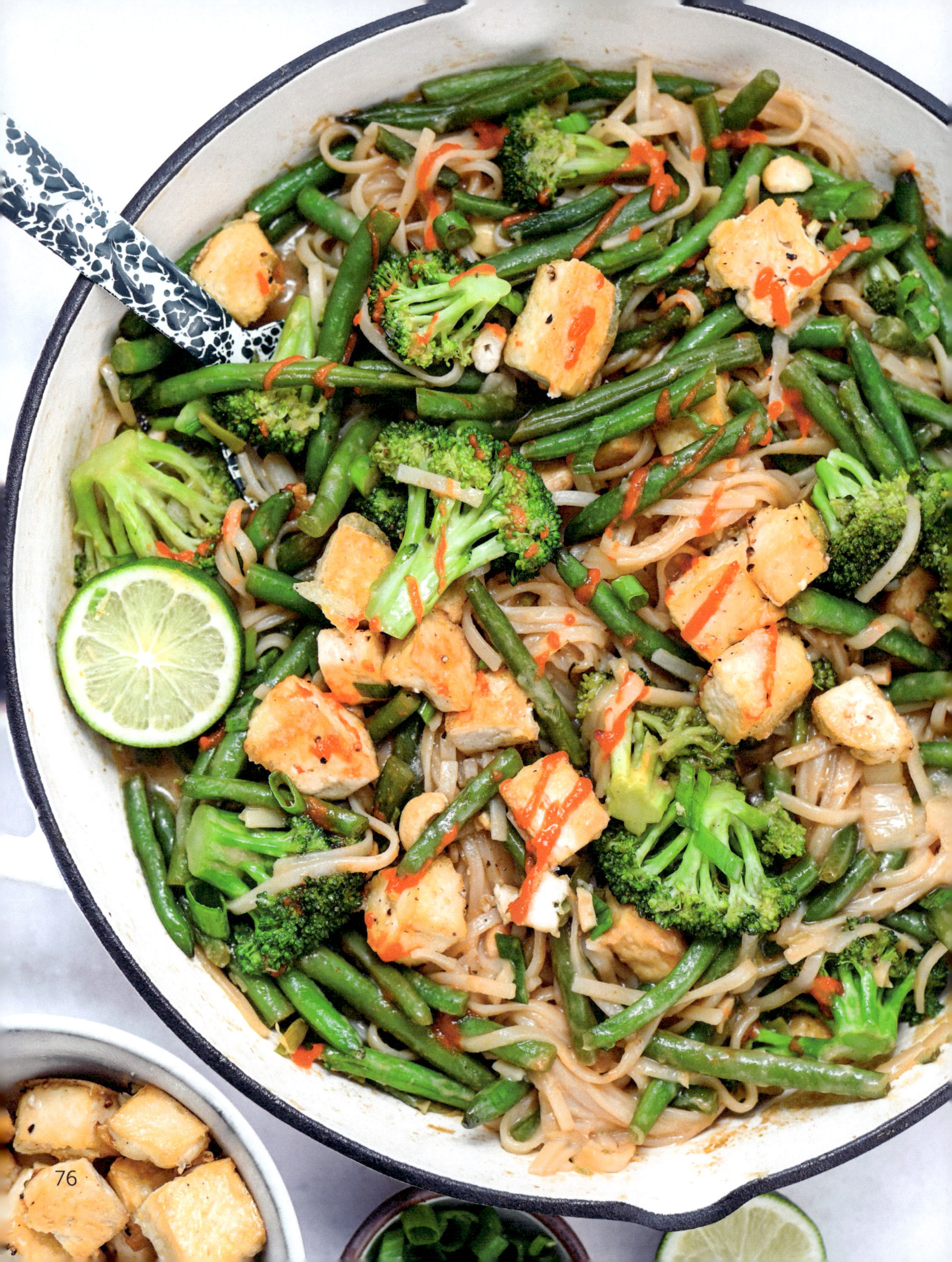

Green Curry Noodle Bowls

45 MINUTES • 4 SERVINGS

This dish is inspired by the late and great restaurant The Grit in Athens, Georgia, which always had a noodle bowl available on the menu. It might be obvious from the green curry paste that this dish is inspired by Thai curry. Other than that, there isn't much traditional about this recipe; that's because the goal of this dish is to deliver a big warming bowl of noodles in weeknight-friendly time, unlike more traditional curry recipes, which tend to be more time-intensive.

BAKED TOFU

1 (14-ounce) block extra-firm tofu, cut into ½-inch cubes
1 tablespoon canola oil
1 tablespoon cornstarch
¼ teaspoon kosher salt
Freshly ground black pepper

GREEN CURRY

1 tablespoon canola oil
12 ounces green beans, trimmed and sliced into 2-inch pieces
1 bunch green onions, sliced; green and white parts separated
¼ teaspoon kosher salt
3 tablespoons green curry paste
1 tablespoon minced garlic
2 teaspoons grated ginger (about 1 inch)
2 cups vegetable broth
1 (13.5-ounce) can coconut milk
1 tablespoon soy sauce
½ teaspoon granulated sugar
7 ounces rice noodles
1 large broccoli crown, sliced into florets
2 tablespoons lime juice (about one small lime)
½ teaspoon lime zest
¼ teaspoon freshly ground black pepper, plus more to taste
Sriracha, for serving (optional)

For the tofu

1. Preheat the oven to 425°F. Line a half sheet pan with parchment paper.

2. In a medium bowl, toss cubed tofu with canola oil, corn starch, salt, and pepper, to taste. Spread tofu in an even layer on the baking sheet. Bake on the middle oven rack at 425°F for 25 to 30 minutes, or until golden and crisp.

For the curry

3. Heat a 12-inch skillet over medium heat. Drizzle with oil. Once hot, add the green beans, the white parts of the green onions, and the salt. Sauté for 3 to 4 minutes, until the green beans are vivid green but still firm.

4. Add the green curry paste, garlic, and ginger to the pan. Cook, stirring frequently, until the garlic is fragrant and golden, about 2 to 3 minutes. If needed, deglaze the pan with a splash of vegetable broth.

5. Pour in the remaining vegetable broth along with the coconut milk, soy sauce, and sugar. Bring to a rapid simmer over medium-high heat. Stir in the rice noodles so that they are fully covered in liquid. Top with the broccoli florets. Cover the pot tightly with a lid. Cook until the noodles are tender and the broccoli is vivid green, about 4 to 5 minutes. Stir as needed to keep the noodles from sticking to each other.

6. Remove the lid. Just before serving, stir in lime juice, lime zest, black pepper, remaining green onions, baked tofu, and a drizzle of sriracha.

> **Note:** I like to use my 12-inch braising pan or 12-inch cast iron skillet for this recipe. The sides are low enough to allow the vegetables to brown and high enough to fit pasta.

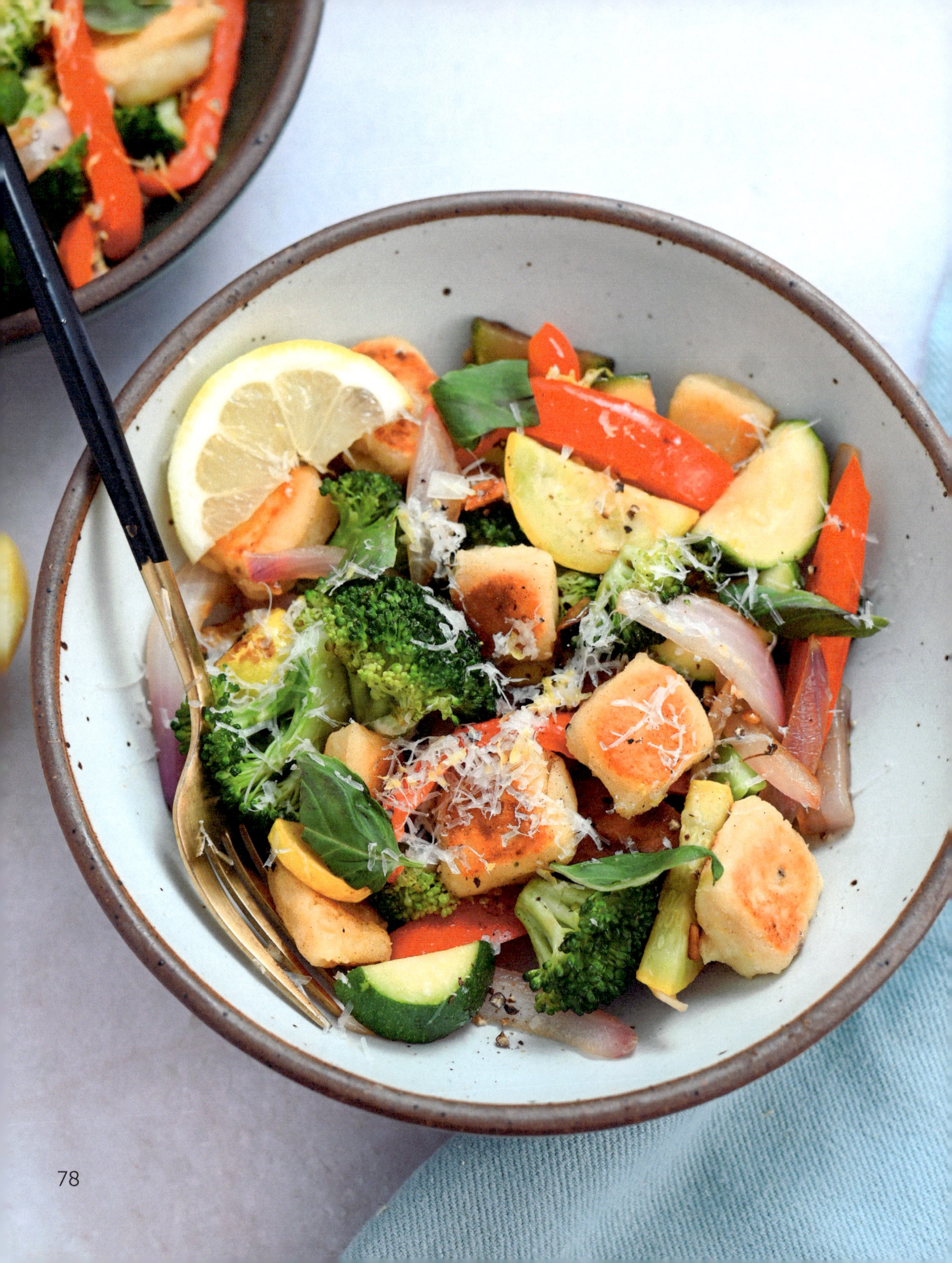

Ricotta Gnocchi Primavera

50 MINUTES • 3 TO 4 SERVINGS

I'll be the first to admit that this is one of the more intimidating recipes in the cookbook, despite the simple ingredient list. The result is pillowy soft, heavenly gnocchi. It's so worth making, with a few notes in mind: It is very important that the ricotta is strained for at least 30 minutes, or the dough will be too difficult to work with. If you have time, an overnight strain is best. This is one of the few recipes in the cookbook that can't be veganized without significant changes.

RICOTTA GNOCCHI

1 (15-ounce) container whole milk ricotta
1 large egg
1 large egg yolk
¼ cup finely grated Parmesan
1 teaspoon lemon zest (from about one small lemon)
¼ teaspoon kosher salt
⅛ teaspoon black pepper
1 ½ to 2 cups all-purpose flour
2 tablespoons unsalted butter

VEGETABLES AND ASSEMBLY

2 tablespoons extra virgin olive oil
1 medium red bell pepper, sliced into ½-inch strips
1 medium red onion, sliced into ¼-inch strips
1 medium head broccoli, cut into small florets
1 medium yellow squash, sliced into ¼ inch half moons
1 medium zucchini, sliced into ¼-inch half moons
½ teaspoon kosher salt
4 cloves garlic, minced
2 tablespoons lemon juice (about one small lemon)
1 teaspoon lemon zest
Fresh basil leaves, Parmesan, and freshly ground black pepper, for serving

1. Start by straining the ricotta to remove excess liquid. Place a medium fine-mesh strainer over a mixing bowl. Line the strainer with cheesecloth or a layer of paper towels. Add the ricotta. Gently press the ricotta into an even layer. Cover loosely with a towel or plastic wrap and refrigerate for at least 30 minutes, but ideally overnight. Discard the strained liquid.

2. In a medium bowl, mix together the strained ricotta, egg, egg yolk, Parmesan, lemon zest, salt, and pepper. Add in 1 cup of flour, mixing until well combined. The dough should be wet but manageable. Add an extra ½ to 1 cup of flour if the dough is too sticky to work with. *Note: The longer the ricotta is strained, the less flour is needed. Gnocchi with less flour is more delicate.*

3. Turn the dough out onto a lightly floured surface. Use a bench scraper or knife to slice the dough into long strips 1-inch wide. Slice each strip into ½-inch gnocchi-sized pieces. *Note: As I slice the dough, I like to transfer the gnocchi to a piece of parchment paper. This just makes them easier to manage because the dough is still a little delicate at this point.*

4. Heat a large skillet over medium heat. Add the butter. Once melted, add in about ⅓ of the gnocchi. Pan fry until golden, then flip over, about 2 minutes on each side. Repeat until all gnocchi is cooked.

5. While the gnocchi cooks in one skillet, heat another large skillet over medium heat. Drizzle with olive oil. Once hot, add the vegetables and salt. Cook for 8 to 10 minutes, stirring occasionally, until the veggies are mostly tender. Stir in the garlic and continue cooking until golden and aromatic, about 2 minutes.

6. Add the pan-fried gnocchi to the vegetables. Before serving, top with lemon juice, lemon zest, basil, ample fresh Parmesan, and black pepper.

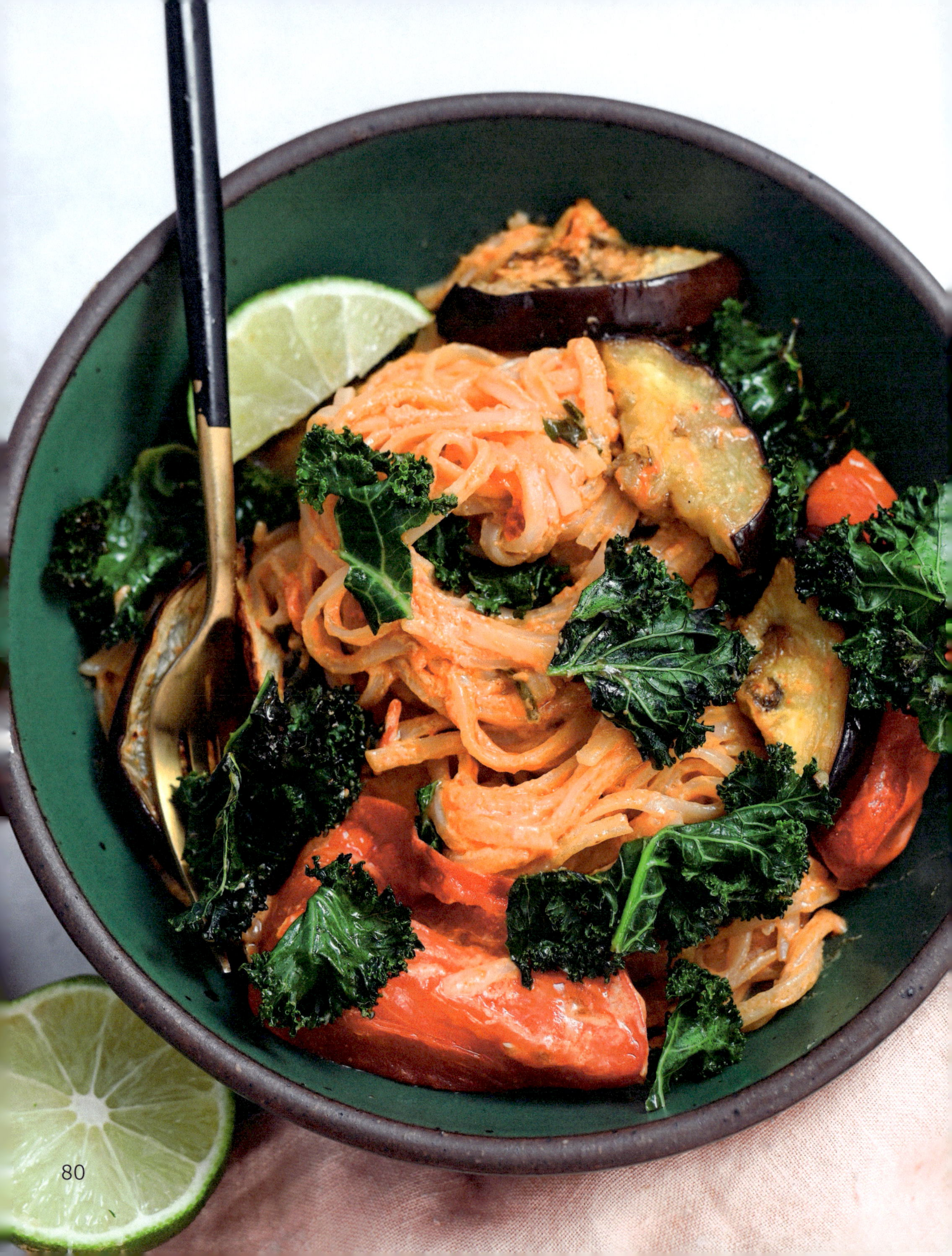

Tahini Noodles with Roasted Vegetables

50 MINUTES • 4 SERVINGS

One of my best friends is allergic to most nuts, which means tahini has to do a lot of heavy lifting to replace nut-based dishes like peanut noodles. She cooked a variation of this dish for me soon after she moved into her new home, and ever since I've been in love with tahini-based pasta dishes. This is also one of my favorite ways to cook eggplant. The result is jammy, melt-in-your mouth eggplant.

ROASTED VEGETABLES

1 medium eggplant, sliced into half moons
4 Roma tomatoes, quartered
1 tablespoon + 1 teaspoon extra virgin olive oil, divided
¾ teaspoon kosher salt, divided
½ teaspoon ground coriander
1 bunch curly kale, torn into bite-sized pieces

TAHINI NOODLES

8 ounces rice noodles
1 tablespoon extra virgin olive oil
1 inch ginger, grated
1 to 2 tablespoons harissa, adjust based on spice preference
¼ cup fresh chopped parsley, plus more for serving
½ cup tahini
3 tablespoons soy sauce
1 tablespoon tomato paste
2 teaspoons honey
¾ cup cooked rice noodle water
1 medium lime, sliced in half

1. Preheat the oven to 425°F. Line a large sheet pan with parchment paper or foil. Set aside.

2. In a large bowl, toss the eggplant and tomatoes with 1 tablespoon oil, ½ teaspoon salt, and coriander. Spread out in an even layer on the sheet pan. Roast for 20 minutes at 425°F. The vegetables will not be completely cooked at this point.

3. Toss the torn kale pieces with the remaining 1 teaspoon of oil and ¼ teaspoon salt. Sprinkle the kale pieces across the top of the eggplant and tomatoes. Return to the oven to roast for an additional 8-10 minutes, or until the kale pieces are mostly dry and crisp.

4. While the vegetables roast, cook rice noodles according to package instructions. **Reserve at least 1 cup of pasta water before draining the noodles.**

5. In a large skillet, heat olive oil over medium heat. Once hot, add ginger, harissa, and parsley. Cook until the ginger is golden and fragrant, about 2 minutes.

6. Reduce heat to medium-low. Add in the tahini, soy sauce, tomato paste, and honey. Whisk in the reserved pasta water to thin the sauce.

7. Add cooked noodles to the tahini sauce. Toss to coat with the sauce. Squeeze juice from a lime over the top just before serving.

8. Serve the tahini noodles with roasted vegetables on the side.

Note: The harissa balances out the nutty tahini without providing an overpowering level of spice. Start with 1 tablespoon and adjust the heat based on your heat tolerance.

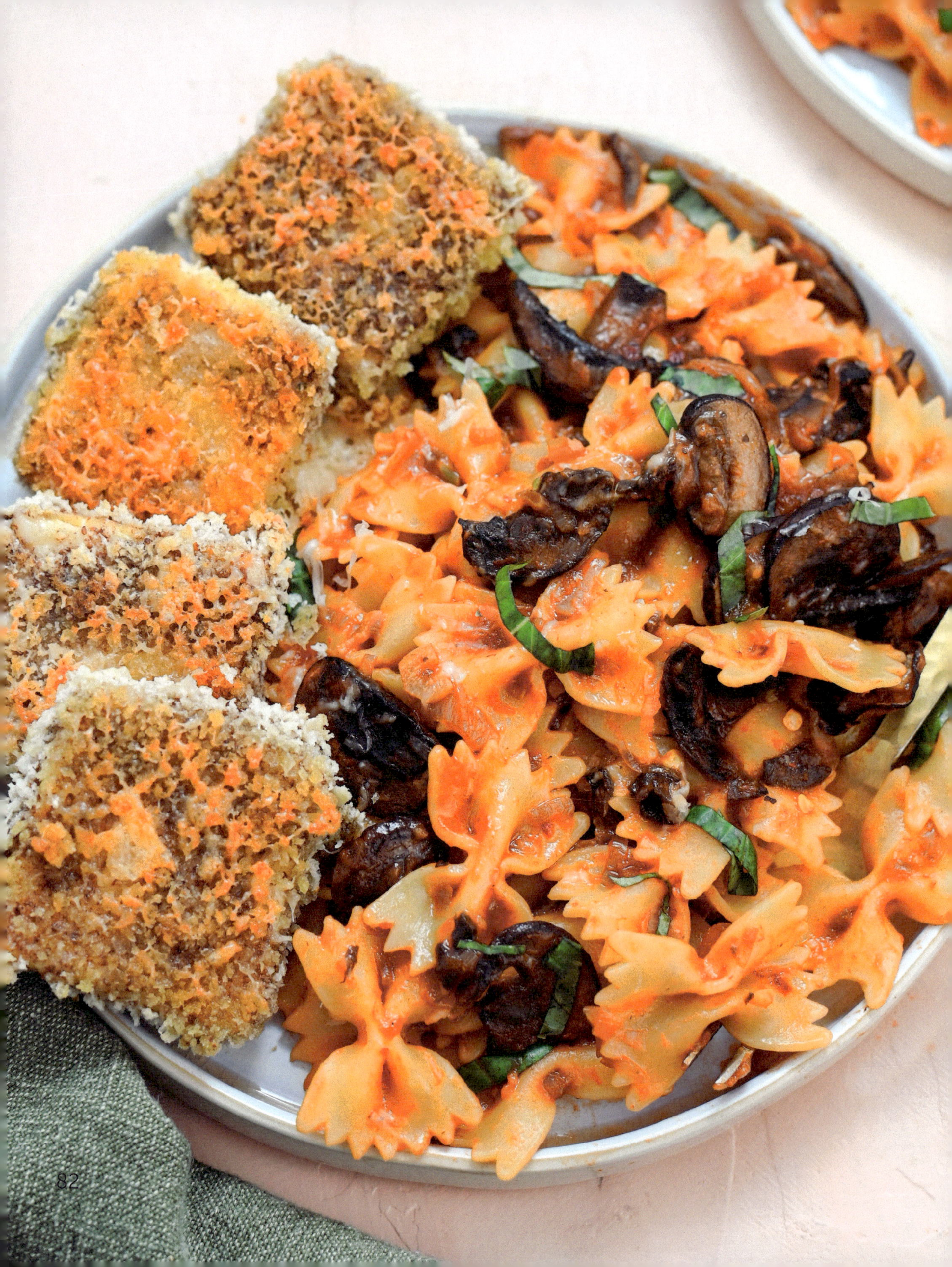

Caramelized Shallot Pasta with Herby Breaded Tofu

1 HOUR 10 MINUTES • 3-4 SERVINGS

This recipe is a great option for dinner parties! A few notes for success: Caramelized shallots and mushrooms can be prepped up to 24 hours in advance and refrigerated until ready to use. If the shallots start to burn, reduce heat further and add a splash of water to the pan.

PASTA

2 tablespoons unsalted butter
6 large shallots, thinly sliced
16 ounces baby bella mushrooms, thinly sliced
½ teaspoon kosher salt
12 ounces bow tie (farfalle) pasta
6 cloves garlic, minced
¼ cup + 2 tablespoons tomato paste
2 teaspoons red pepper flakes
2 tablespoons sherry vinegar
1 ½ cups reserved pasta water
½ cup thinly sliced fresh basil
Freshly grated Parmesan, to taste

TOFU

1 (14-ounce) block extra-firm tofu
2 tablespoons ground flaxseed
¼ cup + 2 tablespoons water
½ cup milk of choice
2 tablespoons soy sauce
1 cup all-purpose flour
1 teaspoon dried parsley
1 teaspoon dried rosemary
½ teaspoon garlic powder
½ teaspoon onion powder
½ teaspoon table salt, divided
1 ½ cups panko breadcrumbs
Cooking spray (optional)
½ cup (½ ounce) shredded Parmesan

For the pasta

1. Heat a large skillet over medium heat. Add butter. Once melted, add the shallots, mushrooms, and salt. Sauté for just 3 to 4 minutes, until the shallots start to turn golden. Reduce heat to medium-low. Continue cooking for 30 to 40 minutes, stirring only every 10 minutes.
2. When the shallots are almost done, start cooking the pasta in well-salted water until al dente. **Reserve at least 1 ½ cups of water from the cooked pasta.**
3. Once the shallots are caramelized, increase heat to medium and stir in garlic, tomato paste, and red pepper flakes. Cook until the garlic is golden, about 3 minutes.
4. Deglaze the pan with sherry vinegar. Whisk in the reserved pasta water to form a sauce. Stir in the pasta.

For the tofu

5. Preheat the oven to 400°F. Start prepping the tofu after turning the heat on the shallots to medium-low. Press the tofu for 10 minutes. In a small bowl, whisk together the ground flaxseed and water to form a flax egg. Let rest 5 minutes, then stir in the milk.
6. Cut the pressed tofu into 12 thin squares. Drizzle with 2 tablespoons of soy sauce.
7. In a shallow bowl, whisk together the flour, parsley, rosemary, garlic powder, onion powder, and ¼ teaspoon salt. Add panko to another bowl with the remaining ¼ teaspoon salt.
8. Coat each slice of tofu in the flour mixture, then flax egg, then panko. Place tofu on a baking sheet. Optionally, spray tofu with cooking spray so that it becomes golden.
9. Bake tofu at 400°F for 25 minutes, or until golden. Remove from the oven and flip the tofu. Sprinkle each piece of tofu with shredded Parmesan. Return to the oven for 5 minutes, or until the Parmesan is melted.
10. Divide baked tofu between each serving of pasta. Top with basil and Parmesan, to taste.

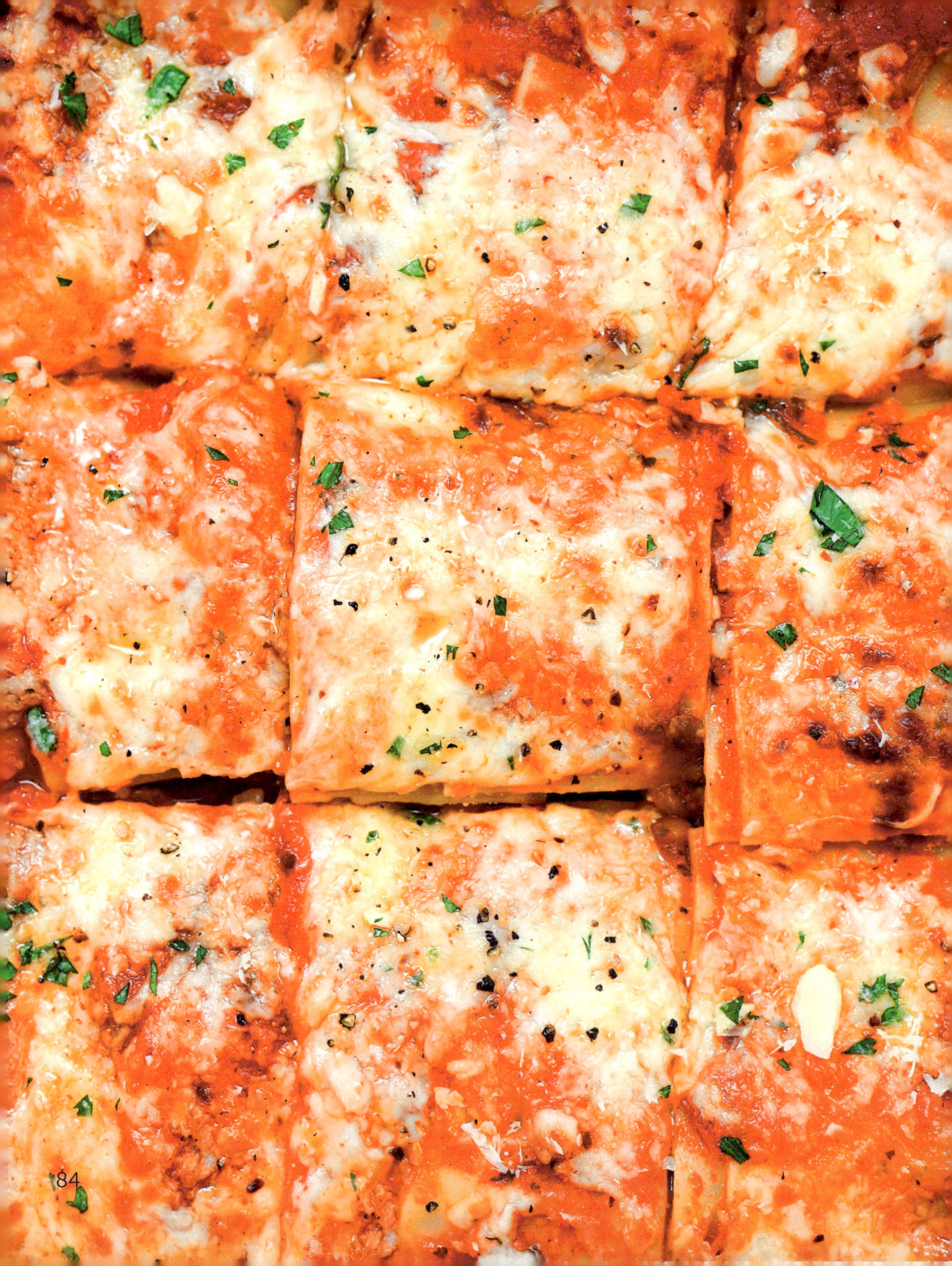

Big Veggie & Lentil Lasagna

1 ½ TO 2 HOURS • 6 SERVINGS

When I set about writing a book about vegetarian dinners, I knew that I had to include a lasagna recipe. I'll admit that lasagna isn't my favorite recipe to cook, because there's really no way around it taking a whole lot of time to make. When developing this lasagna, I tried to take shortcuts, but in the end I admitted that you might just have to spend a couple of hours in the kitchen if you want a delicious homemade lasagna. The result is a nutritious but comforting lasagna which features four vegetables, two types of cheese, and homemade tomato sauce. It's totally worth making and freezes well.

TOMATO SAUCE

1 (28-ounce) can crushed tomatoes
1 (15-ounce) can tomato sauce
¼ cup tomato paste
2 teaspoons Italian seasoning
1 teaspoon dried basil
½ teaspoon kosher salt
¼ teaspoon black pepper

VEGETABLE FILLING

1 cup dry brown lentils, rinsed
3 cups vegetable broth
¾ teaspoon kosher salt, divided
8 ounces baby bella mushrooms
1 medium yellow bell pepper
1 medium yellow onion
1 large zucchini
1 tablespoon extra virgin olive oil
5 cloves garlic, minced
1 teaspoon dried basil
1 teaspoon dried parsley

ASSEMBLY

12 lasagna noodles (do not use no-boil noodles)
1 (15-ounce) container whole milk ricotta
1 large egg
Pinch of nutmeg
2 cups (8 ounces) shredded mozzarella
1 cup (1 ounce) shredded Parmesans

1. **Sauce:** To a medium pot, add the crushed tomatoes, tomato sauce, tomato paste, Italian seasoning, dry basil, salt, and pepper. Cover and simmer over medium-low heat, stirring occasionally, for at least 20 minutes or until all of the other lasagna components are ready.

2. **Cook the lentils:** Combine the lentils, vegetable broth, and ¼ teaspoon salt in a medium pot. Bring to a rapid simmer over medium-high heat. Reduce to a gentle simmer and cover. Simmer until tender, about 20 to 25 minutes. Drain off excess liquid and set aside.

3. **Filling:** Finely dice the vegetables, aiming for ¼-inch pieces. Heat a large skillet over medium heat. Drizzle with oil. Once hot, add the vegetables. Sauté for 10 minutes, stirring occasionally. Add the minced garlic, basil, parsley, and remaining salt. Cook for 10 more minutes, until the veggies are very reduced. Stir in the cooked and drained lentils.

4. **Other steps:** Preheat the oven to 375°F. Bring a large pot of well-salted water to a boil. Add the lasagna noodles and cook until al dente. Drain and set aside. In a medium bowl, whisk together the ricotta, egg, and pinch of nutmeg.

5. **Assembly:** Spread ½ cup of the tomato sauce in a 9x13 inch baking dish. Top with 4 lasagna noodles. Spread with half of the ricotta. Top with ½ cup mozzarella, ¼ cup Parmesan, half of the veggie filling, and 1 ½ cups sauce. Top with 4 noodles, the remaining ricotta, ½ cup mozzarella, ¼ cup Parmesan, remaining veggie filling, and 1 ½ cups sauce. Top with the last 4 noodles and the remaining sauce. Spread the sauce to cover the noodles. Sprinkle with the remaining shredded cheese.

6. Cover the lasagna tightly with foil. Bake at 375°F on the middle oven rack for 30 minutes, then remove the foil and continue baking for 15 to 20 minutes, or until the cheese is golden and bubbly. Remove from the oven and let cool for at least 10 minutes before slicing and serving.

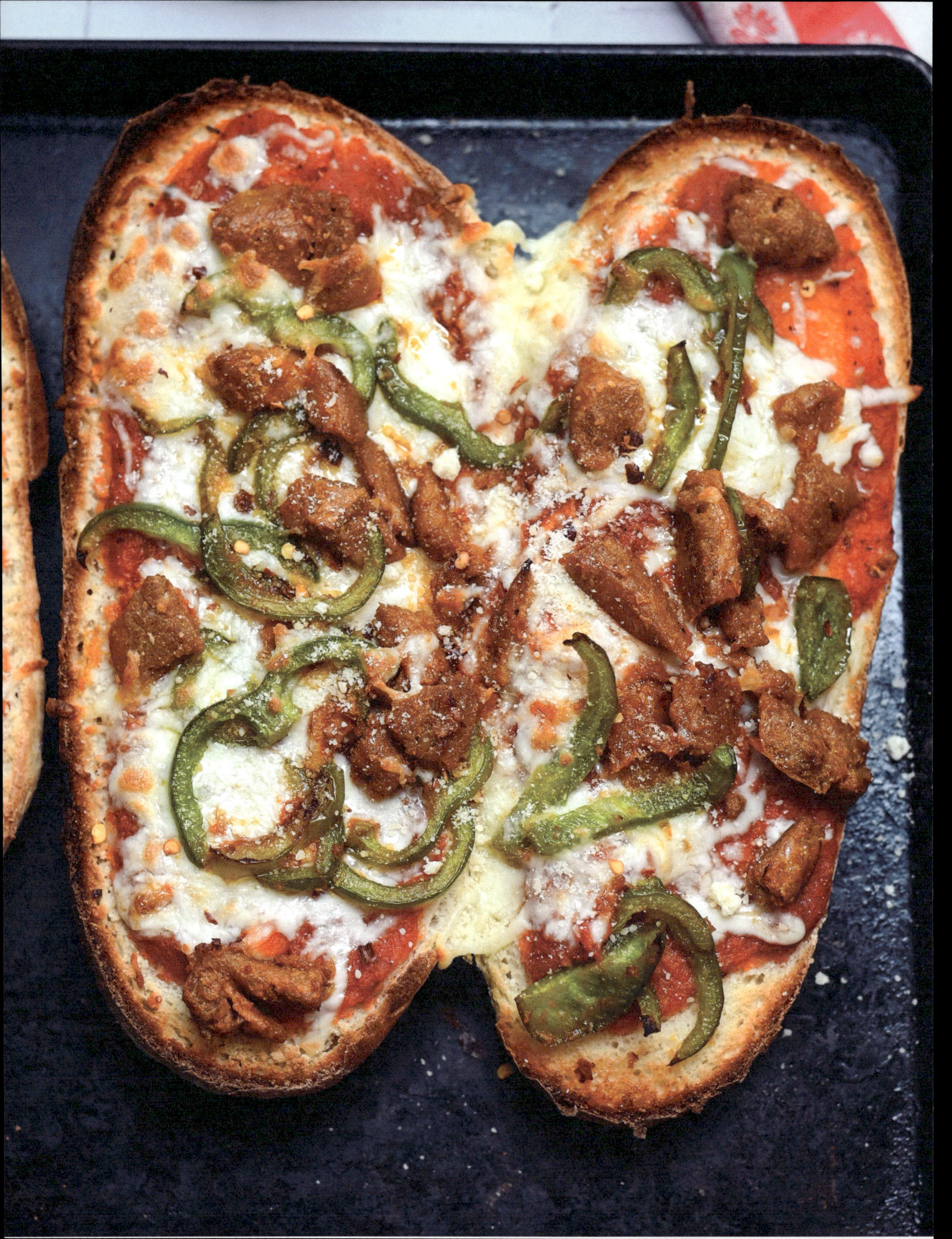

Chapter 4:
Handhelds & Sandwiches for Dinner

When I started eating vegetarian, one of the things that I missed most was sandwiches and subs with deli meat. These days, it's easy to find meatless lunch meat, but there's also a whole world of sandwiches out there that feature tofu and tempeh. When this was originally a comfort food cookbook, I had a section called "Diner Food." You'll find that a lot of these sandwiches still fit naturally in that section, though I also include a few options that work well for light lunches.

Cassidy's Favorite: Pizza Bread (p. 105)

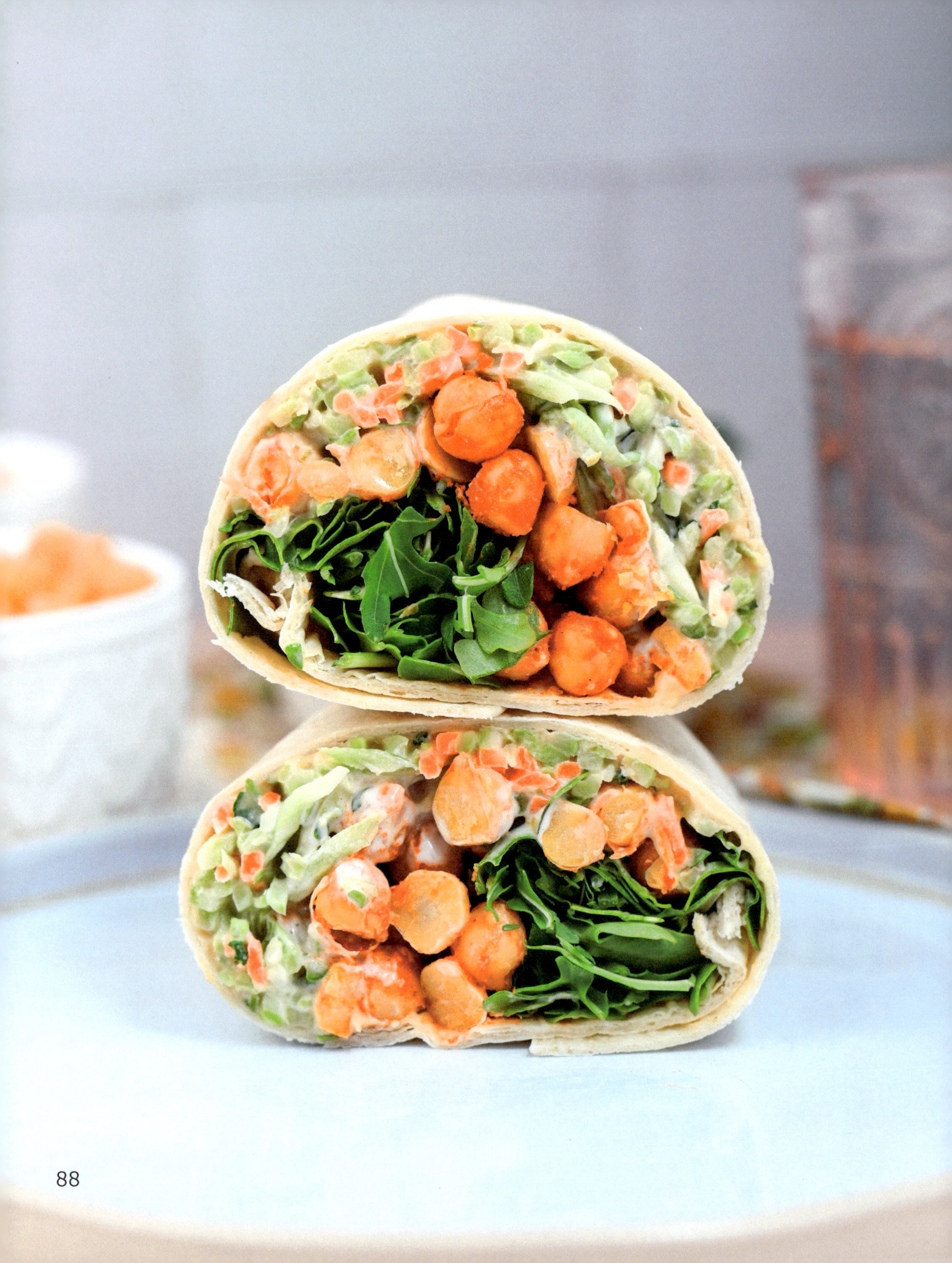

Buffalo Chickpea Wraps with Broccoli Slaw

15 MINUTES • 3-4 SERVINGS

This is one of the simplest recipes in the cookbook, making it perfect for lunch and meal prep. Cholula is my go-to hot sauce, but any kind of vinegar-based sauce works here. Because these wraps are on the spicy side, I recommend adjusting hot sauce to taste.

BUFFALO CHICKPEAS

1 tablespoon unsalted butter
2 cloves garlic, minced
1 (15-ounce) can chickpeas, drained and rinsed
2 to 3 tablespoons hot sauce
¼ teaspoon onion powder
¼ teaspoon kosher salt
⅛ teaspoon freshly ground black pepper

BROCCOLI SLAW

8 ounces broccoli slaw
¼ cup mayonnaise
2 tablespoons lime juice (about one medium lime)
1 teaspoon lime zest (from the medium lime)
1 teaspoon honey
¼ teaspoon kosher salt

ASSEMBLY

4 (10-inch) tortillas or wraps
Hummus and arugula, for serving

1. In a medium skillet, melt butter over medium heat. Once melted, add the garlic. Sauté until golden and fragrant, about 2 minutes.

2. Reduce heat to medium-low. Add the chickpeas, hot sauce, onion powder, salt, and pepper. Cook uncovered for 4 to 5 minutes, stirring occasionally.

3. Meanwhile, make the slaw. Add the broccoli slaw to a medium bowl. In a separate small bowl, whisk together the mayonnaise, lime juice, lime zest, honey, and salt. Pour this onto the broccoli slaw. Use tongs to toss the broccoli slaw in the sauce.

4. To make a wrap, spread a thin layer of hummus across the center of a tortilla. Top with a handful of arugula, a scoop of slaw, and a scoop of chickpeas. Roll into a burrito. Serve sliced in half. Repeat with the remaining tortillas and filling.

> **Note:** Broccoli slaw usually contains matchstick carrots and broccoli. Regular coleslaw mix also works here.

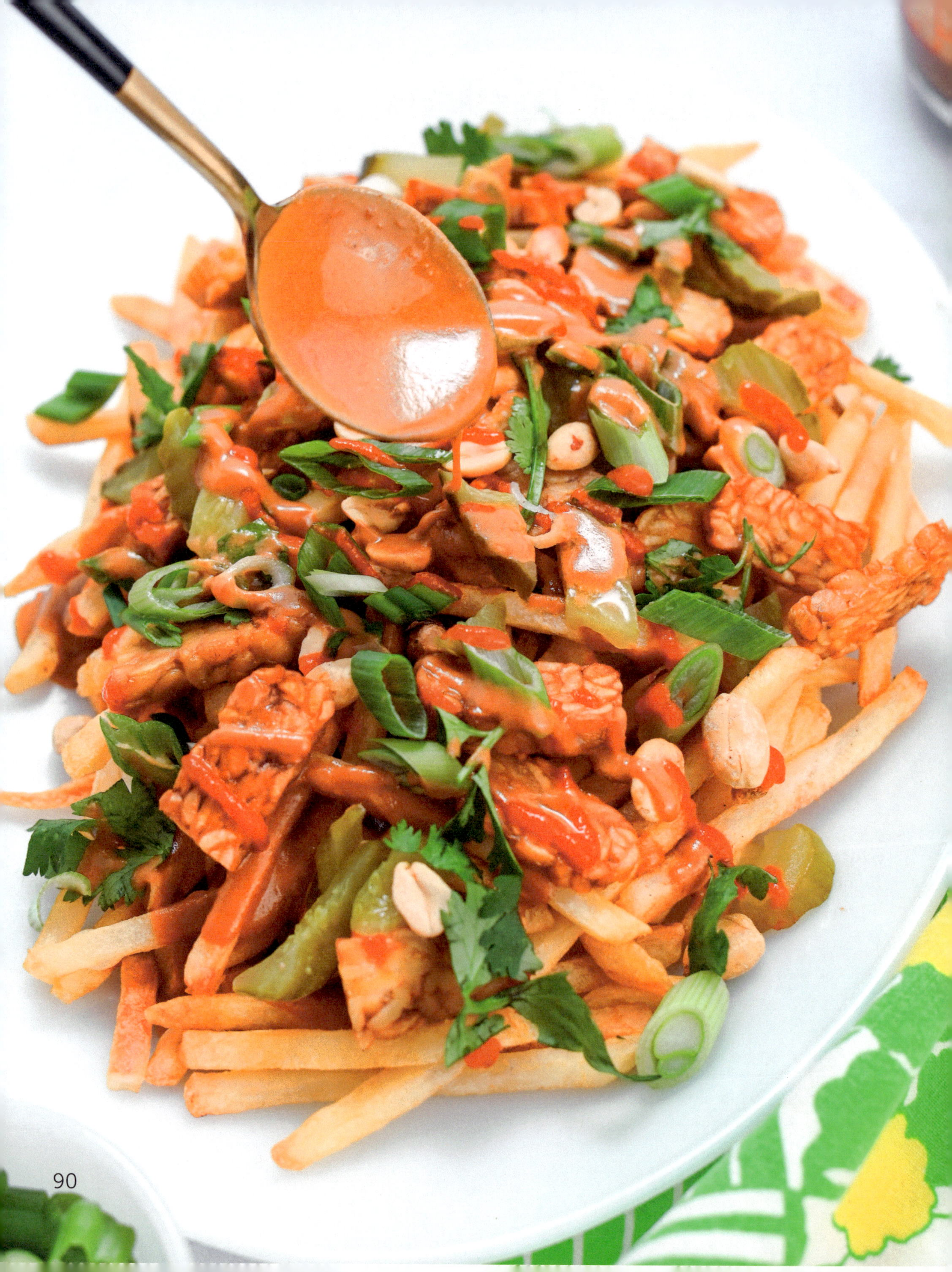

Loaded Fries with Peanut Sauce and Fried Tempeh

30 MINUTES • 4 SERVINGS

These fries are inspired by the Dandan fries served at Basilisk in Portland, Oregon, where I lived for two years after college. Traditional Dandan recipes are made with minced pork and Sichuan peppers, neither of which appear in these fries. The inspiration for these fries is more based on the restaurant and less based on what you might actually expect from Chinese Dandan-style dishes. These fries have a spicy peanut sauce, zesty pickles (yes, pickles!), and crispy fried tempeh. This is easily one of my top 10 favorite cookbook recipes.

ASSEMBLY

1 (32-ounce) package regular-cut frozen french fries (about 8 cups)
Salt, to taste
1 (8-ounce) package tempeh
Canola oil, for frying
1 tablespoon soy sauce
Sriracha, to taste
1 bunch green onions, sliced
¾ cup chopped sandwich pickles
½ cup roasted peanuts
½ cup fresh chopped cilantro
Lime wedges, for serving

PEANUT SAUCE

¼ cup creamy peanut butter
2 tablespoons rice vinegar
2 tablespoons soy sauce
1 tablespoon sriracha
1 tablespoon black vinegar
½ teaspoon toasted sesame oil
1 to 4 tablespoons vegetable broth or water, as needed

1. Cook the frozen french fries according to package instructions, or until golden and crisp. Season with salt, if needed.

2. Slice the tempeh into about 16 thin strips. Cut each strip in half to make two smaller 1-inch pieces, or about 32 pieces of tempeh total. Set aside.

3. **To make the peanut sauce:** In a small bowl, whisk together the peanut butter, rice vinegar, soy sauce, sriracha, black vinegar, and toasted sesame oil. The sauce should have a pourable, dressing-like consistency. If needed, add 1 tablespoon of vegetable broth or water at a time to thin.

4. **For the tempeh:** Heat a large Dutch oven or skillet over medium-high heat. Add ½ inch of oil. Once shimmering and hot, add the sliced tempeh. The tempeh should be completely covered by the cooking oil. Fry until golden and crisp, about 6 to 8 minutes. Using a slotted spoon, remove tempeh from the oil, and place on a paper-towel lined plate. Drizzle with 1 tablespoon of soy sauce.

5. **To assemble the fries:** Divide the fries between 4 to 5 plates. Drizzle with peanut sauce and sriracha, to taste. Top each portion with tempeh, sliced green onions, pickles, peanuts, cilantro, and a squeeze of lime. Alternatively, assemble the fries and toppings on one large serving platter.

> **Note:** Black vinegar is a sweet, multi-dimensional Chinese vinegar. You can find it in the international aisle at most grocery stores or at Asian supermarkets. Try adding a splash to tahini noodles (p. 81) or stir fries (p. 131).

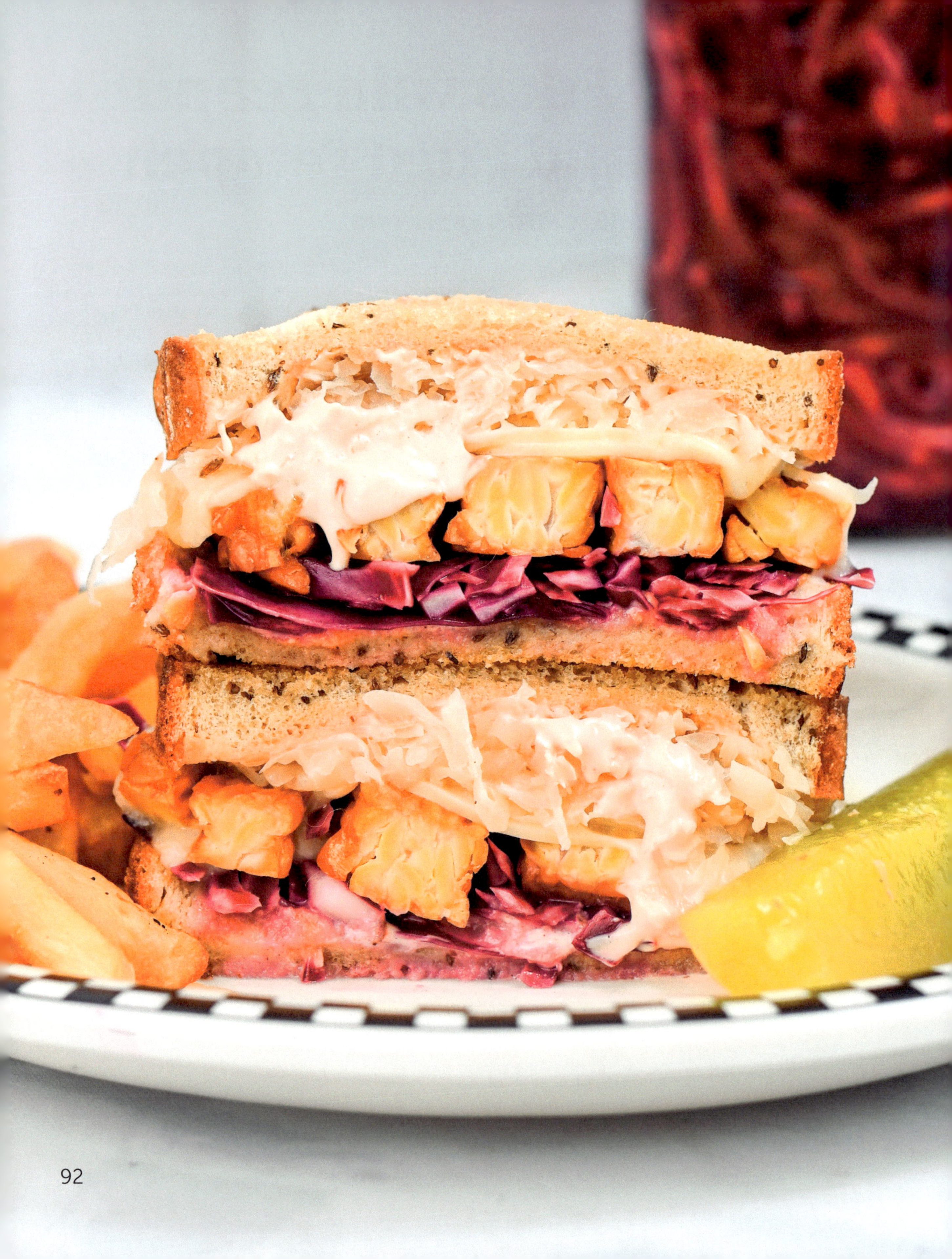

Tempeh & Red Cabbage Reuben

30 MINUTES (PLUS 1 HOUR INACTIVE TIME) • 2 SANDWICHES

This recipe combines two of my favorite takes on vegetarian Reuben sandwiches from two of my favorite restaurants in my town. One of the restaurants fries their tempeh (Hi-Lo Lounge) and the other uses pickled cabbage in place of the meat (Trappeze). I use both of these ingredients for a sandwich that is high in protein and filled with crunch.

PICKLED CABBAGE

¼ small red cabbage, cored and sliced into ¼-inch strips (about 4 cups shredded cabbage)
1 cup red wine vinegar
1 cup water
1 tablespoon kosher salt
2 teaspoons granulated sugar

SANDWICHES

1 to 2 cups canola oil for frying
1 (8-ounce) block tempeh, sliced into 12 pieces
¼ cup mayonnaise
2 teaspoons ketchup
1 teaspoon lemon juice
½ teaspoon vegan Worcestershire sauce
¼ teaspoon onion powder
1 clove garlic, grated
4 slices dark rye bread
Freshly ground black pepper, to taste
⅓ cup sauerkraut
3 slices Swiss cheese
1 tablespoon unsalted butter (oil also works here)

> **Note:** Leftover pickled cabbage is good for at least a week and is a great addition to sandwiches and grain bowls.
>
> If frying in a smaller amount of oil, the tempeh needs to be flipped in order to completely fry each side.

For the cabbage

1. Add the shredded cabbage to a quart-sized mason jar or another heat-safe container. Set aside.

2. In a medium pot, heat the red wine vinegar, water, salt, and sugar over medium-high heat. Once simmering, remove from heat and stir vigorously to dissolve the salt and sugar.

3. Pour the hot liquid onto the cabbage. If the cabbage isn't completely covered, top it off with additional vinegar or water (choose based on preferred tanginess). Let cool to room temperature, then refrigerate for at least an hour but preferably 4 hours.

For the sandwiches

4. Add 1 inch of oil to a medium skillet. Heat to 350°F, or over medium to medium-high heat if you don't have a frying thermometer. Once hot, add half of the tempeh, working in batches as needed. Shallow fry the tempeh until it reaches a deep golden color, about 5 minutes. Carefully remove from the pan and place on a plate lined with paper towels to drain excess oil.

5. In a small bowl, whisk together the mayonnaise, ketchup, lemon juice, Worcestershire sauce, onion powder, and grated garlic. Adjust seasonings to taste.

6. **To assemble:** Spread a thin layer of the dressing on each piece of rye. Take one slice, and over the dressing, add a layer of pickled cabbage, a few cracks of freshly ground black pepper, half of the sauerkraut, half of the tempeh, and 1 and ½ slices of Swiss cheese. Finish off with one more slice of bread, dressing-side down.

7. Heat a medium skillet over medium heat. Add butter. Once the butter is melted, add the sandwiches. Toast until golden, just a few minutes. Flip the sandwiches and reduce heat to low. Cover with a lid and cook until the cheese is melted and the sandwiches are golden, another 2 to 3 minutes. Serve immediately.

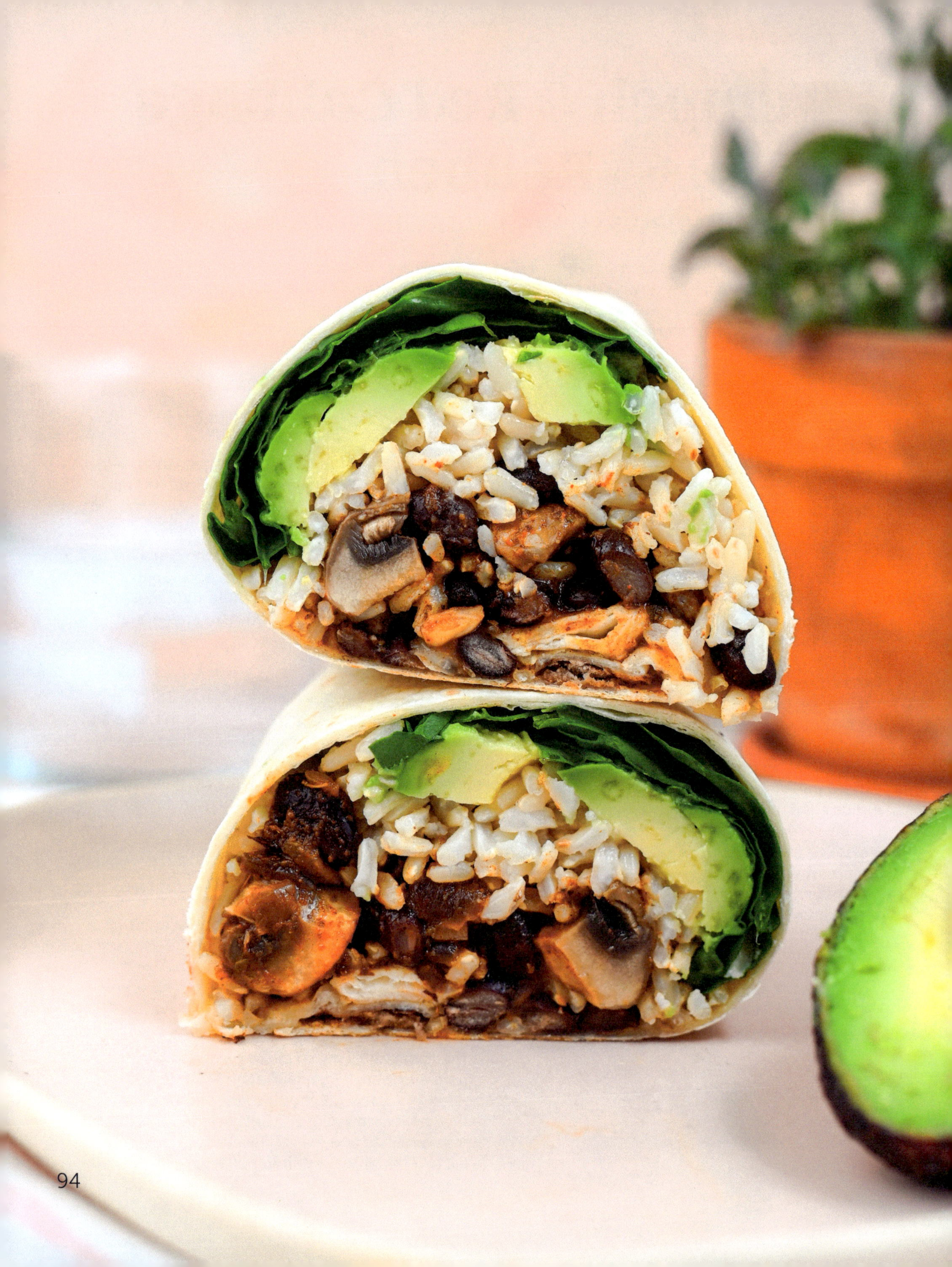

Mushroom & Black Bean Burritos

40 MINUTES • 4 BURRITOS

Although these burritos are great for dinner, they're just as delicious for work lunch or as a grab-and-go freezer meal. Different versions of adobo are used across Latin American, Caribbean, and Spanish cooking, and some varieties of adobo seasoning are available at the grocery store. My homemade adobo blend adds robust, hearty flavor to the mushroom and black bean filling.

ADOBO SEASONING

1 teaspoon chili powder
1 teaspoon dried oregano
½ teaspoon ground cumin
½ teaspoon kosher salt
½ teaspoon onion powder
½ teaspoon paprika
½ teaspoon smoked paprika
¼ teaspoon black pepper
¼ teaspoon garlic powder

FILLING & ASSEMBLY

1 tablespoon extra virgin olive oil
8 ounces white mushrooms, quartered
1 cup diced red onion (about ½ medium onion)
3 cloves garlic, minced
1 tablespoon soy sauce
1 (15-ounce) can black beans, drained and rinsed
¼ cup vegetable broth
4 (12-inch) tortillas
2 cups spinach, torn into bite-sized pieces
½ cup salsa verde
1 large avocado, sliced
1 cup cooked brown rice

1. In a small jar, whisk together the chili powder, oregano, ground cumin, kosher salt, onion powder, paprika, smoked paprika, black pepper, and garlic powder. Set aside.

2. Heat a medium skillet over medium heat. Drizzle with olive oil. Once hot, add the mushrooms and onions. Sauté for 10 to 12 minutes, or until onions are browned and mushrooms are softened.

3. Add minced garlic. Sauté for an additional 2 to 3 minutes, until the garlic is golden and aromatic. Add soy sauce and the adobo seasoning blend to the mushrooms and onions. Toast the seasonings for 30 seconds, stirring constantly.

4. Stir in the black beans and vegetable broth. Reduce to a gentle simmer over medium-low heat. Simmer, uncovered, for 10 minutes.

5. To assemble the burritos, add torn spinach to the center of each tortilla. Top with 2 tablespoons salsa verde and ¼ avocado. Top with ¼ cup brown rice and ¼ of the mushroom and bean mixture. Fold in edges to touch the center, then roll into a burrito.

6. Heat a clean skillet over medium heat. Add burritos to the skillet seam-side down. Cook until golden, just 2 to 3 minutes. Enjoy immediately.

To assemble burritos for freezing: First, let the mushrooms, beans, and rice cool to room temperature. Fill burritos according to step 5. Wrap each burrito in foil, then place in an airtight freezer container or freezer bag.

To reheat frozen burritos: Remove from foil and place on a plate. Microwave for 1 minute. Flip and microwave an additional 1 to 2 minutes, until heated through.

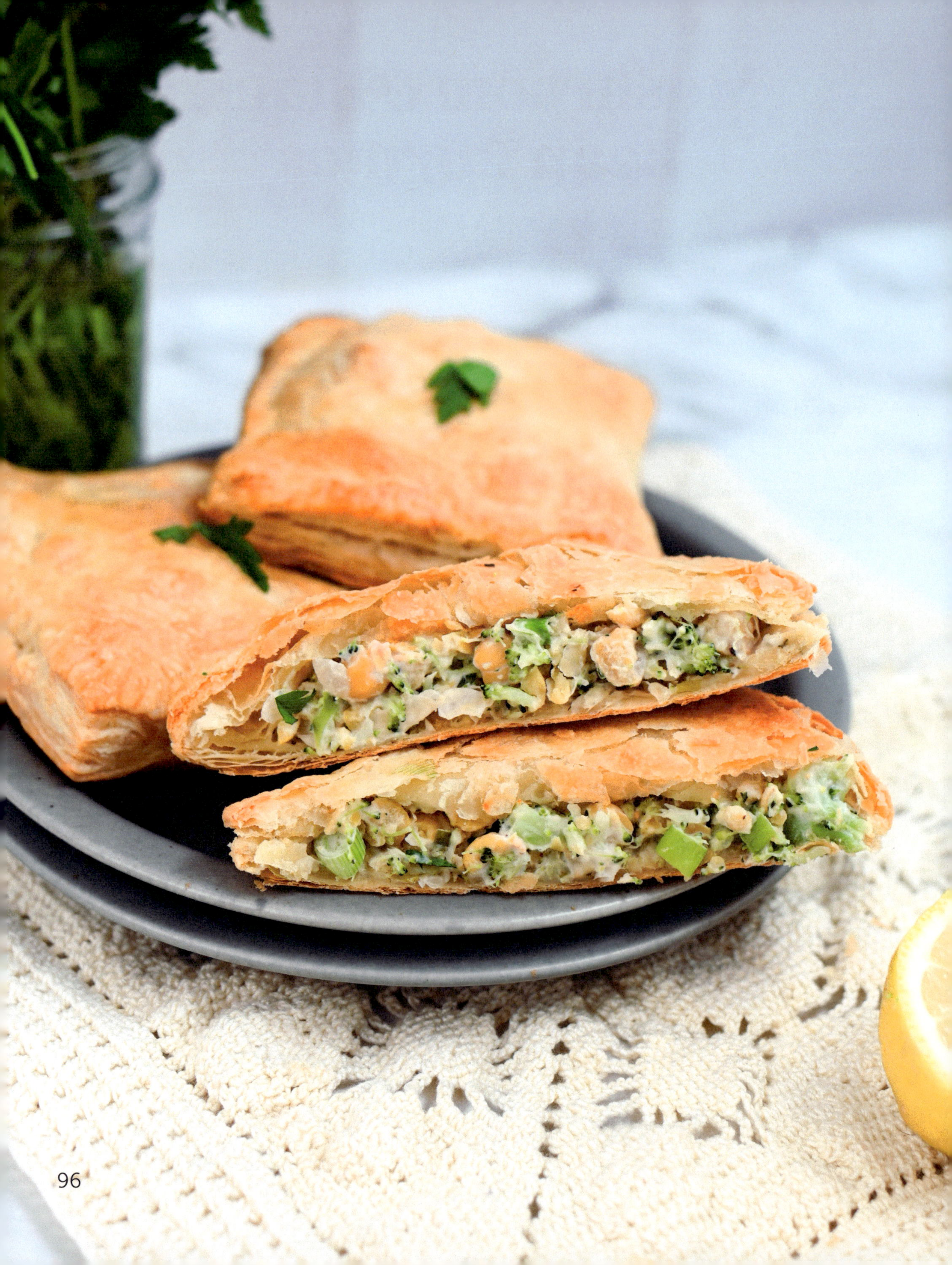

Puff Pastry Broccoli & Chickpea Rollovers

40 MINUTES • 6 PASTRIES

I grew up eating a version of this recipe that used canned chicken and crescent rolls. A true Reeser family classic, and one that I know my mom liked to make because it was quick, easy, and my brothers and I loved it. My veg-friendly version features canned chickpeas and puff pastry, which are just as convenient as the original ingredients. The result is puffy, crispy little pockets of comfort.

- 1 (17-ounce) package frozen puff pastry, thawed (I use Pepperidge Farms brand)
- 2 cups roughly chopped broccoli florets (from about 1 medium broccoli crown)
- 1 (15-ounce) can chickpeas, drained and rinsed
- 4 ounces Neufchâtel cream cheese (lite cream cheese)
- ¼ cup sliced green onions
- 1 tablespoon lemon juice (about half a small lemon)
- 1 tablespoon milk of choice
- 1 teaspoon dried parsley
- ½ teaspoon onion powder
- ¼ teaspoon garlic powder
- ¼ teaspoon kosher salt
- ⅛ teaspoon black pepper

1. Set the puff pastry out to thaw for at least 20 minutes.
2. Meanwhile, place chopped broccoli in a steamer basket over simmering water. Cover with a lid and steam until vivid green and tender, about 6 to 8 minutes.
3. Preheat the oven to 400°F.
4. Place the chickpeas in a medium bowl. Mash with a fork or potato masher until mostly broken down, leaving about ¼ of the chickpeas intact. Stir in the cream cheese, green onions, lemon juice, milk, parsley, onion powder, garlic powder, salt, and pepper. Fold in the steamed broccoli. Set aside.
5. On a lightly floured surface, slice each puff pastry sheet along the fold line to make 3 pieces per sheet, which will make 6 pieces total. Use a rolling pin to roll out each piece so that the rectangle doubles in width.
6. Divide the chickpea filling between the bottom half of each rectangle. Fold half of the puff pastry over so that the filling is covered. Press the edges with a fork to seal the pastry. Repeat with the 5 remaining pastries.
7. Transfer the pastries to a large sheet pan lined with parchment paper. Bake at 400°F° for 18 to 20 minutes, or until the pastry is puffy and golden. Let cool for 5 minutes before serving.

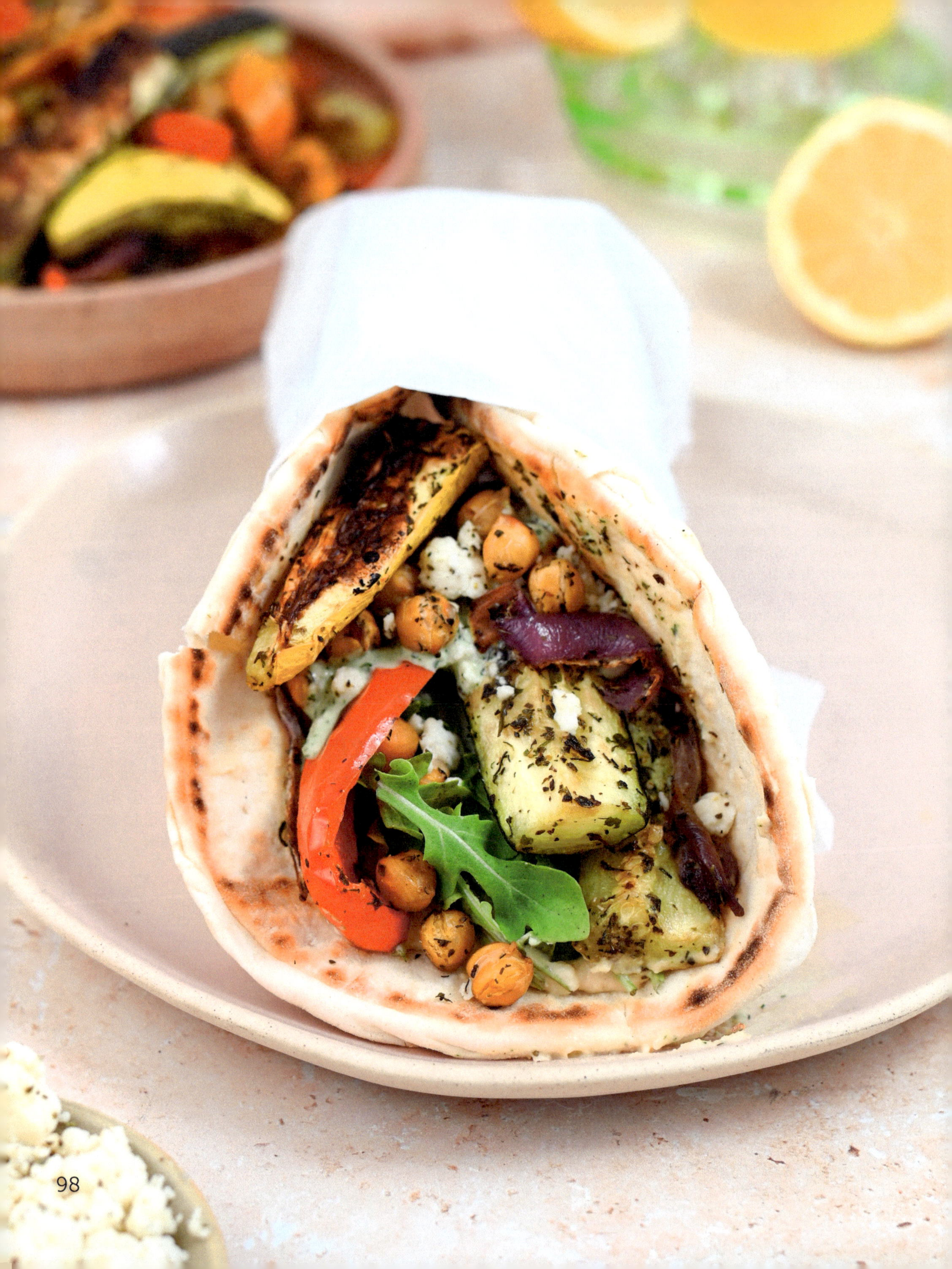

Roasted Vegetable & Chickpea Wraps

45 MINUTES • 4 SERVINGS

During my last summer in college, I worked at a loosely Mediterranean restaurant (loosely because they serve pimento cheese and potato chips as a side). I ate a wrap similar to this on every break, often paired with strongly lemon-flavored roasted potatoes, which I loved. My rendition adds chickpeas for protein, and I won't judge you if you want to serve this with a scoop of pimento cheese and chips on the side.

ROASTED VEGETABLES AND ASSEMBLY

- 1 medium orange bell pepper, sliced in thin strips
- 1 medium red bell pepper, sliced into thin strips
- 1 medium yellow squash, cut into 3-inch wedges
- 1 medium zucchini, cut into 3-inch wedges
- ½ medium red onion, cut into thin wedges
- 1 (15-ounce) can chickpeas, drained and rinsed
- 1 tablespoon canola oil
- 1 tablespoon dried oregano
- 2 teaspoons dried basil
- 1 teaspoon dried dill
- 1 teaspoon dried parsley
- ½ teaspoon garlic powder
- ½ teaspoon kosher salt
- ½ teaspoon onion powder
- ⅛ teaspoon black pepper
- Flatbread or pita bread, hummus, arugula, and crumbled feta, for serving

PESTO AIOLI

- 1 cup fresh basil leaves
- ½ cup mayonnaise
- 2 tablespoons lemon juice (about 1 small lemon)
- 1 teaspoon lemon zest (about 1 small lemon)
- 1 clove garlic, roughly chopped
- Pinch of salt

1. Preheat the oven to 425°F. To a large bowl, add the peppers, squash, zucchini, onion, and chickpeas. Toss with the oil and seasonings: oregano, basil, dill, parsley, garlic powder, kosher salt, onion powder, and pepper.

2. Place the vegetables and chickpeas on a large sheet pan. Try not to overlap any pieces. Roast at 425°F for 25 to 30 minutes, or until the vegetables are tender and golden.

3. Meanwhile, make the pesto aioli. Add the basil, mayo, lemon juice, lemon zest, chopped garlic, and a pinch of salt to a blender. Blend until mostly smooth and green.

4. To assemble a wrap, spread a piece of flatbread with the pesto aioli and hummus. Top with a handful of arugula, roasted vegetables, chickpeas, and a sprinkle of feta.

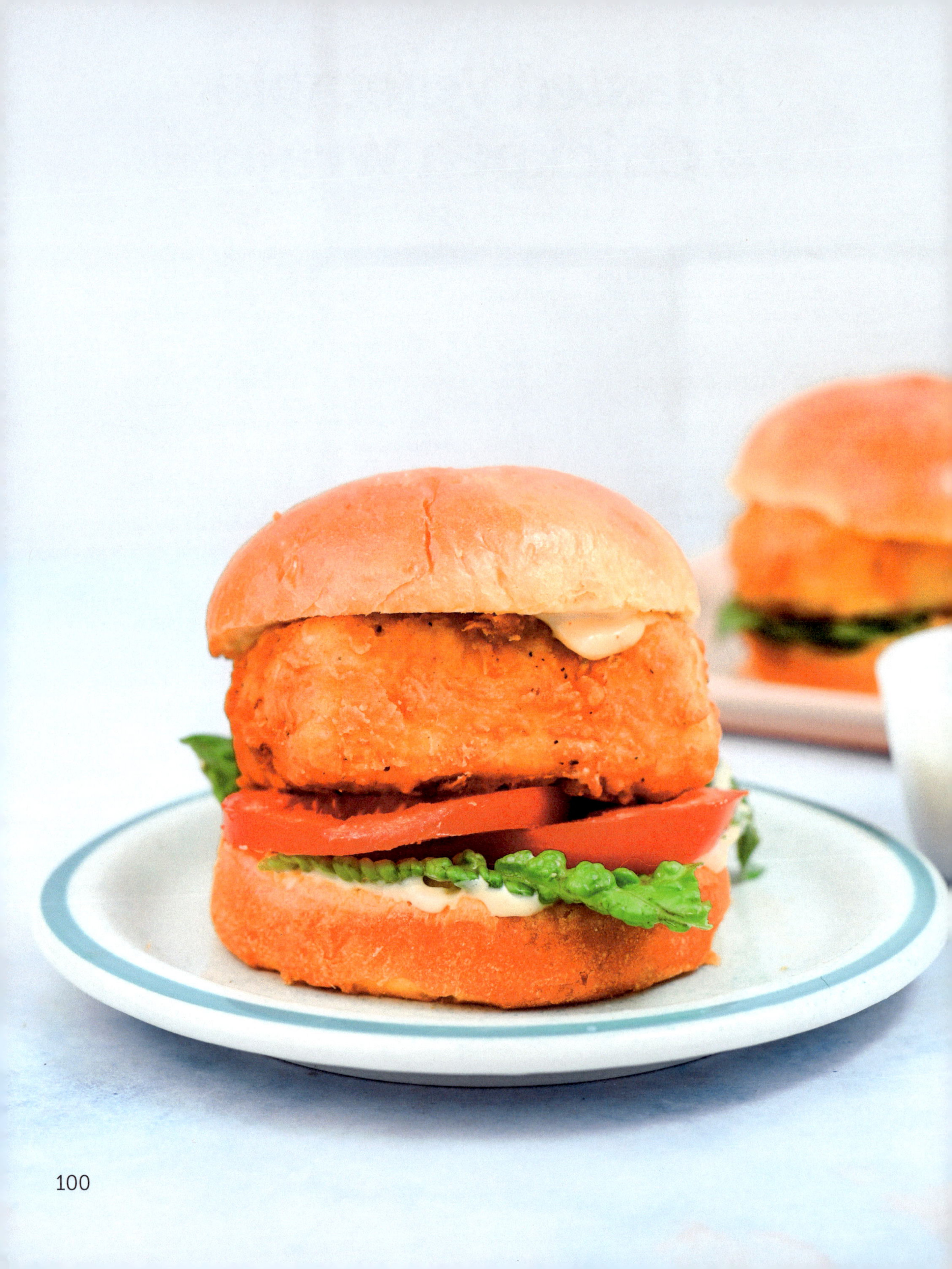

Fried Tofu Sandwich

1 HOUR • 4 SANDWICHES

If this cookbook had a section titled "pure comfort," this would be its first recipe. Living in the South, or maybe just being from the U.S. in general, I love fried food. This is a chicken sandwich dupe, with a hearty crisp and crunchy battered block of tofu and sweet and spicy burger sauce. Recipe testers noted that this recipe is also fantastic as tofu nuggets!

TOFU MARINADE

1 (16-ounce) block super-firm tofu
½ cup unsweetened soy milk or oat milk
¼ cup pickle juice, from a jar of sandwich pickles
1 teaspoon paprika
½ teaspoon garlic powder
½ teaspoon onion powder
¼ teaspoon kosher salt
¼ teaspoon black pepper

TOFU BREADING

1 cup all-purpose flour
1 teaspoon baking powder
1 teaspoon Old Bay seasoning
½ teaspoon black pepper
½ teaspoon garlic powder
½ teaspoon onion powder
¼ teaspoon kosher salt

ASSEMBLY

2 to 3 cups canola oil, for frying
1 tablespoon unsalted butter
4 burger buns
½ cup mayonnaise
2 teaspoons Dijon mustard
2 teaspoons honey
2 teaspoons sriracha
Romaine lettuce and sandwich pickles, for serving

> **Note:** Unlike a few other recipes in the cookbook, this recipe only works with shallow or deep frying. Try to keep the oil at 325°F-350°F during frying. If you don't have a frying thermometer, this step will take some guesswork. The oil should be steadily bubbling.

1. Slice the tofu in half length-wise then width-wise to make 4 thick slices of tofu. Set aside.
2. In a medium bowl, whisk together the soy milk, pickle juice, paprika, garlic powder, onion powder, salt, and pepper. Add the blocks of tofu and marinate for at least 30 minutes, but ideally overnight. After marinating, remove tofu and **reserve the marinade**. Gently pat the tofu dry with a paper towel to remove excess moisture. Set aside.
3. To make the breading, whisk together the flour, baking powder, Old Bay seasoning, black pepper, garlic powder, onion powder, and salt in a shallow dish wide enough to fit the tofu.
4. Use one hand to dip each tofu slice in flour, then the other hand to place the tofu in the reserved marinade. Shake tofu to remove any big drops of liquid. Return it to the flour to coat once again. Repeat until all pieces of tofu are double-battered.
5. Add at least 3 inches of oil to a large skillet or Dutch oven. Heat oil over medium to medium-high heat to a temperature of 350°F. Carefully add two pieces of breaded tofu at a time, careful not to overcrowd the pot. The tofu should be fully covered by oil. Fry until crisp and golden, about 8 to 10 minutes.
6. Carefully remove tofu from the pot and place on a plate lined with paper towels to drain.
7. Meanwhile, heat a medium skillet over medium heat. Add a small sliver of butter. Once melted, place burger buns cut-side down on the skillet. Toast until golden, just 1 to 2 minutes.
8. Make the sriracha sauce by whisking together the mayonnaise, Dijon mustard, honey, and sriracha in a small bowl.
9. Assemble sandwiches by spreading each bun with the sauce. Top with a romaine lettuce leaf, the fried tofu, and pickles. Enjoy immediately.

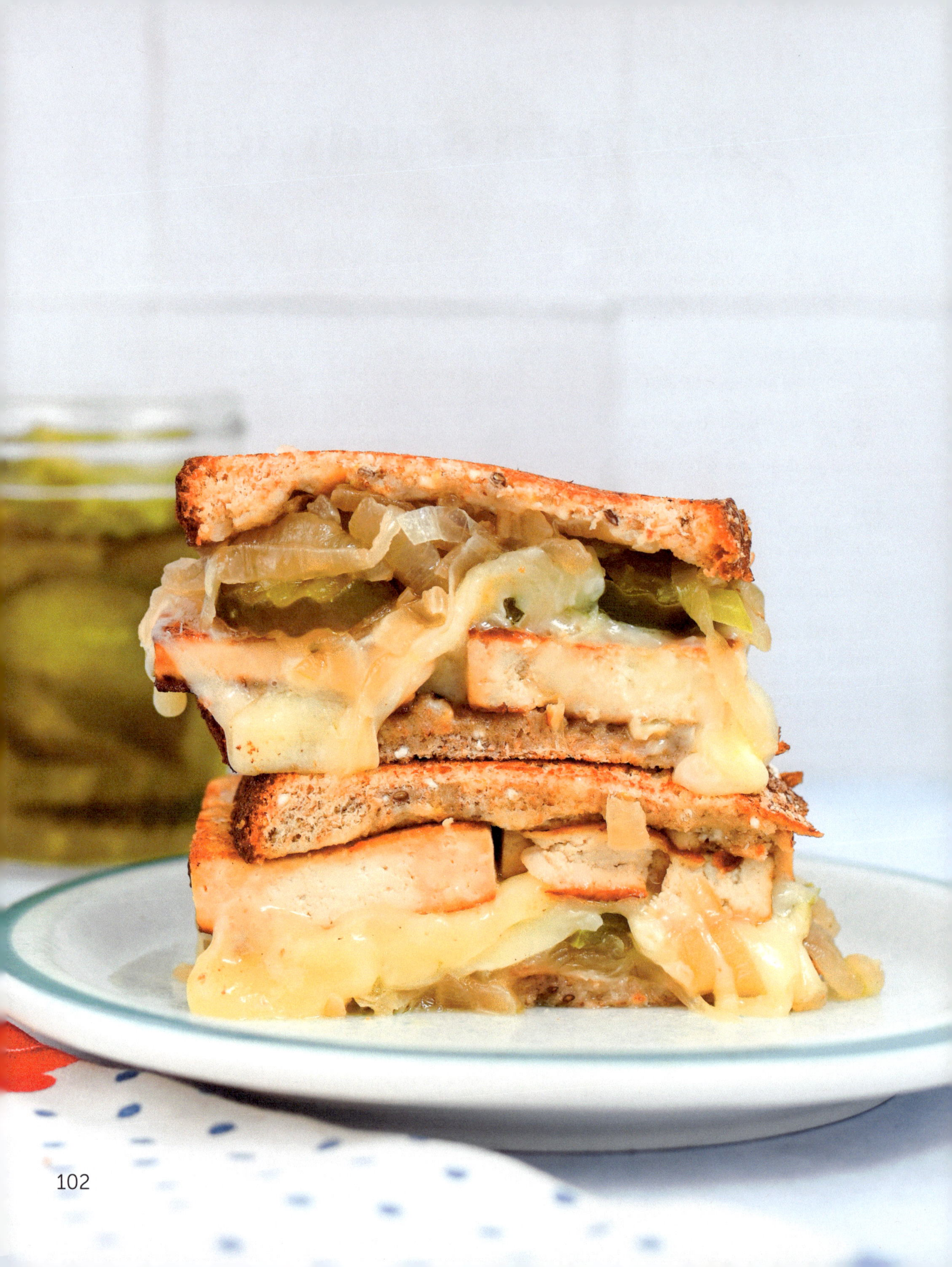

Tofu Patty Melt

1 HOUR • 4 SANDWICHES

While caramelized onions keep this from being a quick and easy sandwich, I promise that the sweet jammy flavor they add is worth the effort. Maggi sauce is a very concentrated but high-impact umami flavor enhancer. A small amount goes a long way, and I highly recommend keeping it on hand for tofu marinades. It's available in most grocery stores in the international aisle.

- 1 tablespoon extra virgin olive oil, more as needed
- 3 small yellow onions, sliced into very thin strips
- ¼ teaspoon kosher salt
- ⅛ teaspoon granulated sugar
- 1 (14-ounce) block extra-firm tofu
- ½ cup vegetable broth
- 1 tablespoon nutritional yeast
- 1 tablespoon soy sauce
- 1 teaspoon Maggi sauce
- ½ teaspoon garlic powder
- 8 slices white bread (whole wheat bread also works)
- ¼ cup mayonnaise
- 6 slices sharp white cheddar cheese
- ½ cup dill pickle sandwich chips
- 1 tablespoon unsalted butter

1. Heat a large skillet over medium heat. Drizzle with a thin layer of oil. Once hot, add the onions. Sprinkle with salt and sugar. Cook for 5 to 6 minutes, until the onions begin to turn golden and soften. Reduce heat to medium-low. Continue cooking for 35 to 40 minutes, stirring only every 8 to 10 minutes. The goal is soft, golden brown caramelized onions. *Note: If the onions are burning or cooking too quickly, reduce heat further and add a splash of water to the skillet.*

2. Meanwhile, press the tofu block for 10 minutes. After pressing, slice the tofu into 12 thin rectangles. In a medium bowl, whisk together the vegetable broth, nutritional yeast, soy sauce, Maggi sauce, and garlic powder. Marinate tofu in a shallow dish for at least 20 minutes and up to overnight. If the tofu isn't completely covered in marinade, flip it halfway through.

3. Heat another skillet over medium heat. Drizzle with a thin layer of oil. Add the marinated tofu, cooking in batches as needed. Cook until golden on each side, about 8 to 10 minutes total.

4. To assemble the sandwiches, first spread two pieces of bread with a thin layer of mayonnaise. Top with ¼ of the caramelized onions, then top with ¼ of the tofu. Top with 1 ½ slices of cheese and a few sandwich pickles. Close the sandwich.

5. Heat a skillet over medium heat. Add the butter. Once melted, add the sandwich. Once golden on one side, flip the sandwich and reduce heat to medium-low. Cover with a lid and cook until the cheese is completely melted. Repeat with each sandwich. Enjoy immediately.

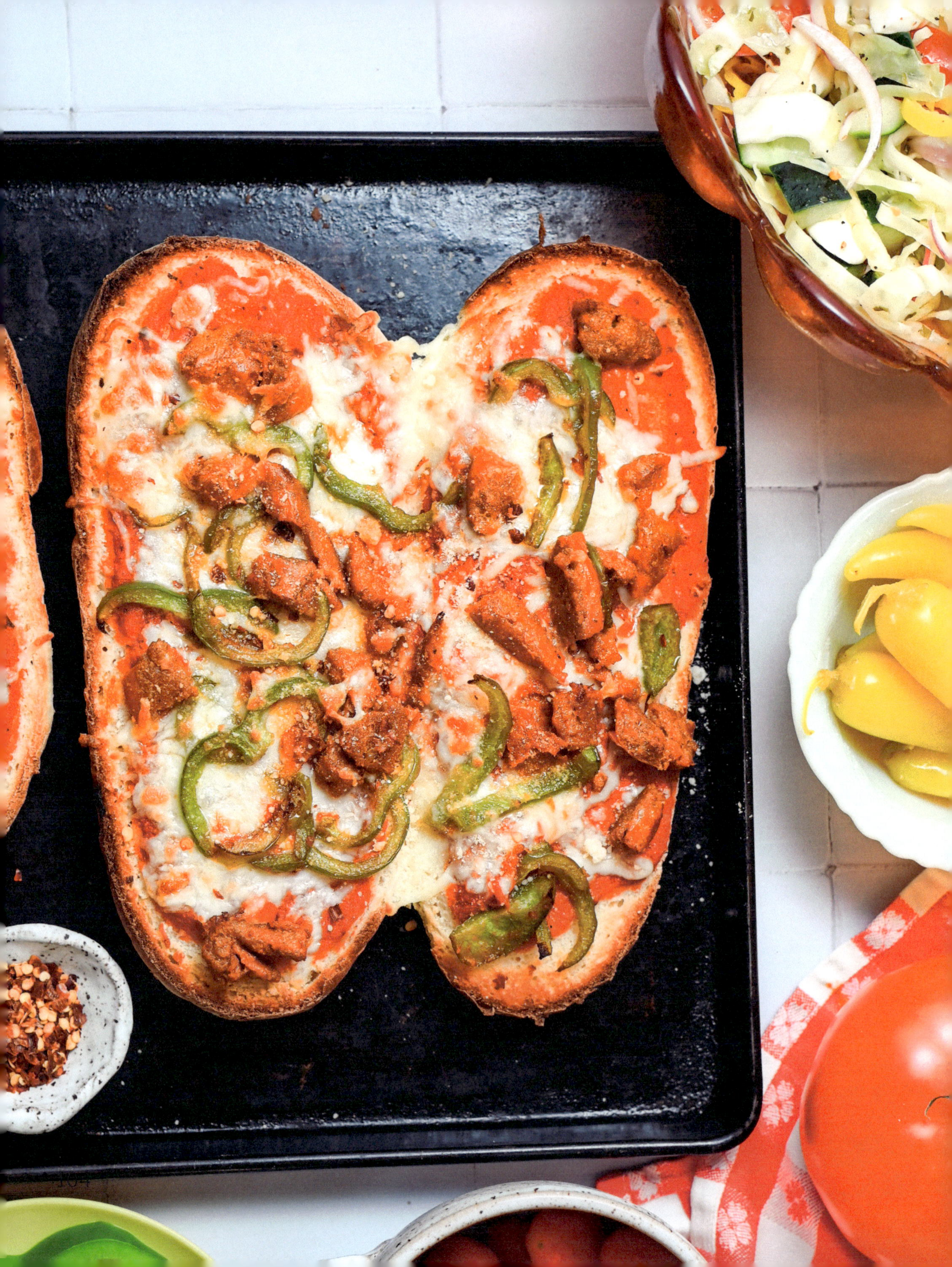

Pizza Bread

3 HOURS (30 MINUTES ACTIVE TIME) • 4-8 SERVINGS

In Normal, Illinois (yes, I'm originally from a town called Bloomington Normal), there's a restaurant called Avanti's. They make the most wonderful homemade bread that they turn into gondolas (sub sandwiches, basically), pizza burgers (meatball subs), and pizza bread. I haven't lived in Illinois since I was a child, but that didn't stopped me from developing my own homemade Avanti's bread recipe. It's sweet, tender, and makes the perfect base for all kinds of sub sandwiches.

BREAD

1 ½ cups water
1 package instant yeast (2 ¼ teaspoons yeast)
½ cup granulated sugar
1 large egg
1 tablespoon canola oil
½ teaspoon table salt
4 ½ to 5 cups all-purpose flour

ASSEMBLY

1 (24-ounce) jar marinara sauce
1 teaspoon extra virgin olive oil
1 medium green bell pepper, sliced
2 cups (8 ounces) shredded mozzarella cheese
1 tablespoon fresh chopped oregano (or 1 teaspoon dried oregano)
Other topping ideas include veggie sausage, onion, hot peppers, or tomatoes

Notes: If you don't have a thermometer, aim for "bathwater" temperature, which is cool enough that you can tolerate the water, but hot enough that it is significantly warm. Water that is too hot kills the yeast and water that is too cool prevents the yeast from activating. A "warm area" for resting the dough changes depending on the season. In the summer, the countertop is usually fine. On cooler days, I preheat the oven to the lowest setting for 5 minutes, then turn it off and place the dough bowl inside with the oven door cracked.

1. Heat water to 105°F on the stove or with an electric kettle.

2. To a large mixing bowl, add the warm water, instant yeast, sugar, egg, canola oil, salt, and 1 ½ cups flour. Stir with a large spoon until combined. Stir in flour one cup at a time, until a total of 4 and ½ cups are added. The dough should be easy to work with and slightly sticky.

3. Transfer dough to a lightly floured surface. Knead until smooth and elastic, about 8 to 10 minutes. Add additional flour if the dough is too sticky to handle. Lightly oil a large bowl. Add the dough, tossing to coat. Cover with a clean towel and let rest in a warm area until doubled in size, about 1 to 1 ½ hours, depending on the kitchen temperature.

4. Punch down the dough to deflate it. Knead a few times on the same lightly floured surface. Divide the dough into 4 equally sized pieces. Using a rolling pin or your hands, gently roll each piece of dough into roughly 9x2 inch loaves resembling small sub rolls. Transfer to two half sheet pans. Cover with a clean dish cloth or plastic wrap. Let rise until doubled in size, about 30 minutes. During the last 10 minutes of rising, preheat the oven to 350°F.

5. Once doubled in size, bake the bread at 350°F for 20 to 25 minutes, or until golden brown on top. Remove from the oven and let cool while preparing the toppings.

6. Add marinara sauce to a medium pot. Cover with a lid and heat over medium heat until hot and simmering. Meanwhile, heat a skillet over medium heat. Drizzle with olive oil. Once hot, add the sliced bell pepper and any other desired toppings. Sauté until golden, about 6 to 8 minutes.

7. Increase the oven temperature to 375°F. Slice the bread loaves in half as you would a sub roll. Spread about ¼ cup of marinara sauce over each half. Top each side with ¼ cup shredded mozzarella, a sprinkling of sautéed peppers, and a sprinkle of the fresh chopped oregano.

8. Return to the oven to bake at 375°F for 10 minutes, or until the cheese is golden and bubbly. Remove from the oven and serve hot.

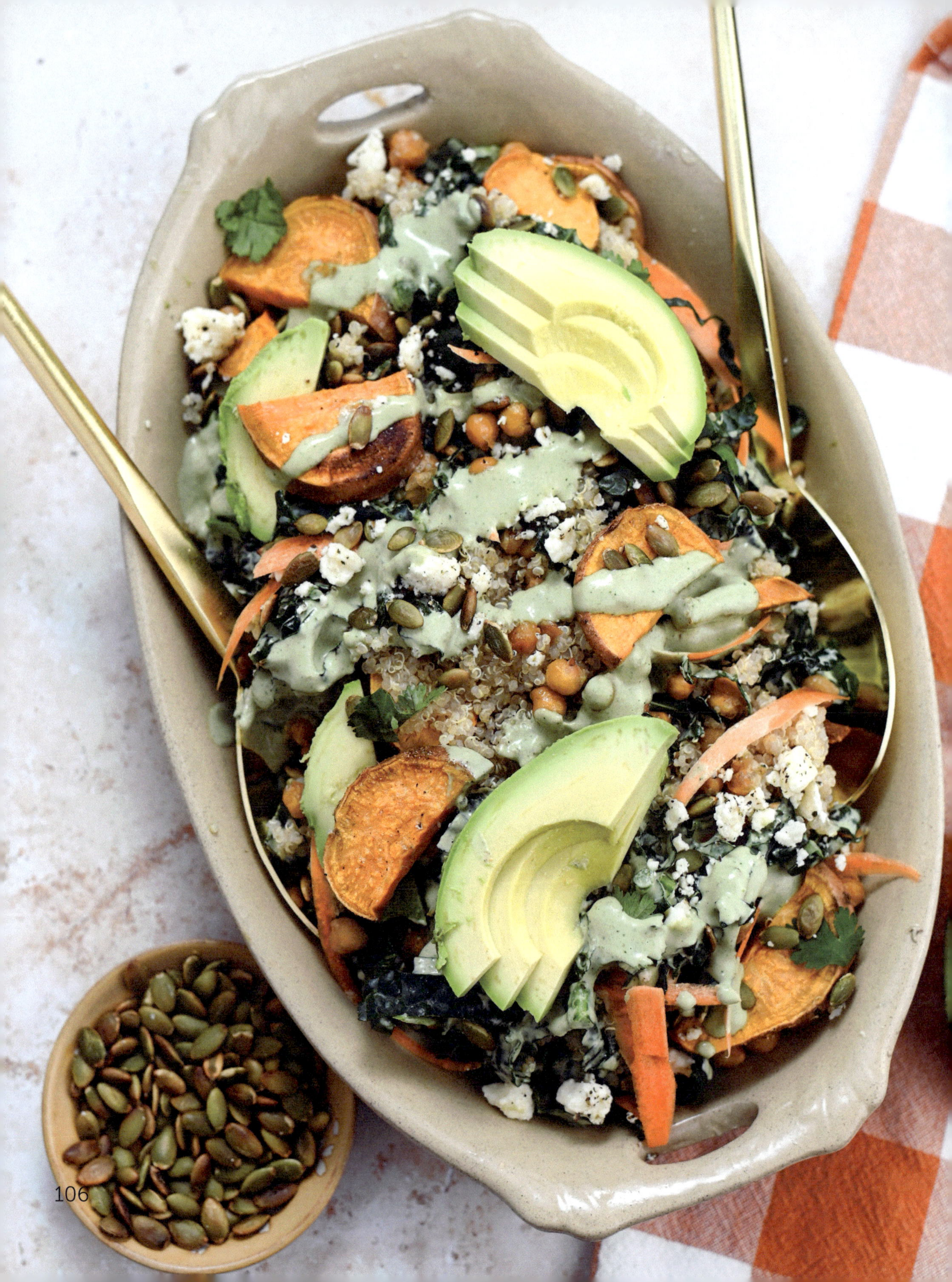

Chapter 5: Soup & Salad for Dinner

In a sea of hot dinner casseroles, bowls, and pasta dishes, this section is a refuge of lighter, meal-worthy salads and simple soups. Many of these soups and salads pair well with the previous section's sandwiches, but they are also hearty enough to serve as meals on their own. This is a great section for my gluten-free folks because all but a few of these recipes are gluten-free.

Cassidy's Favorite: Roasted Sweet Potato Salad with Jalapeño Dressing (p. 113) and White "Chicken" Chili (p. 119)

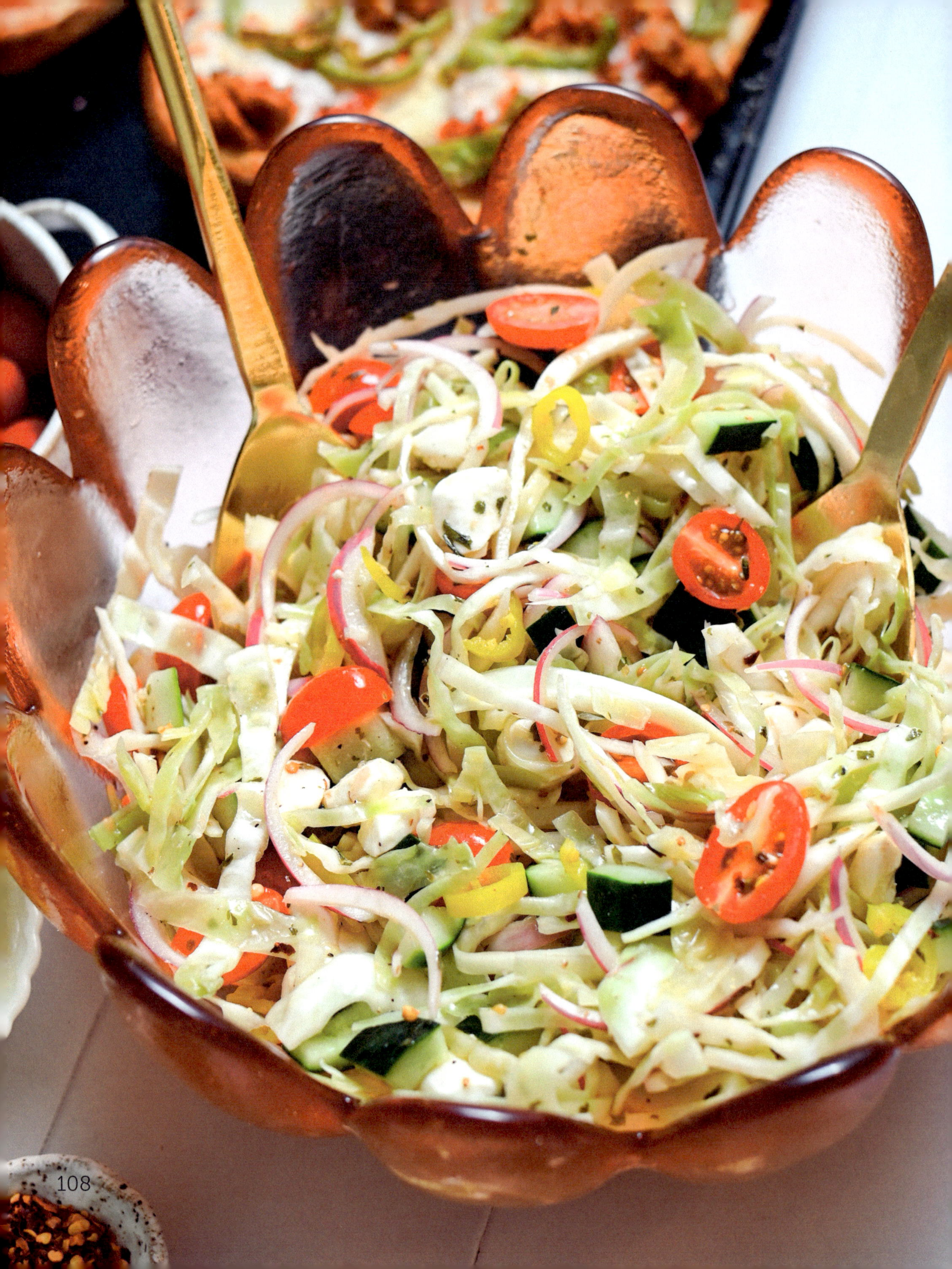

Chopped Pizza Salad

20 MINUTES • 4-6 SERVINGS

I love the concept of salad that's made just for pizza. This one is crisp, crunchy, tangy, and perfectly balances out soft pizza, especially Pizza Bread (p. 105) or Spicy Sausage Pizza (p. 61). I opt for thinly sliced cabbage for a whole lot of crunch, but cabbage skeptics can make this salad with an equal amount of shredded romaine lettuce instead.

RED WINE VINAIGRETTE

⅓ cup extra virgin olive oil
¼ cup red wine vinegar
1 teaspoon dried parsley
1 teaspoon Dijon mustard
½ teaspoon dried oregano
½ teaspoon honey, plus more to taste
¼ teaspoon table salt
1 clove garlic, grated

SALAD INGREDIENTS

½ small green cabbage, thinly shredded (about 8 cups shredded cabbage)
½ large red onion, very thinly sliced
½ cup chopped banana peppers
1 pint cherry tomatoes, sliced in half
4 ounces mozzarella pearls
1 medium cucumber, diced
Freshly ground black pepper, to taste
Red pepper flakes, for serving

1. In a medium bowl or jar, make the vinaigrette by whisking together the olive oil, red wine vinegar, parsley, Dijon mustard, oregano, honey, salt, and garlic. Adjust seasonings to taste.

2. Add the shredded cabbage to a large bowl. Toss with the red wine vinaigrette. Add in the onion, banana peppers, tomatoes, mozzarella pearls, and cucumber. Toss to combine. Season with freshly ground black pepper and red pepper flakes, to taste. Cover and chill for at least an hour before serving. This salad is even better the next day.

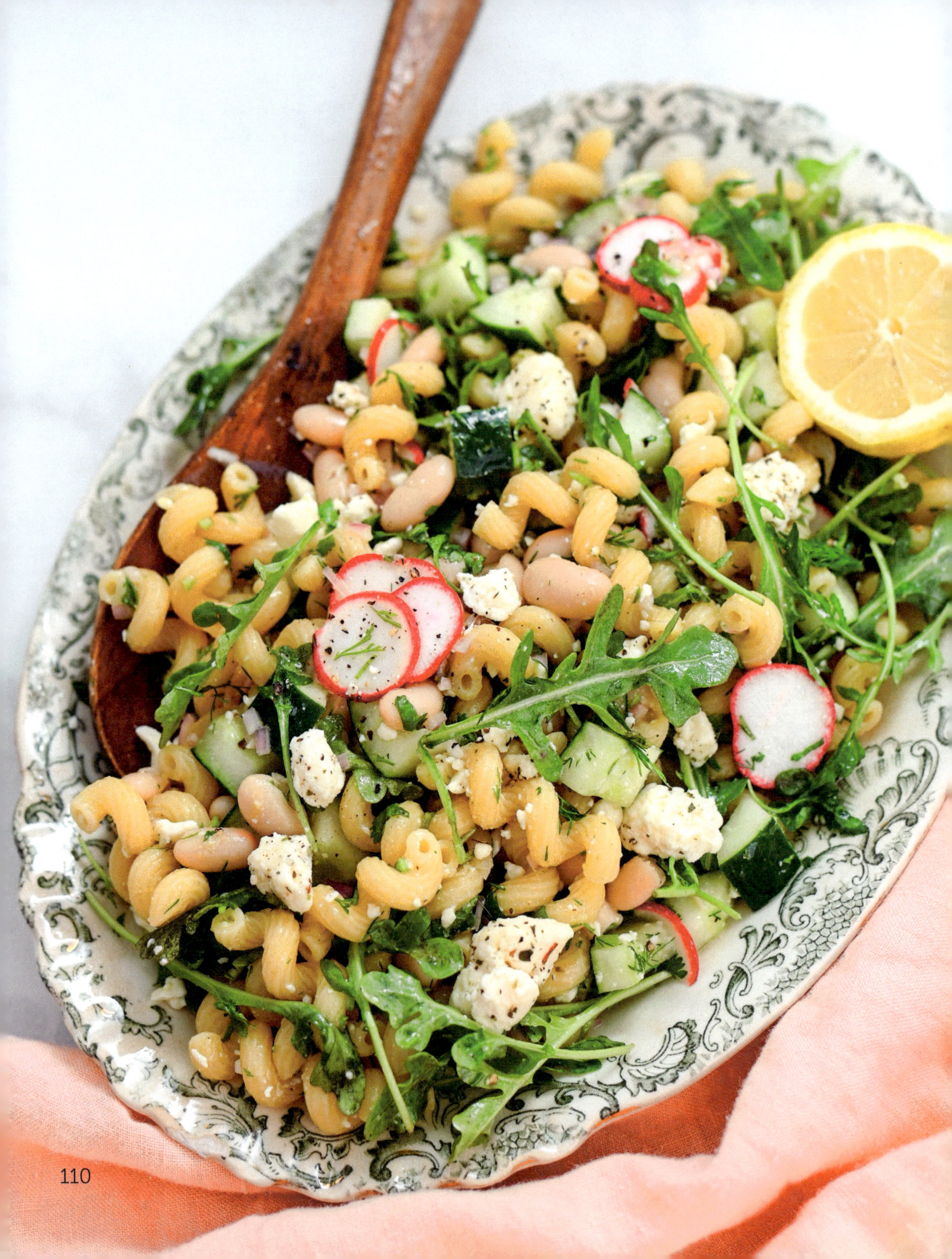

Spring Pasta Salad with Lemon Vinaigrette

25 MINUTES • 4-6 SERVINGS

I absolutely adore the lemon vinaigrette used as the base of this pasta salad. It's a great recipe to keep on hand for all kinds of salads, and it pairs well with crisp radishes and cucumbers. This recipe is great for dinner parties or picnics.

PASTA

8 ounces cavatappi pasta
1 cup (4 ounces) crumbled feta
3 handfuls arugula
1 (15-ounce) can cannellini beans, drained and rinsed
2 medium cucumbers, seeded and diced
1 cup thinly sliced red radishes
¼ cup fresh chopped cilantro
¼ cup fresh chopped dill

LEMON VINAIGRETTE

1 medium shallot, finely diced
5 tablespoons extra virgin olive oil
¼ cup lemon juice (about 2 medium lemons)
2 teaspoons honey
1 teaspoon Dijon mustard
1 heaping teaspoon lemon zest (about 1 medium lemon)
½ teaspoon kosher salt
⅛ teaspoon black pepper

1. Cook cavatappi in well-salted water until al dente. Drain and rinse well under cool running water. This is a quick way to cool pasta, but if you prefer a more "traditional" route, toss the pasta with a bit of oil, cover, and transfer it to the fridge to chill for an hour.

2. While the pasta cooks, prep the remaining ingredients. Make the vinaigrette in a small jar or bowl by whisking together the diced shallot, olive oil, lemon juice, honey, Dijon mustard, lemon zest, salt, and pepper.

3. Toss the pasta with the lemon vinaigrette, crumbled feta, arugula, cannellini beans, diced cucumber, sliced radish, cilantro, and dill. Cover and chill until ready to serve.

> **Note:** If making in advance, wait to dress the pasta with the vinaigrette until just before serving. The pasta absorbs the vinaigrette over time, which can result in a dry salad. Add the arugula just before serving.

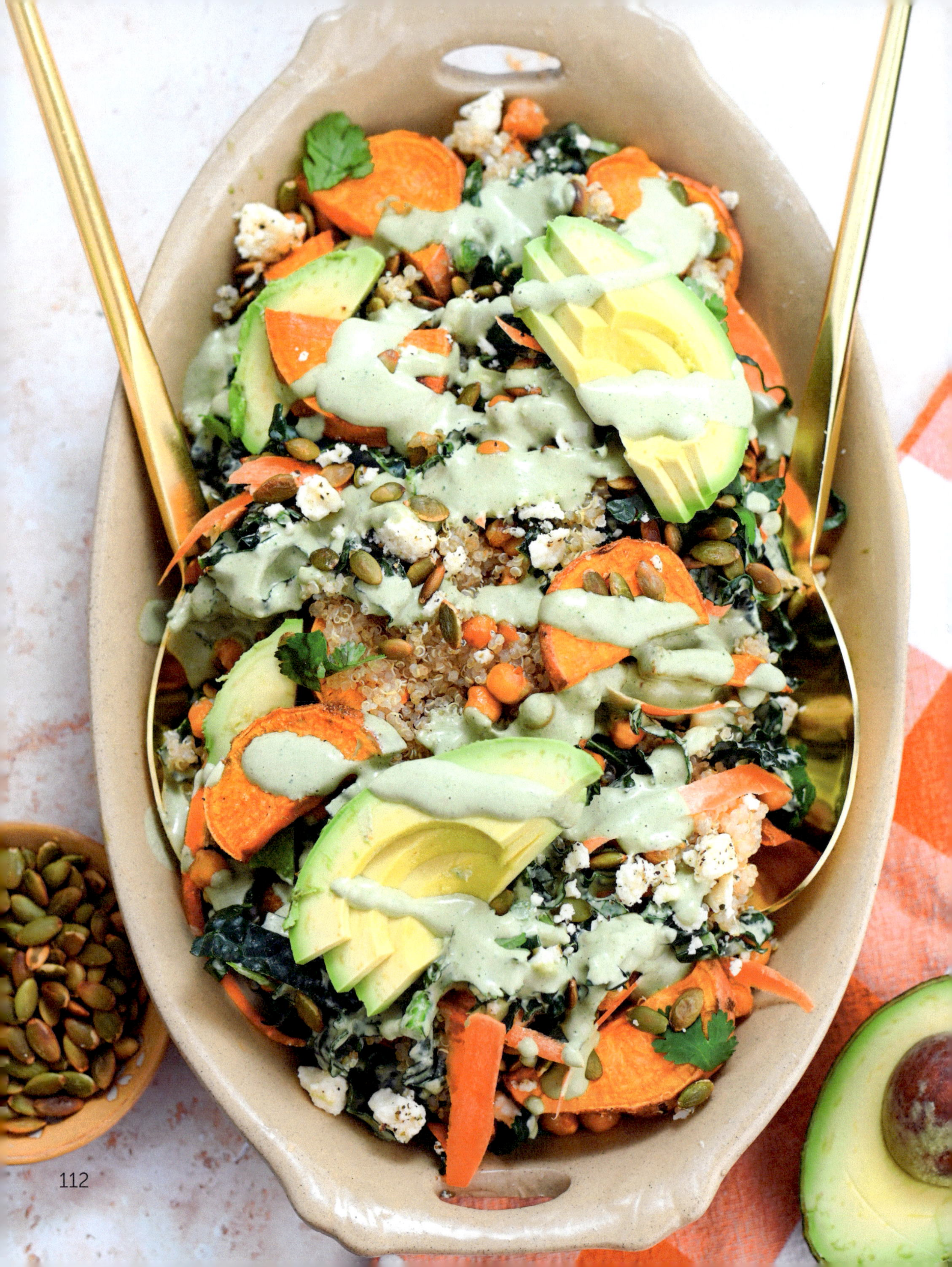

Roasted Sweet Potato Salad with Jalapeño Dressing

50 MINUTES • 4 MAIN SALADS OR 6 SIDE SALADS

This is proof that when made right, salads can be filling enough to be a main dish. This recipe is great for meal prep lunches and dinner parties. I like to serve it with a mix of warm (roasted sweet potatoes and hot quinoa) and cold ingredients (massaged kale and carrots), but leftovers are just as delicious served chilled from the fridge.

ROASTED INGREDIENTS

2 medium sweet potatoes, sliced into ¼-inch half moons
2 (15-ounce) cans chickpeas, drained and rinsed
2 tablespoons canola oil, plus a little more for the jalapeño
½ teaspoon each: ground coriander, garlic powder, ground ginger, kosher salt
1 to 2 medium jalapeños, adjust to taste

ASSEMBLY

⅔ cup dry quinoa
1 ⅓ cup vegetable broth or water
¼ teaspoon kosher salt, more as needed
2 bunches lacinato kale, sliced into ½-inch strips
1 teaspoon extra virgin olive oil
3 large carrots, grated
½ cup (2 ounces) crumbled feta
½ cup roasted pumpkin seeds
¼ cup fresh chopped cilantro
1 large avocado, sliced

JALAPEÑO LIME DRESSING

2 roasted jalapeños (see step #4)
⅔ cup tahini
⅔ cup water
½ cup fresh chopped cilantro
¼ cup lime juice (about 2 small limes)
1 teaspoon honey
¼ teaspoon kosher salt
Water, as needed

For the roasted ingredients

1. Preheat the oven to 400°F. Line a large sheet pan with parchment paper or foil.

2. In a large bowl, toss the sliced sweet potato and chickpeas with canola oil, coriander, garlic powder, ginger, and salt. Spread into a single layer on the sheet pan. Try to avoid overlapping.

3. Toss the jalapeño with a small amount of oil and pinch of salt. Place on the sheet pan. Roast at 400°F for 35 to 40 minutes, until the sweet potatoes are tender and chickpeas are crisp and almost crunchy. The jalapeño will be golden brown, almost blackened.

4. **To make the dressing:** Remove the stem from the roasted jalapeño. To a blender, add the roasted jalapeños, tahini, water, cilantro, lime juice, honey, and salt. The dressing should be a smooth, pourable consistency. If needed, add water 1 tablespoon at a time to thin.

For the salad & assembly

5. While the vegetables roast, cook the quinoa. Rinse quinoa in a fine-mesh sieve. Transfer to a medium sauce pot with water and ¼ teaspoon salt. Bring to a rapid simmer, then reduce to a gentle simmer over medium-low heat. Cover and simmer until the liquid is fully absorbed, about 15 minutes. Turn off heat and fluff quinoa with a fork.

6. Transfer the sliced kale to a large bowl. Gently massage sliced kale with 1 teaspoon olive oil for a full minute.

7. Use tongs to toss the kale with roasted jalapeño dressing. Add the quinoa, sweet potatoes, chickpeas, carrots, feta, pumpkin seeds, cilantro, and avocado. Gently toss to combine. Serve as one large salad or divide into smaller salads.

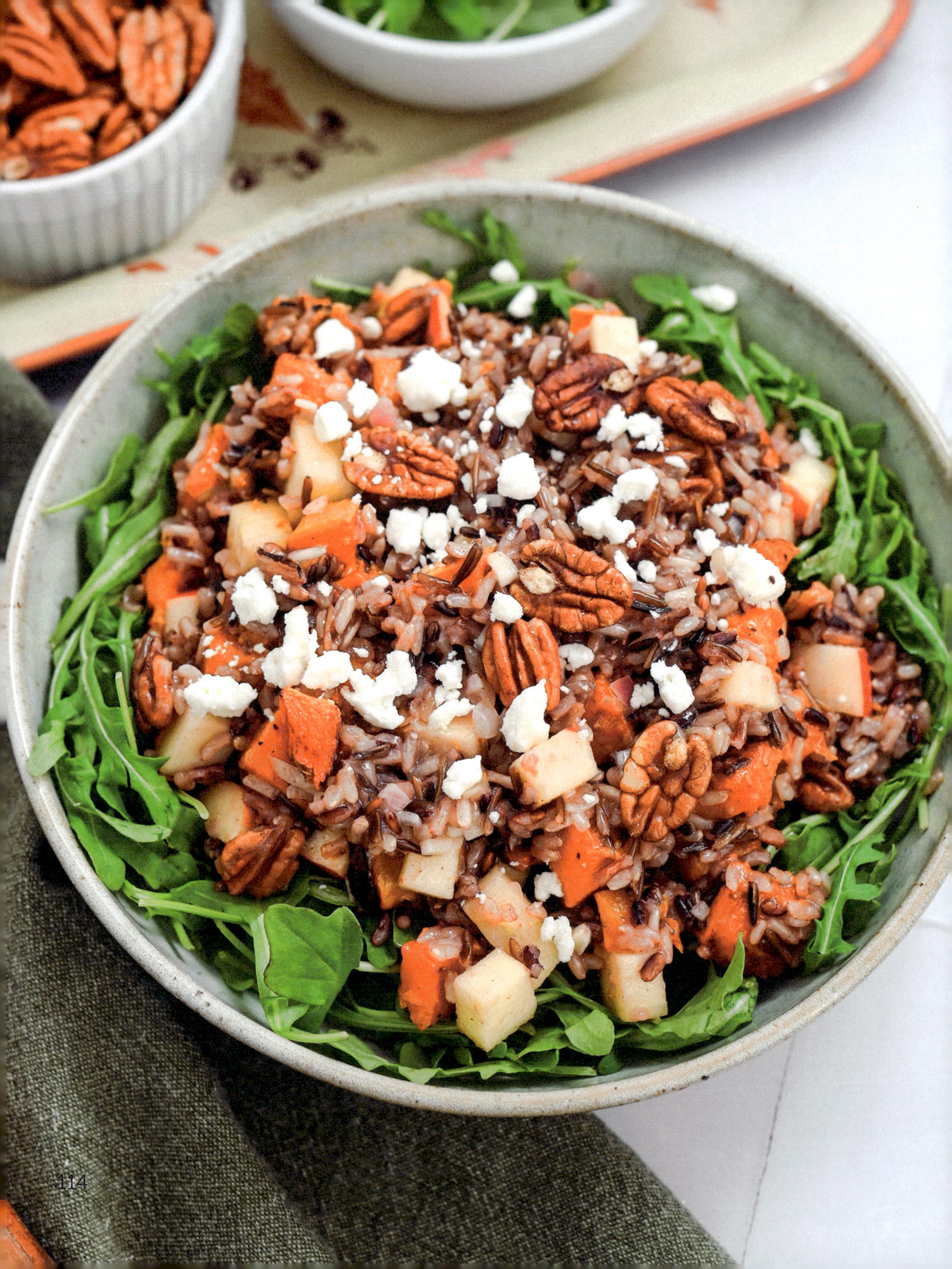

Wild Rice Salad with Apple Cider Vinaigrette

1 HOUR • 4 SERVINGS

This salad was made with fall in mind. It is the perfect addition to Thanksgiving spreads, thanks to the sweet and earthy combination of roasted butternut squash, pecans, wild rice, and a refreshing apple cider vinaigrette.

ASSEMBLY

1 cup wild rice blend
1 ¾ cup vegetable broth
¼ teaspoon table salt
5 ounces arugula
1 medium honeycrisp apple, diced
1 cup (4 ounces) crumbled goat cheese

ROASTED BUTTERNUT SQUASH

1 ½ pounds butternut squash
1 tablespoon canola oil
½ teaspoon kosher salt
¼ teaspoon black pepper
¼ teaspoon dried ground thyme
¼ teaspoon garlic powder
¼ teaspoon onion powder
½ cup pecans

APPLE CIDER VINAIGRETTE

1 small shallot, finely diced
5 tablespoons extra virgin olive oil
¼ cup apple cider vinegar
1 teaspoon Dijon mustard
¼ teaspoon kosher salt

1. Preheat the oven to 425°F.

2. Rinse the rice well in a fine-mesh strainer. Add the rinsed rice, vegetable broth, and salt to a medium pot. Bring to a boil over high heat, then reduce to a gentle simmer over low to medium-low heat. Cover and simmer until the rice is tender, about 45 to 50 minutes. Fluff with a fork. The rice should be chewy but cooked through. Drain off excess water, if needed.

3. Meanwhile, peel skin from the butternut squash. Cut the squash in half lengthways, then scoop out the seeds. Dice the squash into ½-inch cubes. Toss with oil, salt, black pepper, dried thyme, garlic powder, and onion powder.

4. Spread the squash into an even layer on a large parchment paper or foil-lined sheet pan, careful not to overlap pieces. Roast at 425°F for 30 minutes, or until golden and tender. At the 30-minute mark, add the pecans to the sheet pan. Cook an additional 5 minutes, or until the pecans are toasted and the squash is starting to blacken in some spots.

5. While the rice and squash cook, make the vinaigrette in a small bowl or jar by whisking together the diced shallot, olive oil, apple cider vinegar, Dijon mustard, and salt. Taste for seasonings.

6. In a large bowl, toss the arugula with the vinaigrette. Add the rice, roasted butternut squash, pecans, diced apple, and goat cheese. Toss to combine. Serve warm.

> **Note:** Wild rice blends usually contain a variety of rice types. I use Lundberg brand wild rice blend. I don't recommend using plain wild rice for this recipe.

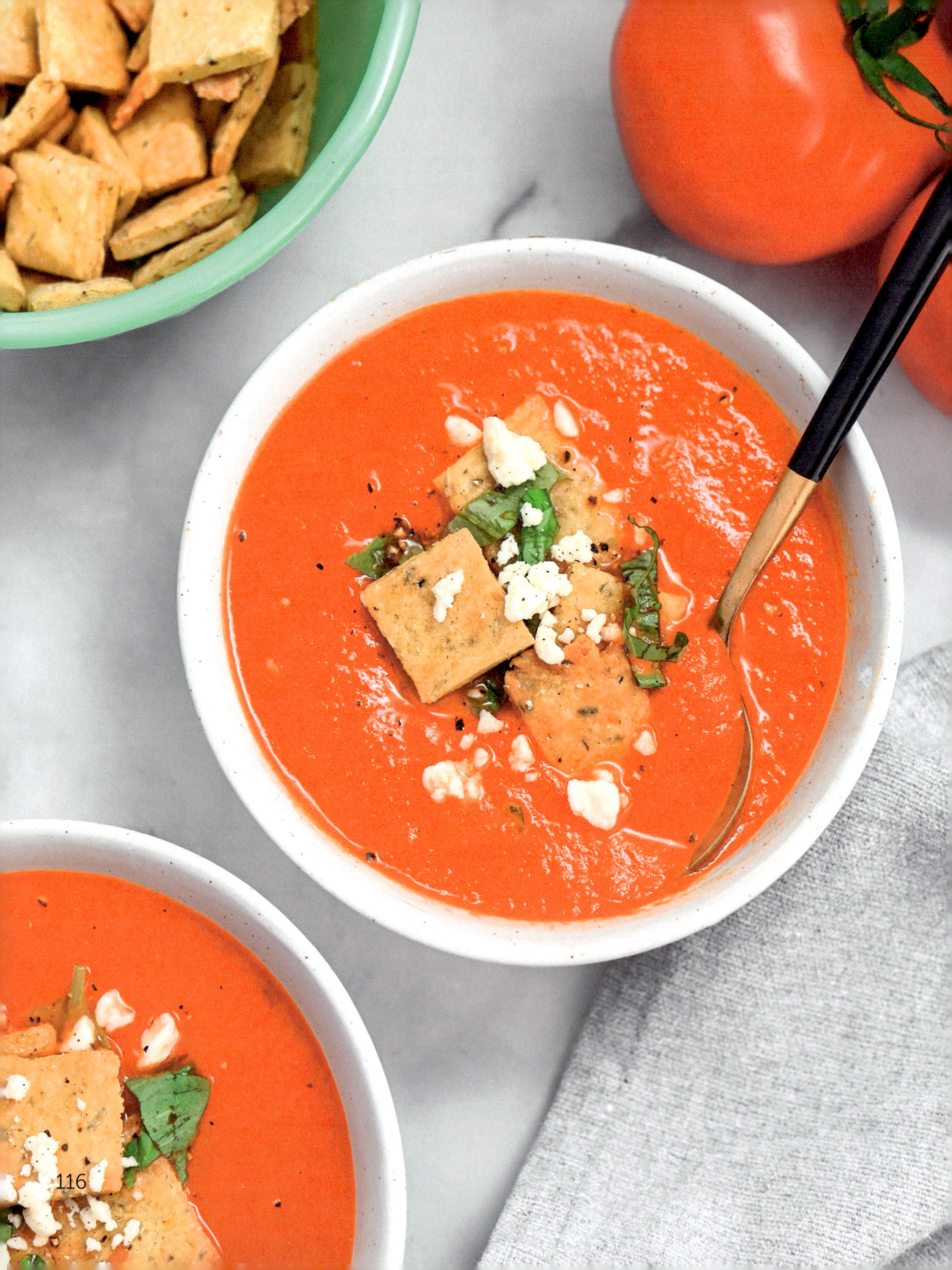

Year-Round Pantry Tomato Soup with Herby Crackers

20 MINUTES SOUP • 30 MINUTES CRACKERS • 4 SERVINGS

Maybe this is just me, but the irony of tomato soup is that it's most enjoyable on cold days, but in season during the hottest days of summer. In the summer, I do love to make tomato soup using fresh, ripe tomatoes from my own garden or from the farmer's market. In the winter, I rely on pantry ingredients. This is the perfect soup to pair with grilled cheese or a tofu patty melt (p. 103).

TOMATO SOUP
- 2 tablespoons extra virgin olive oil
- 1 cup diced yellow onion (about ½ medium onion)
- ¾ teaspoon kosher salt
- 3 cloves garlic, roughly chopped
- 2 tablespoons tomato paste
- 1 (28-ounce) can whole, peeled tomatoes
- ½ cup vegetable broth
- ½ teaspoon dried basil
- ¼ teaspoon granulated sugar

HERBY CRACKERS
- 1 ¼ cup all-purpose flour
- 3 tablespoons nutritional yeast
- 1 teaspoon dried rosemary
- 1 teaspoon dried thyme
- ¼ teaspoon table salt
- ¼ teaspoon black pepper
- ¼ cup extra virgin olive oil
- 4 to 5 tablespoons ice cold water, as needed

> **Note:** Smaller crackers bake more quickly than larger crackers. Be sure to check the crackers frequently, especially toward the end of the bake time, as they burn quickly.

For the tomato soup

1. Heat a medium pot over medium heat. Drizzle with olive oil. Once hot, add the onions and salt. Sauté until softened and golden, about 6 to 8 minutes. Add the garlic and tomato paste. Sauté, stirring frequently, until the garlic is golden and aromatic, about 2 minutes.

2. Add the whole, peeled tomatoes with juices, vegetable broth, basil, and sugar. Carefully transfer to a blender and blend until puréed, or immersion blend in the pot until smooth.

3. Return to the stove. Simmer over medium-low heat for at least 10 minutes, or while prepping the crackers. Taste for salt and sugar. Serve with crackers.

For the crackers

4. Preheat the oven to 350°F. Line a large sheet pan with parchment paper.

5. In a medium mixing bowl, stir together the flour, nutritional yeast, rosemary, thyme, salt, and pepper. Stir in the olive oil, using a spoon to combine. The mixture will be crumbly. Add in 1 tablespoon of water at a time, mixing with your hands, until a ball forms and holds together.

6. Lightly dust a clean surface with flour. Using a rolling pin, roll out the dough on a baking mat or between two sheets of wax paper. Roll until the dough is a very thin sheet. Use a pizza cutter or knife to slice into 1-inch squares.

7. Place cracker-dough squares on the baking sheet, careful not to overlap pieces. Use a toothpick to poke 1 to 2 holes in each cracker.

8. Bake at 350°F for 15 to 20 minutes, or until lightly browned. Remove from oven and allow to cool on racks before serving on the tomato soup.

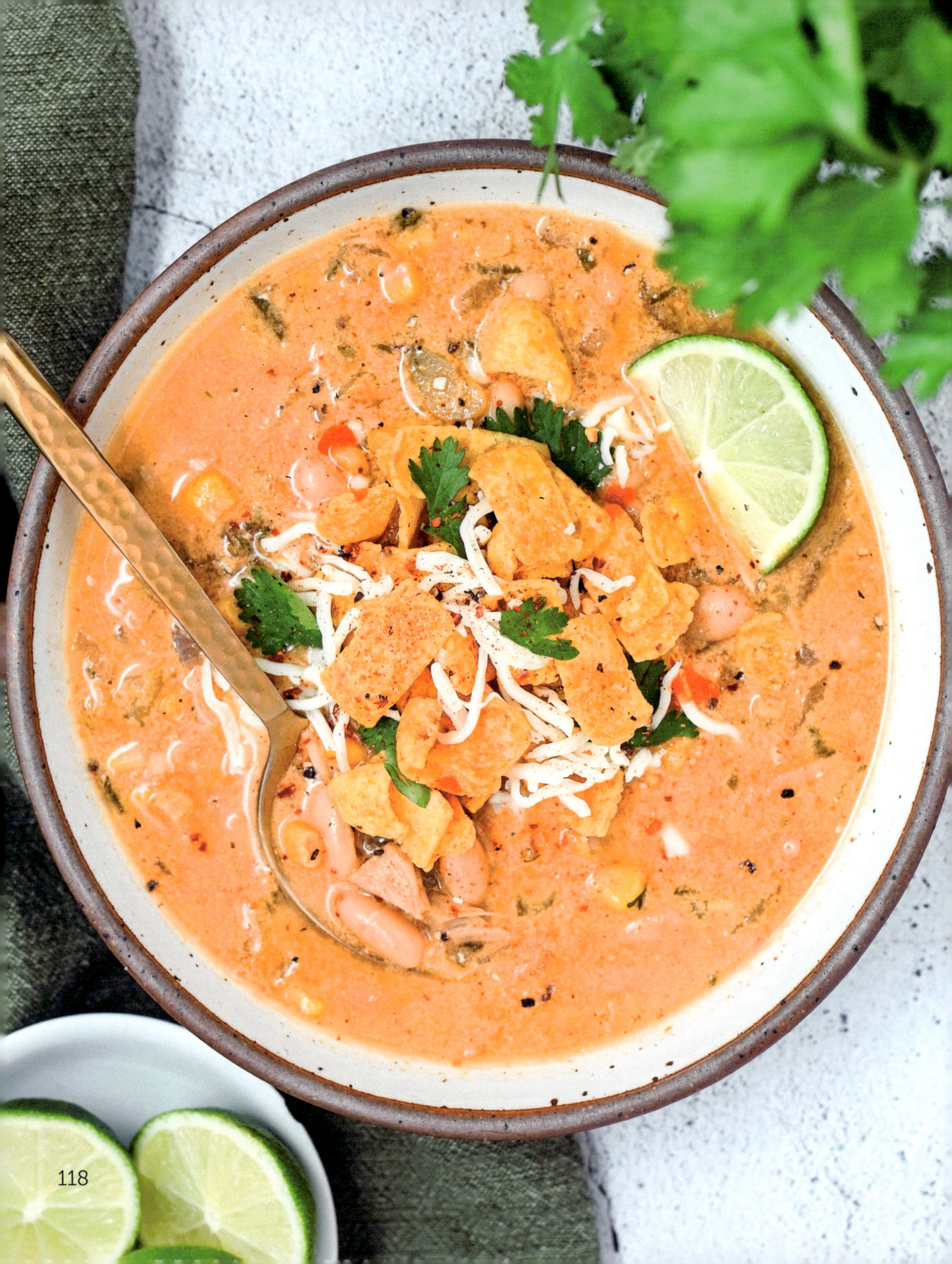

White "Chicken" Chili

35 MINUTES • 6 SERVINGS

When I first started assembling this cookbook, I had five recipes that featured some kind of chili, which isn't too egregious for someone from a Midwestern family that grew up on near-weekly Steak 'n Shake chili consumption. I eventually wheedled it down to 3 recipes, and this one reminds me most of a recipe that I grew up eating. Traditionally made with shredded chicken, this meatless version uses shredded jackfruit for a similar texture, with white beans to keep the protein per serving relatively high. A creamy white broth and a base of salsa verde and green chiles make this chili more like tortilla soup than any chili that you'd expect to find at a chili cook-off.

4 ounces Neufchâtel (low-fat) cream cheese, cubed
1 (20-ounce) can jackfruit, drained
1 tablespoon extra virgin olive oil
2 cups diced sweet yellow onion (about 1 medium onion)
1 cup diced celery (about 2 ribs)
½ teaspoon kosher salt
3 cloves garlic, minced
2 teaspoons chili powder
½ teaspoon ground cumin
½ teaspoon dried oregano
½ teaspoon paprika
5 cups vegetable broth
2 (15-ounce) cans cannellini beans, drained and rinsed
1 (15-ounce) can supersweet golden corn, drained
1 (4-ounce) can diced green chiles with juices
½ cup salsa verde
Fresh chopped cilantro, corn chips, lime wedges, and shredded mozzarella cheese, for serving

1. Set the cream cheese out to come to room temperature while the soup cooks. To prep the canned jackfruit, roughly chop it so that it resembles shredded chicken. Set aside.

2. Heat a 6-quart Dutch oven or stock pot over medium heat. Drizzle with 1 tablespoon of oil. Once hot, add the onion, celery, and salt. Sauté, stirring occasionally, until the onion is softened, about 6 to 8 minutes.

3. Add the shredded jackfruit and garlic. Continue cooking for 2 to 3 minutes, or until the garlic is golden. Stir in the chili powder, cumin, oregano, and paprika. Toast for 30 seconds to bloom the spices, stirring consistently.

4. Add in the vegetable broth, cannellini beans, corn, green chiles with juices, and salsa verde. Bring to a rapid simmer over medium-high heat, then reduce to a gentle simmer over medium-low heat. Simmer, uncovered, for at least 15 minutes and up to an hour.

5. Just before serving, stir in the room-temperature cream cheese. Stir until it melts into the soup. For a creamier soup, blend 2 cups in a blender, then add back into the pot or briefly blend with an immersion blender.

6. Serve garnished with cilantro, corn chips, a lime wedge, and shredded mozzarella.

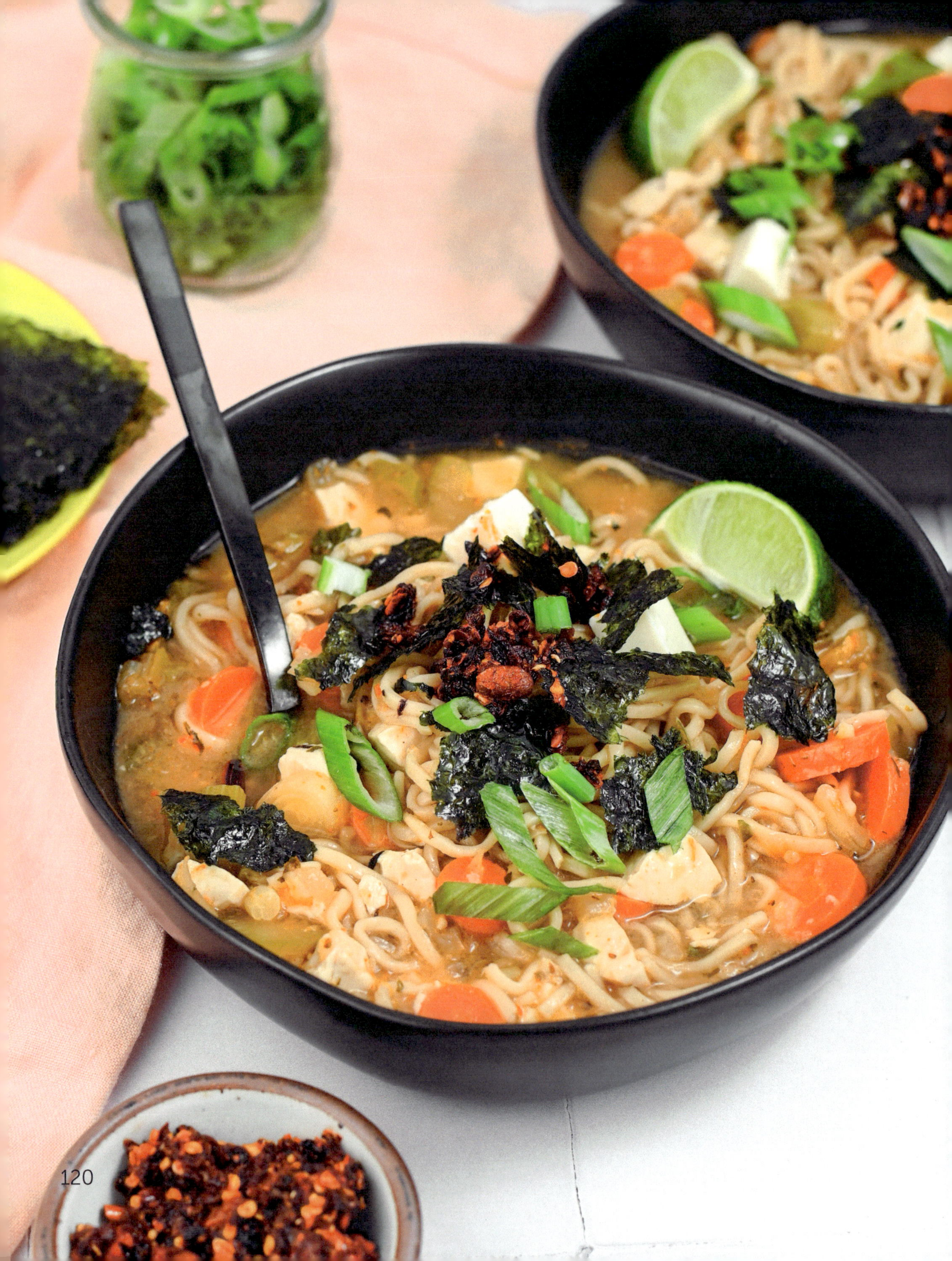

Not-Chicken Miso Noodle Soup

45 MINUTES • 4-6 SERVINGS

This recipe started out as a "chicken" noodle soup recipe and slowly morphed into the ramen noodle soup fusion that you find here. Miso is a salty fermented soybean paste traditional to Japan, and just a small amount of it served alongside ramen noodles lends a really hearty, cozy twist to an otherwise classic chicken noodle soup. This is the soup to make when you're sick and just want a big bowl of salty but nourishing comfort.

1 tablespoon yellow miso
1 tablespoon water
2 tablespoons unsalted butter
1 medium yellow onion, diced
3 large carrots, sliced into coins
3 ribs celery, sliced
½ teaspoon kosher salt
5 cloves garlic, minced
2 teaspoons grated ginger (about 1 inch ginger)
1 bunch green onions, sliced with white and green parts separated
1 teaspoon each dried oregano, paprika, parsley, and thyme leaves
6 cups vegetable broth
4 cups water
1 teaspoon garlic powder
1 teaspoon onion powder
¾ teaspoon poultry seasoning
8 ounces ramen noodles
1 (16-ounce) block soft or silken tofu, drained and cubed into ½-inch pieces
Chili crisp, roasted seaweed sheets (nori), for serving

1. In a small bowl, whisk together the miso and water to thin the miso. Set aside.

2. Heat a 6-quart Dutch oven or stock pot over medium heat. Add the butter. Once melted, stir in the onion, carrot, celery, and salt. Sauté until softened and golden, about 11 to 13 minutes.

3. Stir in the garlic, ginger, and white parts of the green onions. Sauté until the garlic is aromatic and golden, another 3 to 4 minutes. Add the oregano, paprika, parsley, and thyme, stirring frequently for 30 seconds to bloom.

4. Deglaze the pot with a splash of vegetable broth, stirring to remove any stuck on bits. Add remaining vegetable broth along with the water, garlic powder, onion powder, poultry seasoning, and thinned miso.

5. Bring to a boil over high heat. Stir in the ramen noodles. Reduce to a gentle simmer over low heat, then stir in the cubed tofu. Simmer very gently over low heat until the ramen is tender, and up to an hour to marry the flavors.

6. Serve in bowls garnished with the remaining green onion, a scoop of chili crisp, and the crushed nori.

> **Note:** Use rice noodles for a gluten-free option.

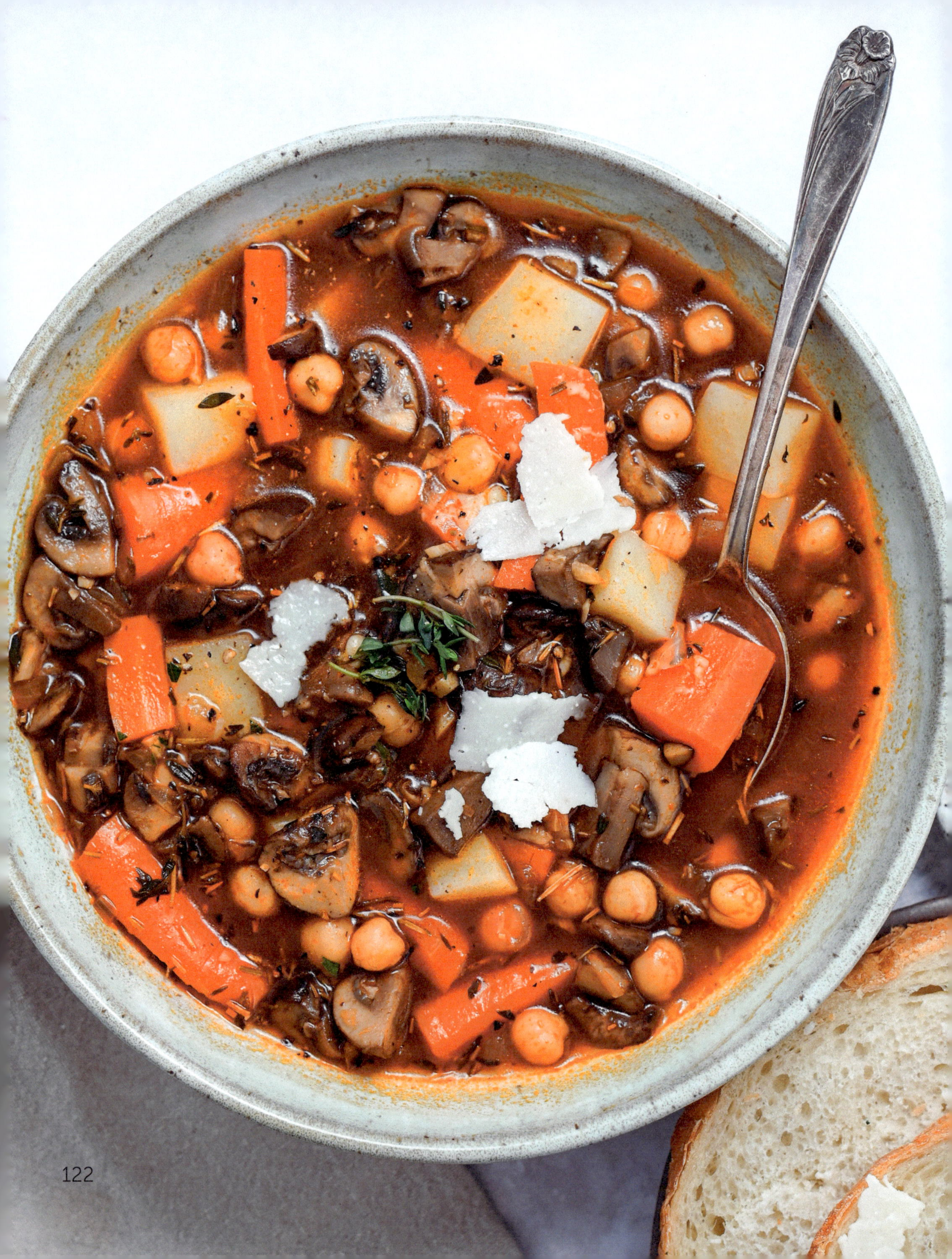

Mushroom & Potato Soup

45 MINUTES • 4-6 SERVINGS

This is my take on beef stew. Because the soup relies on low-maintenance chickpeas and mushrooms, this is much quicker than your classic meat stew. Despite that, it's richly flavored and very hearty. I highly recommend serving it with crusty bread.

8 ounces baby bella mushrooms
4 ounces "gourmet blend" mushrooms, such as shiitake and oyster
2 tablespoons extra virgin olive oil
1 cup diced yellow onion (about ½ medium onion)
3 large carrots, quartered and sliced into 2-inch pieces
1 cup celery (about 2 ribs)
4 cloves garlic, minced
2 tablespoons tomato paste
1 tablespoon fresh chopped rosemary
1 tablespoon fresh chopped thyme
¼ cup dry red wine (Cabernet or Pinot Noir)
4 ½ cups vegetable broth
1 (15-ounce) can chickpeas, drained and rinsed
1 medium russet potato, peeled and diced into ½-inch cubes
2 tablespoons nutritional yeast
1 tablespoon soy sauce
1 teaspoon vegan Worcestershire sauce
¼ teaspoon black pepper
Freshly grated Parmesan, freshly ground black pepper, and crusty bread, for serving

1. Clean the mushrooms and pat dry with a towel. Roughly chop 4 ounces of the baby bella mushrooms and slice the remaining 4 ounces into quarters. Thinly slice the gourmet blend.

2. Heat a 4 quart Dutch oven or pot over medium heat. Drizzle with olive oil. Once hot, add mushrooms. Cook for just 3 to 4 minutes, until the mushrooms start to brown. Add in onion, carrots, and celery. Cook for an additional 6 to 8 minutes, until the onions are starting to turn golden.

3. Stir in the minced garlic, tomato paste, rosemary, and thyme. Stir frequently, cooking until the garlic is golden and aromatic, about 2 minutes.

4. Deglaze the pot with the wine, stirring to remove any stuck-on bits. Add the vegetable broth, chickpeas, diced potato, nutritional yeast, soy sauce, Worcestershire sauce, and black pepper.

5. Bring to a rapid simmer over medium-high heat, then reduce to medium-low heat. Simmer uncovered until the potato is tender, about 15 minutes. Serve topped with Parmesan, black pepper, and a side of crusty bread or herby crackers (p. 117).

Notes: Choose wine that you might enjoy drinking with the meal. Don't use cheap wine that's gone bad — the mushroom soup deserves better than that! For a wine-free option, add 1 tablespoon of balsamic vinegar to the soup just before serving.

Some stores have packages of "gourmet blend" mushrooms, which feature oyster, shiitake, and other less-common mushroom varieties. If this isn't available, just grab shiitake mushrooms.

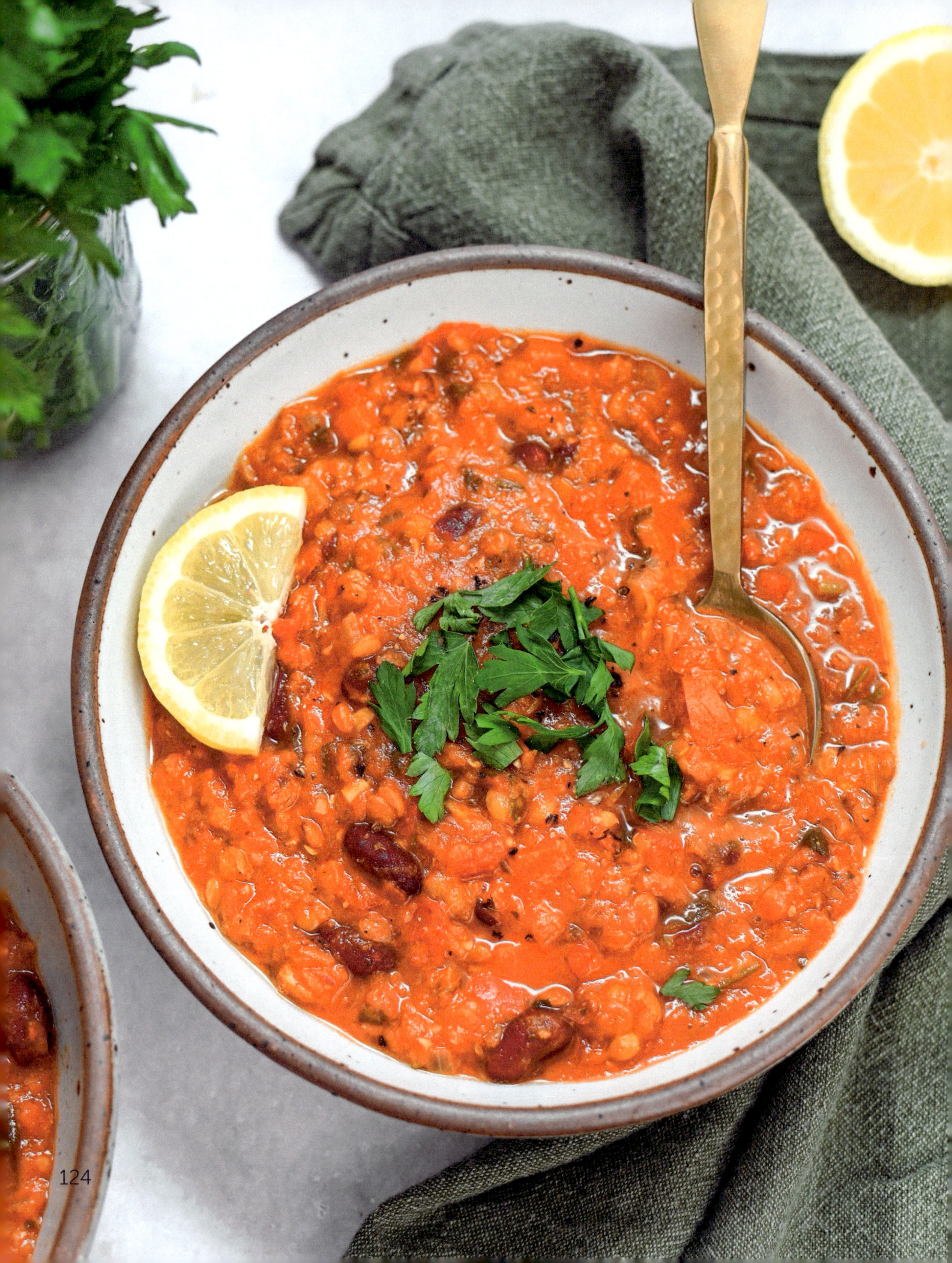

Lemony Lentil Soup

50 MINUTES • 6 SERVINGS

This was originally a chili-style lentil soup, but after one of my aunt's served me a curry and lemon-infused lentil soup during a visit to her house in Arizona, I knew I had to redo the recipe based on my memory of that soup. Curry powder adds complex flavor that is lightened up by bright lemon notes, while the lentils and vegetables make this a hearty meal.

2 tablespoons canola oil
2 cups diced red onion (about 1 medium onion)
1 medium red bell pepper, diced
2 large carrots, diced
4 cloves garlic, minced
½ teaspoon kosher salt
2 tablespoons tomato paste
1 teaspoon curry powder
1 teaspoon dried oregano
1 teaspoon ground cumin
½ teaspoon garlic powder
⅛ teaspoon nutmeg
4 cups vegetable broth
1 (14-ounce) can crushed tomatoes
1 (14-ounce) can fire-roasted diced tomatoes
1 (15-ounce) can light red kidney beans, drained and rinsed
1 cup dry brown lentils, rinsed and sorted
½ cup fresh chopped parsley
¼ teaspoon granulated sugar (optional)
3 tablespoons lemon juice (about 1 large lemon)
1 heaping teaspoon lemon zest (about 1 large lemon)
Fresh chopped parsley, lemon wedges, and crackers, for serving

1. Heat a 4-quart pot or Dutch oven over medium heat. Drizzle with canola oil. Once hot, add the onion, pepper, carrot, garlic, and salt. Cook until the onion is softened and starting to turn golden, about 8 to 10 minutes.

2. Stir in the tomato paste, curry powder, oregano, cumin, garlic powder, and nutmeg. Cook for 30 seconds to toast the spices, stirring frequently. Deglaze the pot with a splash of vegetable broth, stirring to remove any stuck-on bits from the pot.

3. Add in the remaining vegetable broth, crushed tomatoes, fire-roasted tomatoes with juices, kidney beans, brown lentils, parsley, and sugar. Stir to combine.

4. Bring to a rapid simmer over medium-high heat, then reduce to a gentle simmer over medium-low heat. Cover and simmer until the lentils are tender and cooked through, about 20 to 25 minutes.

5. Stir in the lemon juice and lemon zest. Optionally, immersion blend the soup for a few seconds to thicken it. Taste for seasonings and serve garnished with additional fresh parsley, lemon wedges, and crackers.

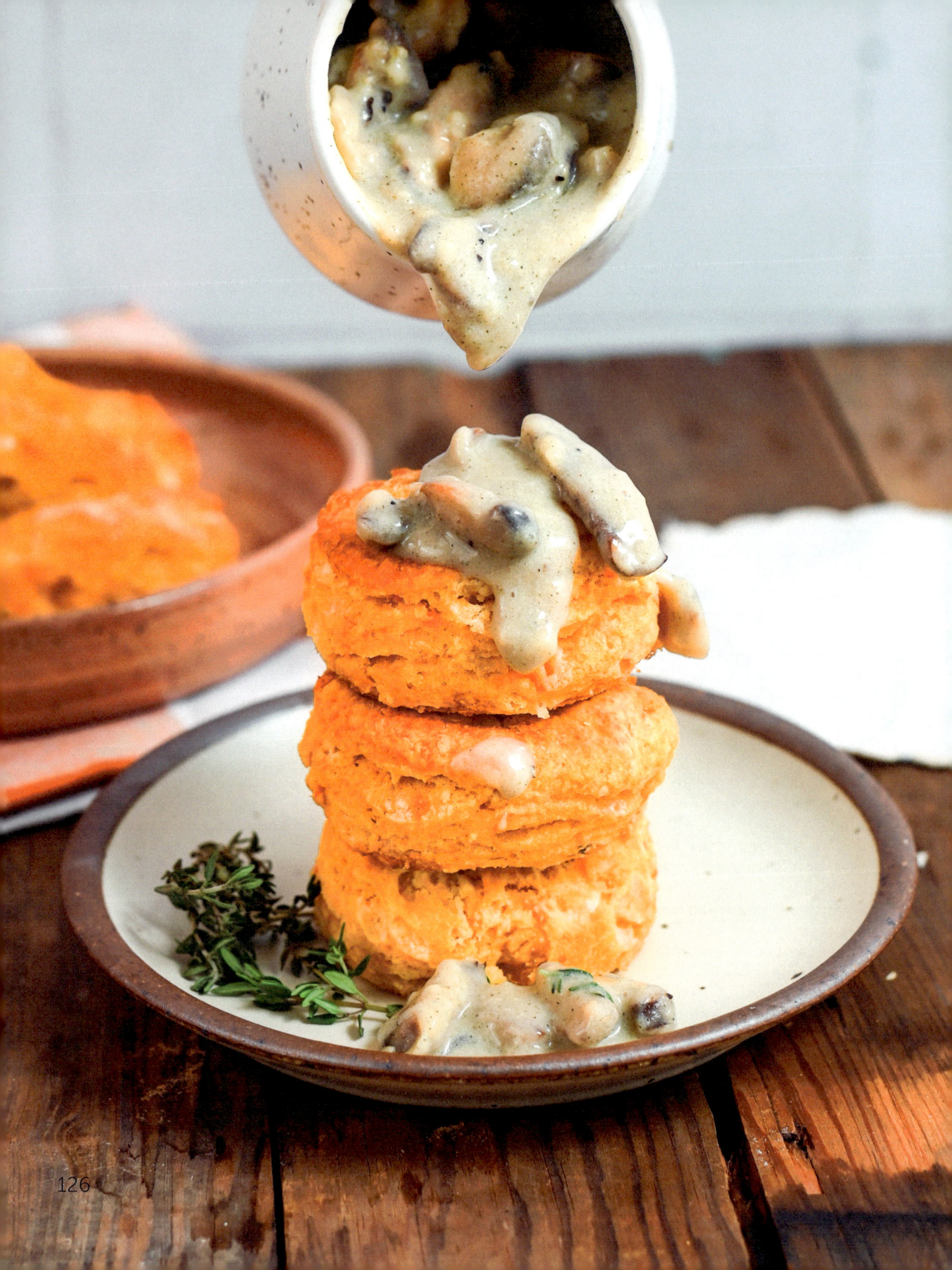

Chapter 6: Breakfast for Dinner

I couldn't write a cookbook all about meals without including breakfast. Often chosen because I don't feel like cooking, or because nothing else sounds very good, Breakfast for Dinner includes some of the closest ingredients you'll find to dessert in this cookbook. It also includes one snack recipe (technically breaking my own self-imposed rule of meals-only recipes) and a few recipes that don't quite fit the "balanced" approach of other sections in this cookbook. That's okay, because rules, especially food rules, are meant to be broken, right?

Cassidy's Favorite: Sweet Potato Biscuits with Mushroom Gravy (p. 145)

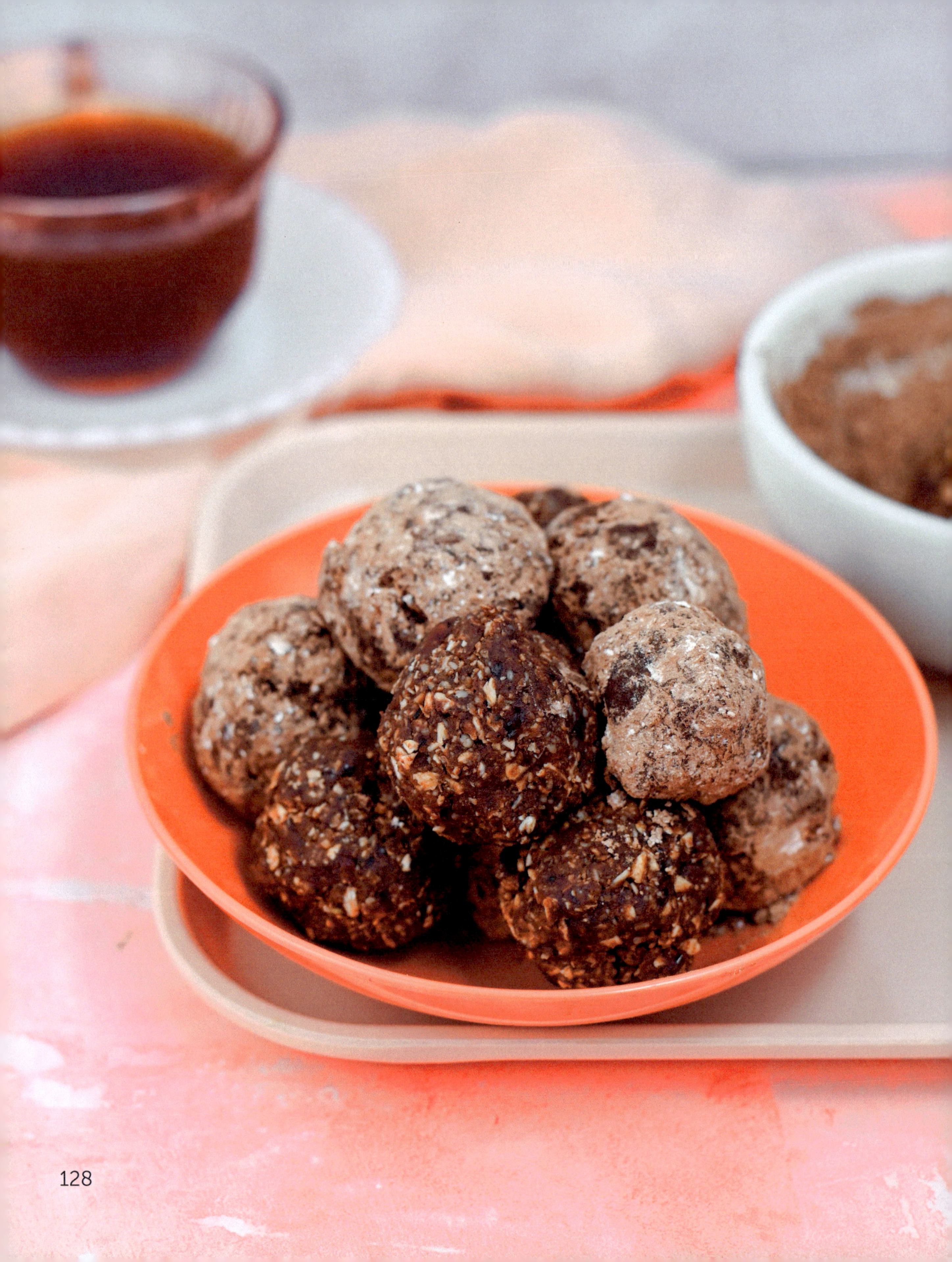

Chocolate Peanut Butter Bites

10 MINUTES • 12 BITES

This recipe doesn't quite cut it as far as dinner is concerned, but it's a wonderful snack to keep on hand for when you need a little between-meal boost. I store these bites in the freezer for a quick pre-workout snack, but they're also great as a post-dinner dessert. You do need a food processor to make this recipe, unless you know from experience that your blender can handle sticky medjool dates.

- 1 cup (10 to 12) pitted medjool dates, sliced in half
- 1 cup old-fashioned oats
- ¼ cup hemp hearts
- ¼ cup creamy peanut butter
- 4 tablespoons cocoa powder, divided
- Pinch or two of salt
- 3 tablespoons oat milk (or milk of choice)
- 2 tablespoons powdered sugar

1. To a food processor with a standard blade attachment, add the sliced dates and oats. Pulse until the dates are mostly broken down and the oats are a sandy texture.

2. Add the hemp hearts, peanut butter, 2 tablespoons cocoa powder, and a pinch or two of salt. Process just a few seconds to combine the ingredients. Add 2 tablespoons milk and process until the "batter" holds together. Add the remaining tablespoon of milk as needed.

3. Roll the batter into 12 balls, each about the size of a ping pong ball.

4. In a small bowl, whisk together the remaining 2 tablespoons of cocoa powder and the powdered sugar. Roll each ball in the powder, tossing to coat. This step is optional but adds an extra touch of chocolate and sweetness.

5. Enjoy immediately or refrigerate to chill. These also freeze well.

Highly recommended flavor variation: For mocha flavor, add ½ teaspoon espresso powder and use strong coffee or cold brew in place of milk. Try adding flaked sea salt to the powdered sugar coating to enhance the cocoa flavor further.

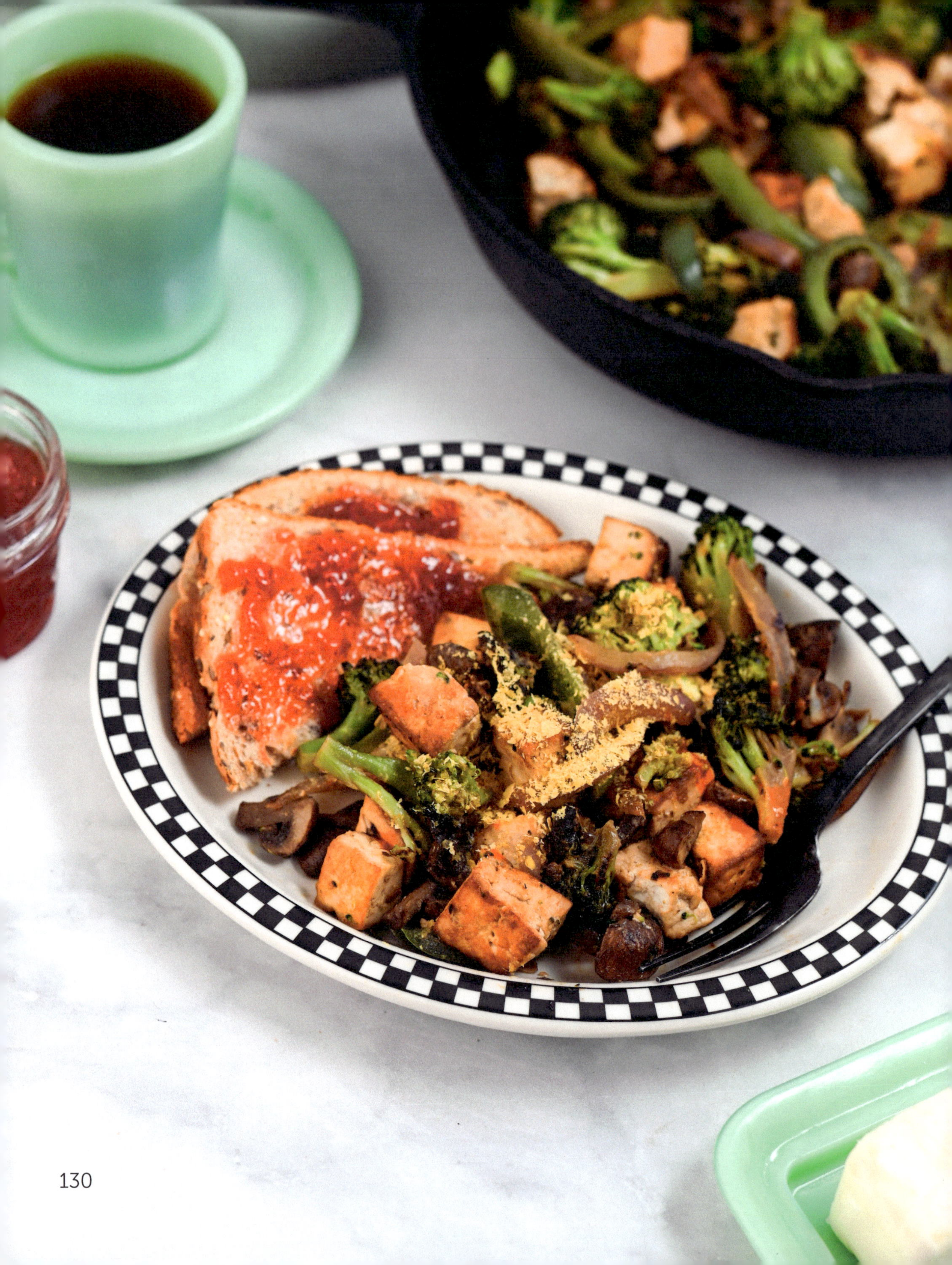

All-Purpose Tofu & Vegetable Stir Fry

25 MINUTES • 3-4 SERVINGS

This recipe is inspired by an Athens vegetarian mainstay that closed in the past year, The Grit. Their golden bowls relied heavily on nutritional yeast and soy sauce as the primary (and only) seasoning. The Grit cookbook published their recipe for tofu, which simply says to add soy sauce and nutritional yeast. The secret to this recipe is the same: when in doubt, add more nutritional yeast or soy sauce.

- 1 (14-ounce) block extra-firm tofu
- 2 tablespoons canola oil, divided
- 2 tablespoons soy sauce, more as needed
- 1 large broccoli crown, florets sliced in half
- 1 large green pepper, sliced into strips
- ½ medium red onion, sliced into strips
- 8 ounces baby bella mushrooms, quartered
- 3 tablespoons nutritional yeast, plus more for serving
- Hot sauce, for serving (optional)

1. Gently squeeze the block of tofu with a paper towel to remove some water. Slice the tofu into ½-inch cubes.

2. Heat a large skillet over medium-high heat. Drizzle with 1 tablespoon of oil. Once hot, add the tofu. Drizzle with 1 tablespoon of soy sauce. Cook until golden on each side, flipping halfway, about 8 to 10 minutes total.

3. Remove tofu from the pan and set aside. Drizzle the same pan with the remaining tablespoon of oil. Add the broccoli florets, green pepper, red onion, and baby bella mushrooms. Drizzle with remaining tablespoon of soy sauce.

4. Cook on medium-high heat until the vegetables are vibrant and tender, about 8 to 10 minutes. Return tofu to the pan. Sprinkle with 3 tablespoons nutritional yeast. Cook an additional 2 to 3 minutes, or until the tofu and veggies are starting to sear and blacken in some places.

5. Serve with additional nutritional yeast and hot sauce, to taste (optional but recommended).

Notes: This recipe works best with a cast iron skillet because it can handle high heat and chars tofu nicely, but any large skillet will do. The tofu does not need to be pressed for this recipe.

Serving ideas: Whole wheat toast, roasted potatoes (p. 143), fried eggs, sweet potato biscuits (p. 145)

132

Georgia Peach Pancakes

25 MINUTES • 9 (4-INCH) PANCAKES

Although most of my family is from Illinois and that's where I spent my earliest years, and although I didn't move to Georgia until high school (after a brief stint in Florida), it took me until recently to decide that Georgia is the place that most feels like home. All of that is to say: Georgia is known for peaches, this cookbook is being written by Miss Cozy Peach (more than one reader has called me that, and I love it), and I absolutely love these pancakes. And there you have it: Georgia Peach Pancakes.

PANCAKES

2 ½ cups all-purpose flour
1 tablespoon baking powder
1 tablespoon light brown sugar
½ teaspoon ground cinnamon
¼ teaspoon table salt
1 ⅓ cup milk (any kind works)
1 (5.3-ounce) container peach-flavored Greek yogurt
1 large egg
½ teaspoon vanilla extract
¼ teaspoon almond extract (optional)
¼ cup melted unsalted butter, plus more for cooking
1 large ripe peach, diced
½ cup toasted pecans, roughly chopped

PEACH TOPPING

1 tablespoon unsalted butter
2 large ripe peaches, sliced
¼ cup toasted pecans
¼ cup maple syrup, plus more for serving
2 tablespoons light brown sugar
¼ teaspoon vanilla extract
Pinch of salt

1. In a medium mixing bowl, whisk together the dry ingredients: flour, baking powder, brown sugar, cinnamon, and salt. In a separate bowl, stir together the milk, yogurt, egg, vanilla extract, and almond extract.

2. Pour the liquids and the melted butter into the dry ingredients. Stir until just combined. The batter should be thick enough that it drips off the mixing spoon in lumps.

3. Heat a large skillet over medium heat. Add enough butter to coat the skillet. Once melted, add ¼ cup of batter to the skillet to make a pancake. Drop a few peach and pecans pieces onto the pancake. Cook until bubbles begin to pop in the batter, then flip. Continue cooking for an additional 2 minutes, or until golden.

4. While the pancakes cook, make the peach topping. Heat a small skillet over medium heat. Add the butter. Once melted, add the sliced peaches and pecans. Sauté until the peaches are golden, just 2 to 3 minutes.

5. Stir in the maple syrup and brown sugar. Reduce heat to low and continue to simmer gently for 2 to 3 minutes. Remove from heat and stir in the vanilla extract and pinch of salt.

6. Serve pancakes garnished with a scoop of the peach topping and additional maple syrup, to taste.

> **Note:** This recipe also works with canned peaches if fresh peaches aren't in season, but the peach flavor won't be as strong. Use a 15-ounce can of whole peaches canned in juice.

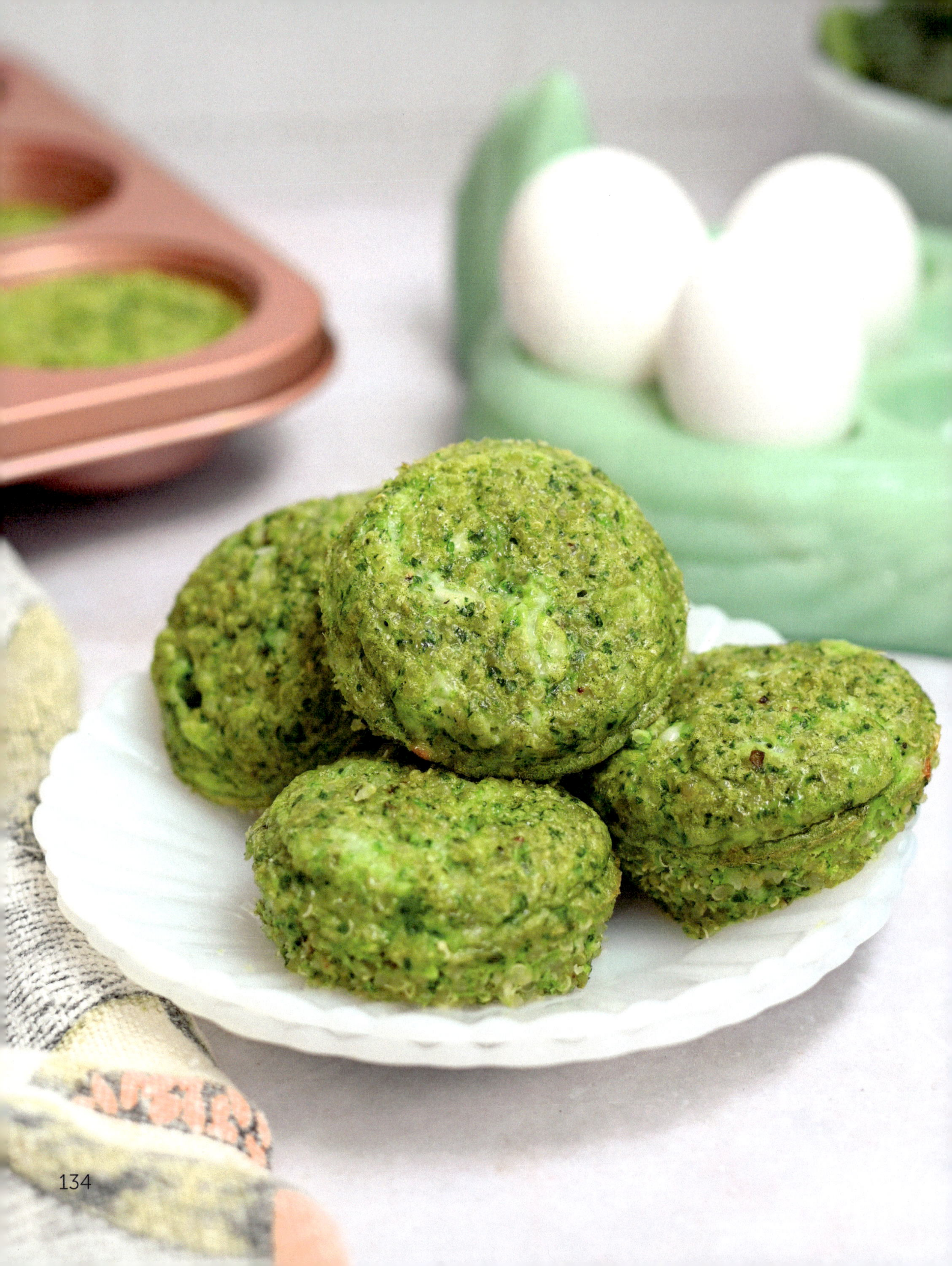

Spinach & Quinoa Egg Muffins

35 MINUTES • 12 MUFFINS • 4-6 SERVINGS

These vivid green muffins are the perfect grab-and-go breakfast or post-workout snack. I like to slice them in half and serve on toast with melted Swiss cheese on top, but they're also great as a side with Georgia Peach Pancakes (p. 133). They freeze well.

½ cup dry quinoa
1 cup vegetable broth or water
¾ teaspoon kosher salt, divided
6 large eggs
3 heaping cups (about 3 ounces) spinach
1 tablespoon extra virgin olive oil
¼ teaspoon garlic powder
¼ teaspoon onion powder
⅛ teaspoon black pepper
½ cup (2 ounces) shredded mozzarella cheese

1. Rinse quinoa well in a fine-mesh sieve. Combine the quinoa, vegetable broth, and ¼ teaspoon salt in a small pot. Bring to a rapid simmer over medium-high heat, then reduce to a gentle simmer over medium-low heat. Cover tightly with a lid and simmer until all of the liquid is absorbed and the quinoa is cooked through, about 15 minutes. Fluff with a fork and drain off excess liquid, if needed.

2. While the quinoa cooks, preheat the oven to 400°F. Line a 12-cup muffin tin with muffin liners.

3. Add the eggs, spinach, olive oil, remaining ½ teaspoon of salt, garlic powder, onion powder, and black pepper to a blender. Blend until the eggs are smooth and the spinach is mostly broken down.

4. In a medium mixing bowl, stir together the egg mixture, cooked quinoa, and shredded mozzarella. Add ¼ cup of the quinoa egg batter to each muffin liner.

5. Bake at 400°F for 10 to 12 minutes, or until the eggs are puffy and a toothpick inserted in the center comes out clean.

Notes: I really wanted the egg bites to work without liners, but they are just better and more user-friendly with them. If you don't have liners, grease the tin very well and note that they will stick a little bit to the muffin tin.

½ cup uncooked quinoa is equivalent to 1 ½ cups cooked quinoa. This recipe works with warm or chilled quinoa.

If you don't have a blender, the spinach can be chopped very finely and the eggs can be whisked by hand.

This recipe is supposed to be super simple, but you can jazz it up by adding sautéed mushrooms, peppers, broccoli, or other vegetables. I recommend using sautéed vegetables instead of raw because the moisture from uncooked vegetables can make the egg bites soggy.

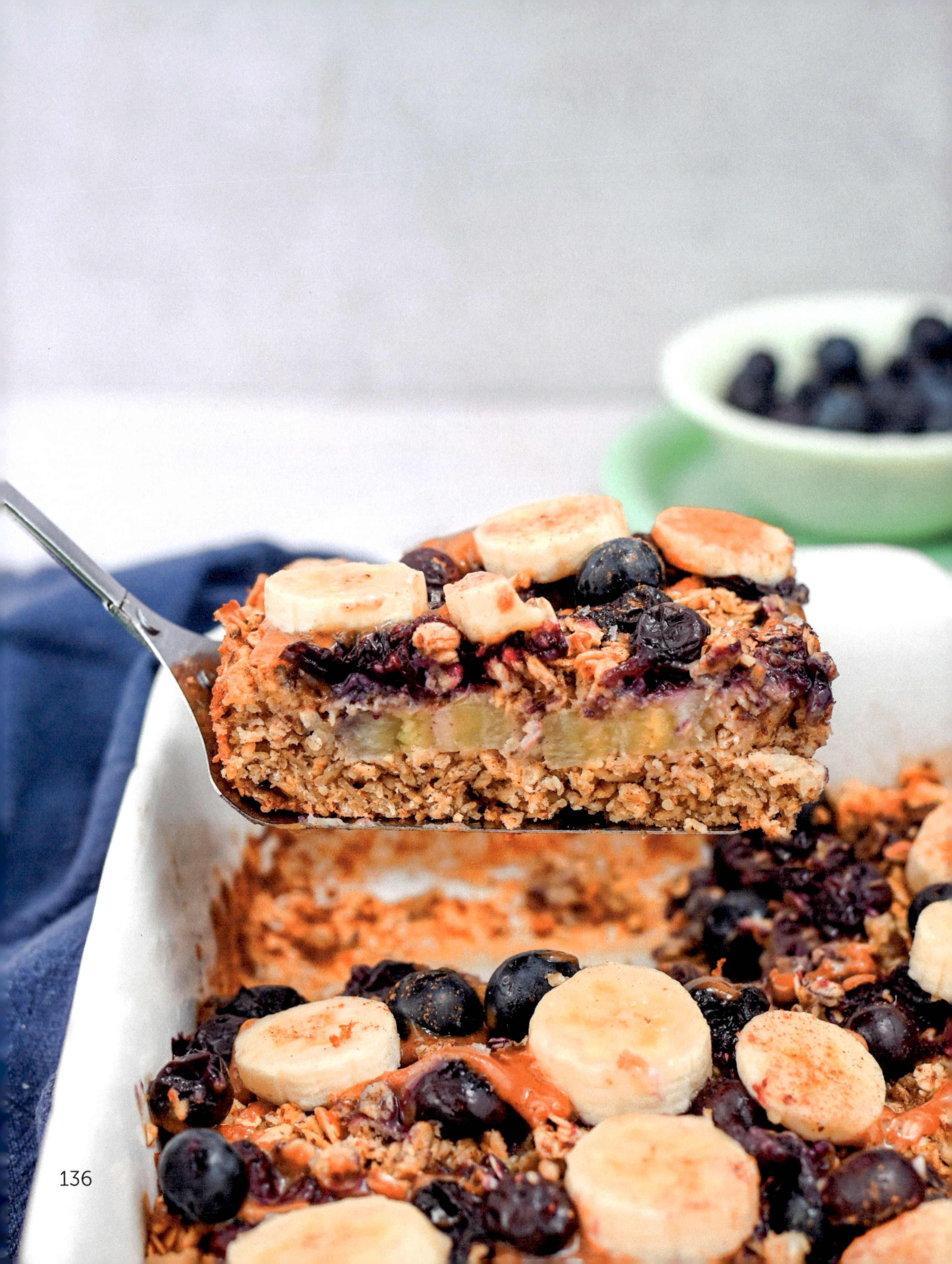

Blueberry Oatmeal Bars with Almond Butter Drizzle

40 MINUTES • 6 SERVINGS

These bars are soft, chewy, and sliceable. They have a layer of bananas and blueberries, and the almond butter topping is absolutely dreamy—as in, you'll want to eat it by the spoonful dreamy. I recommend keeping leftovers refrigerated. This recipe is also great as a snack.

OATMEAL BARS

3 cups old-fashioned oats
2 tablespoons ground flaxseed
2 tablespoons hemp hearts (optional)
1 teaspoon baking powder
1 teaspoon cinnamon
½ teaspoon table salt
1 ¼ cups milk of choice
2 large eggs
¼ cup maple syrup (honey also works)
2 tablespoons canola oil
2 ripe bananas, sliced into coins
1 cup fresh blueberries

ALMOND BUTTER DRIZZLE

3 tablespoons milk, more as needed
3 tablespoons almond butter
2 tablespoons powdered sugar
¼ teaspoon vanilla extract

1. Preheat the oven to 350°F. Lightly oil an 8x8 inch or similarly sized baking dish.

2. In a large mixing bowl, whisk together the oats, ground flaxseed, hemp hearts, baking powder, cinnamon, and salt. In a separate bowl, whisk together the milk, eggs, maple syrup, and oil. Pour wet ingredients into the dry ingredients, whisking until just combined.

3. Spread out half of the oatmeal batter in the greased 8x8 inch dish. Top with sliced bananas. Cover up the bananas with the remaining batter (it's okay if they aren't 100% covered), then top with the blueberries.

4. Bake at 350°F for 35 to 40 minutes, or until firm in the center. A fork or toothpick inserted into the center of the oatmeal should come out clean.

5. Meanwhile, make the almond butter drizzle. In a small bowl, whisk together the milk, almond butter, powdered sugar, and vanilla extract. It should be a smooth, pourable consistency similar to melted chocolate. Add additional milk as needed.

6. Let the oatmeal bars cool at least 10 minutes before drizzling with the almond butter. Slice into 6 rectangles to serve.

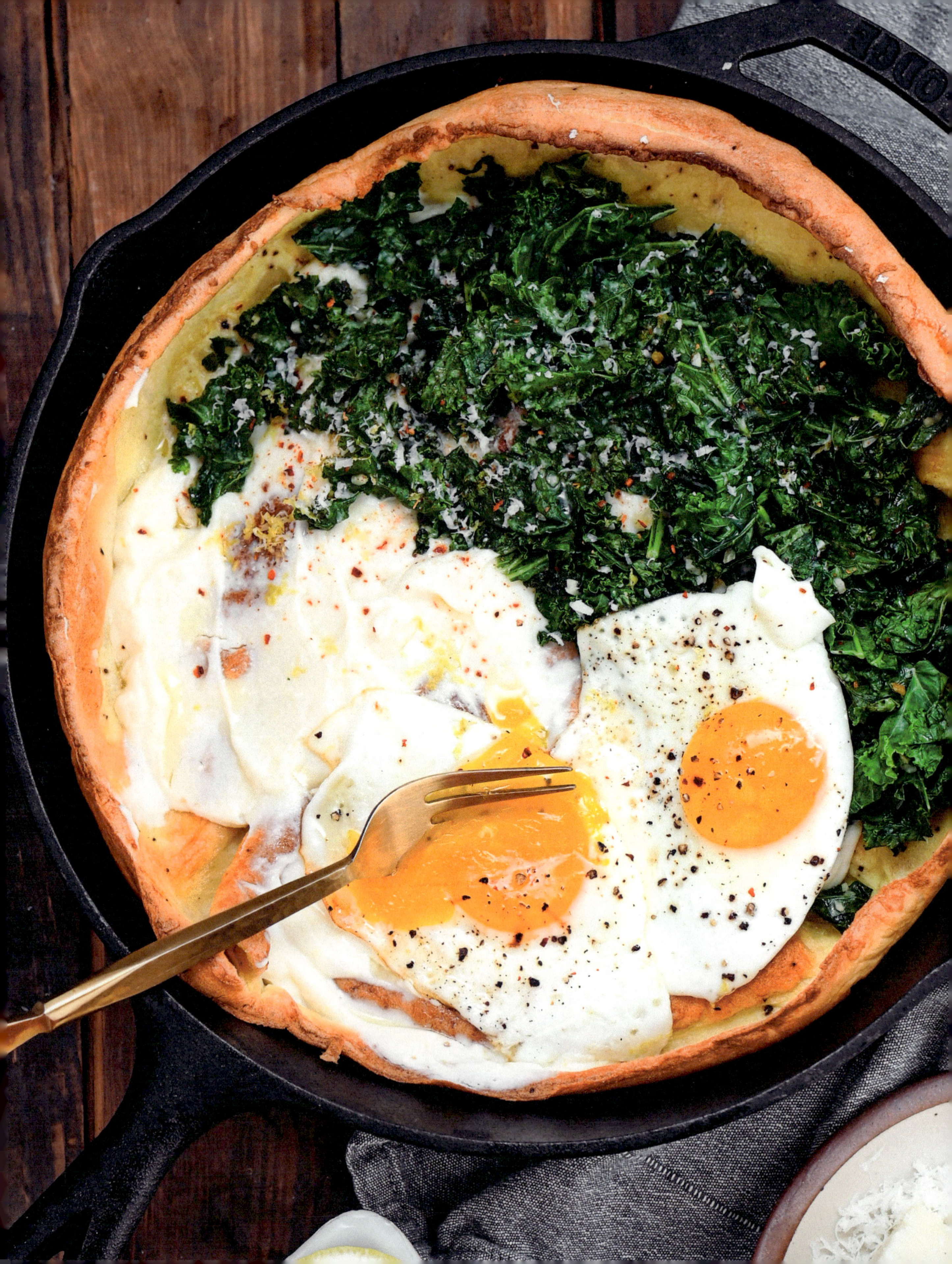

Savory Dutch Baby Pancake with Lemon Ricotta

50 MINUTES • 4 SERVINGS

This giant baked pancake, while more closely resembling a popover than a pancake, is a trendy-yet-satisfying breakfast that just asks to be photographed. My take on a Dutch baby is savory, topped with lusciously creamy lemon ricotta, garlicky kale, and fried eggs with jammy yolks. Don't be tempted to skip preheating the cast iron, as a piping hot pan is required to make a light and fluffy Dutch baby. Conveniently, both the Dutch baby batter and ricotta can be prepped while the pan preheats.

DUTCH BABY

3 large eggs
½ cup 2% milk or milk of choice
3 tablespoons unsalted butter, divided
¼ teaspoon table salt
¼ teaspoon freshly ground black pepper, plus more for serving
½ cup all-purpose flour

LEMON RICOTTA

1 cup whole milk ricotta
3 tablespoons lemon juice (from one large lemon)
1 teaspoon lemon zest (from ½ large lemon)
¼ teaspoon kosher salt

ASSEMBLY

2 teaspoons extra virgin olive oil
4 cups (about 4 ounces) chopped curly kale
2 cloves garlic, minced
¼ teaspoon kosher salt
2 to 4 large eggs (adjust to preference)
Freshly grated Parmesan or Asiago cheese, for serving

1. Place a 10- or 12-inch cast iron skillet or other oven-safe skillet on the middle oven rack. Preheat the oven to 400°F. Heat the skillet in the oven for at least 20 minutes, including preheat time.

2. **Dutch Baby batter:** Meanwhile, make the pancake batter by adding the eggs, milk, 1 tablespoon of melted butter, salt, and pepper to a blender. Blend until smooth. Add the flour and blend until smooth again. Set aside.

3. **Whipped ricotta:** While the skillet heats in the oven, prepare the whipped ricotta. To a food processor with a standard blade attachment, add the ricotta, lemon juice, lemon zest, and salt. Process the ricotta for 2 minutes, until light and fluffy. Taste for lemon and salt.

4. After 20 minutes, remove the skillet from the oven. Add the remaining 2 tablespoons of butter, swirling to fully coat the skillet. Pour in the pancake batter. Return to the oven to bake on the middle rack for 20 to 23 minutes, or until the pancake is puffy and golden-brown. The pancake will start to deflate soon after being removed from the oven.

5. **For the kale:** While the pancake bakes, heat a large skillet over medium heat. Drizzle with olive oil. Once hot, add the chopped kale, garlic, and salt. Sauté, stirring occasionally, until the kale is wilted and vivid green, about 4 to 5 minutes. When the kale is wilted, push it to the side to make space for the eggs. Crack in the eggs and fry until the whites are set and yolks are still runny, about 2 minutes.

6. **To assemble:** Spread ricotta across the pancake. Season with freshly ground black pepper, then top with the kale and eggs. Serve garnished with freshly grated Parmesan cheese.

> **Note:** No food processor? Whip the ricotta with a hand mixer with standard whisk attachment until light and fluffy, about 2 minutes. To make by hand, use a whisk and prepare for tired arms. Whisk until light and fluffy, about 5 minutes.

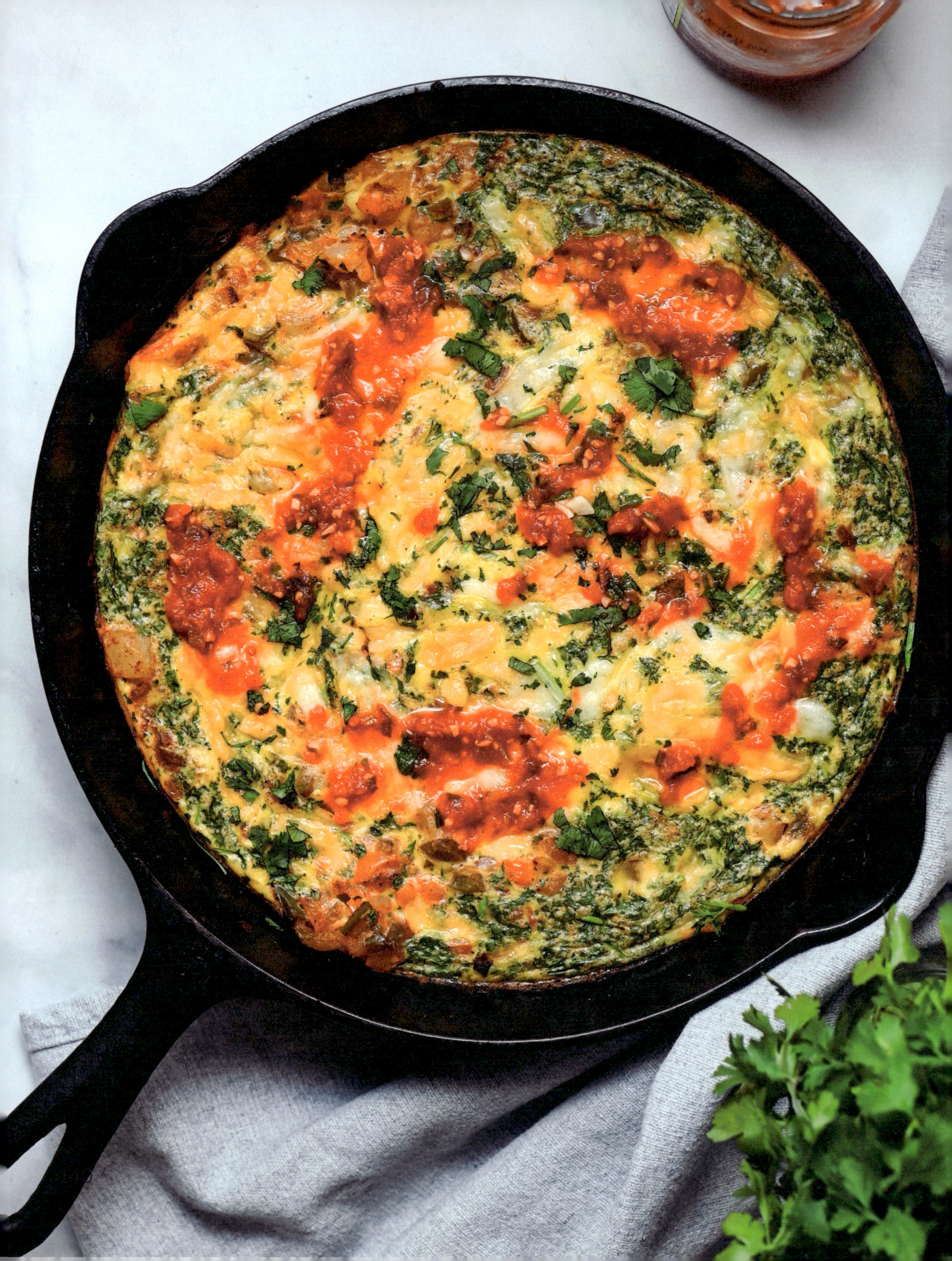

Potato & Pepper Frittata

45 MINUTES • 4-6 SERVINGS

A frittata is like a fancier version of an egg casserole, but it is actually very easy to put together. This recipe does require either a cast iron skillet or another 12-inch oven-safe skillet. Leftovers are great for breakfast or lunch.

1 large russet potato, cut into ½-inch cubes
½ teaspoon table salt
2 tablespoons canola oil
1 cup diced sweet yellow onion (about ½ medium onion)
1 medium green bell pepper, diced
1 medium orange bell pepper, diced
¾ teaspoon kosher salt, divided
¾ teaspoon chili powder
½ teaspoon smoked paprika
¼ teaspoon black pepper
3 cloves garlic, minced
8 large eggs
⅓ cup 2% milk or milk of choice
½ cup fresh roughly chopped cilantro
1 cup (4 ounces) shredded sharp cheddar cheese
Salsa of choice, for serving

1. Add potatoes to a medium pot. Add enough cold water to cover the potatoes by 1 inch. Add ½ teaspoon table salt. Bring to a boil over high heat. Boil until easy to pierce with a fork, about 10 to 12 minutes. Drain the potatoes and set aside.

2. Preheat the oven to 400°F.

3. Heat a 12-inch oven-safe skillet, such as a cast iron skillet, over medium heat. Drizzle with canola oil. Once hot, add the boiled and drained potato, onion, peppers, ½ teaspoon kosher salt, chili powder, smoked paprika, and black pepper. Sauté, stirring occasionally, until the onions and peppers are tender, about 8 to 10 minutes.

4. Stir in the minced garlic. Continue cooking until golden and aromatic, about 2 minutes.

5. Meanwhile, add the eggs, milk, cilantro, and remaining ¼ teaspoon salt to a blender. Blend until the eggs are smooth and the cilantro is mostly broken down.

6. Pour the eggs into the pan with the veggies and potatoes. Sprinkle shredded cheddar over the eggs.

7. Bake in the preheated oven at 400°F on the middle oven rack for 14 to 16 minutes, or until the frittata is puffed up and the edges are pulling away from the pan.

8. Remove the frittata from the oven. It will deflate after just a minute or so. Slice into 6 pieces and serve topped with salsa.

> **Note:** To make this recipe without a blender, just finely chop the cilantro and whisk the eggs, milk, and salt together by hand.

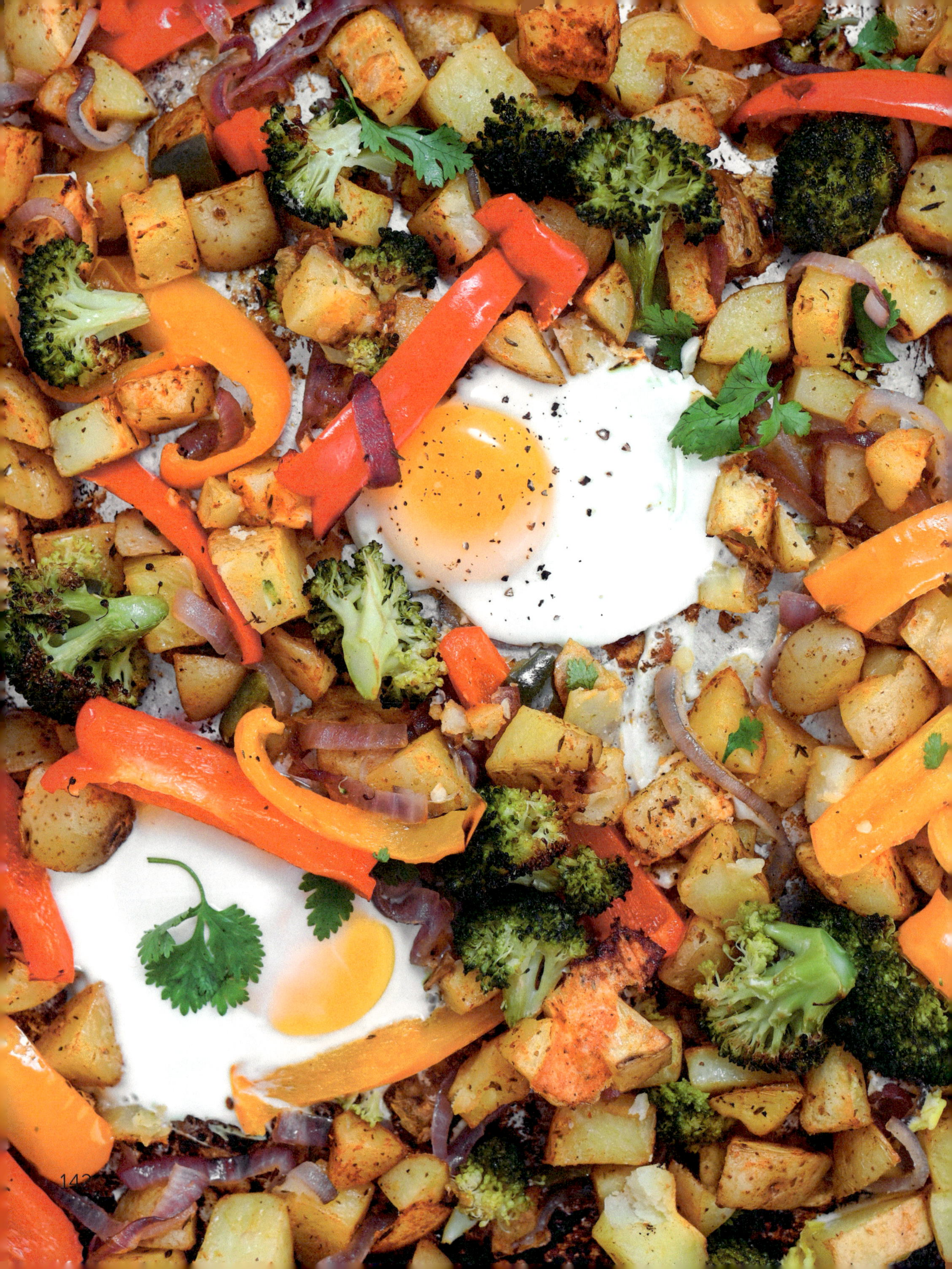

Sheet Pan Breakfast Potatoes & Peppers

50 MINUTES • 3-4 SERVINGS

If there's one recipe that I've made more than any other (in the book and in general), it's these roasted potatoes, or some variation of them. Many of my favorite weeknight meals revolve around roasted potatoes because they are really easy to make and they taste delicious. Toss them with homemade Cajun seasoning and basically any vegetables that you have on hand, and roast until puffy and golden. The fun part of this recipe is that the eggs are cracked directly on the sheet pan, resulting in oven-fried eggs and one less pan to clean!

2 ½ pounds Yukon gold potatoes
2 tablespoons canola oil, divided
1 teaspoon paprika
½ teaspoon garlic powder
½ teaspoon onion powder
1 teaspoon kosher salt, divided
½ teaspoon dried thyme
¼ teaspoon dried oregano
¼ teaspoon white pepper
1 red bell pepper, cut into 1-inch wedges
1 orange bell pepper, cut into 1-inch wedges
1 large red onion, sliced into thin strips
1 large broccoli crown, cut into florets
3 to 4 large eggs, adjust to preference
Fresh chopped cilantro, sliced avocado, hot sauce, for serving

1. Preheat the oven to 425°F. Clean the potatoes well and slice them into 1-inch cubes. I don't peel the potatoes, but you can if you prefer. In a large bowl, toss diced potatoes with 1 tablespoon canola oil, paprika, garlic powder, onion powder, ½ teaspoon salt, thyme, oregano, and white pepper.

2. Transfer the potatoes to a large sheet pan. Roast at 425°F for 15 minutes on the middle oven rack.

3. Meanwhile, toss the bell peppers, onion, and broccoli in the same mixing bowl with the remaining tablespoon of canola oil and ½ teaspoon of salt.

4. After 15 minutes, remove the potatoes from the oven. Stir in the vegetables. Return to the oven for 20 to 25 minutes, or until the vegetables and potatoes are mostly done.

5. Remove from the oven and stir, leaving 4-inch circles open for the eggs. Drizzle a small amount of oil into the open areas. Crack eggs directly onto the oiled sheet pan and season with salt and pepper, to taste. Return to the oven for 2 to 4 minutes, or until the eggs are cooked to your desired preference.

6. Remove from the oven. Serve garnished with fresh chopped cilantro, sliced avocado, and optional hot sauce.

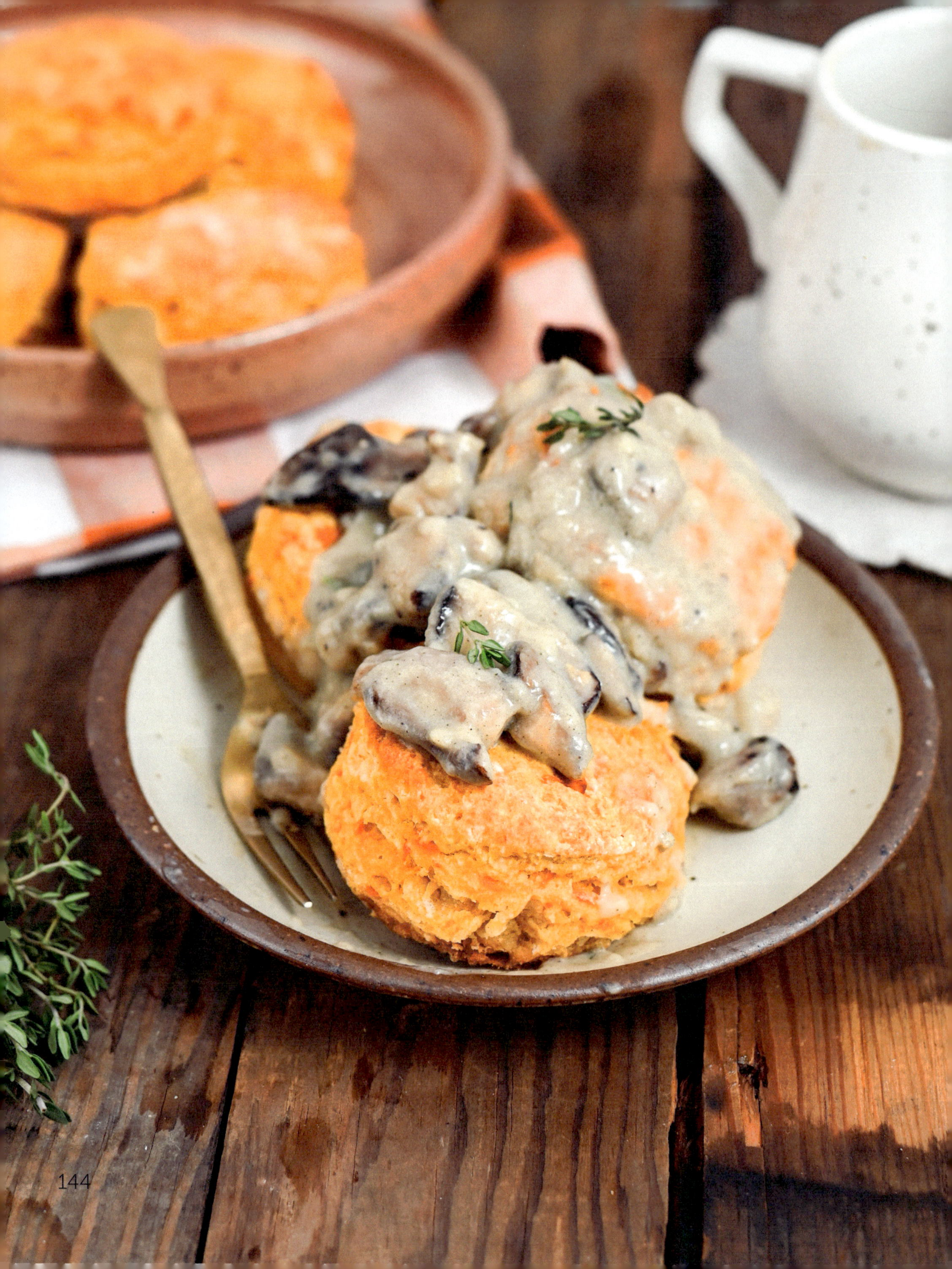

Sweet Potato Biscuits & Mushroom Gravy

1 HOUR 45 MINUTES • 6 SERVINGS

Because I usually make biscuits and gravy on slow weekend mornings, I like to roast the sweet potato the day or night before. This takes the total cook time down to just 30 to 40 minutes, which is much more manageable for a weekend. For an even easier option, use ¾ cup canned sweet potato puree. Because purées tend to be wetter than freshly baked potato, you may need to add extra flour to the biscuit dough.

SWEET POTATO BISCUITS

1 large sweet potato
1 ½ cups all-purpose flour
1 tablespoon baking powder
½ teaspoon table salt
6 tablespoons cold unsalted butter, sliced
⅓ cup whole milk

MUSHROOM GRAVY

2 tablespoons unsalted butter
5 ounces chopped shiitake mushrooms, stems removed
¼ cup all-purpose flour
2 cups whole milk or milk of choice
1 teaspoon dried thyme
½ teaspoon garlic powder
¼ teaspoon dried sage
¼ teaspoon kosher salt
¼ teaspoon freshly ground black pepper

1. Preheat oven to 400°F. Use a knife or fork to poke the sweet potato with a few holes. Place on a pan and roast in the oven at 400°F for 45 minutes to an hour, until completely soft and tender. Remove the skin and place the sweet potato in a bowl. Use a potato masher or fork to mash until completely smooth. Measure out ¾ cup mashed sweet potato.

2. Adjust the oven temp to 425°F and line a sheet pan with parchment paper. Set aside.

3. To a medium mixing bowl, add the all-purpose flour, baking powder, and salt. Stir to combine. Add the sliced butter. Using a pastry cutter or a fork, cut the butter up into pea-sized pieces. Stir in the milk and ¾ cup mashed sweet potato until just combined. The dough should be shaggy but pulling away from the sides of the bowl.

4. Turn the dough out on a lightly floured surface. Gently press it down to about ½-inch thickness, folding the dough over itself 4 to 5 times. Add flour 1 tablespoon at a time if it is too tacky to work with.

5. Cut out biscuit shapes using a 3-inch biscuit cutter or a knife. Place biscuits on the baking sheet with their edges touching. Bake at 425°F for 12 to 15 minutes, until golden and fluffy.

6. While the biscuits bake, heat a large skillet over medium heat. Add the butter. Once melted, add the chopped mushrooms. Cook for 8 to 10 minutes, or until the mushrooms are golden and reduced in size.

7. Sprinkle with ¼ cup flour. Toast until golden, stirring frequently, about 2 to 3 minutes. Slowly whisk in the milk, then add the thyme, garlic powder, sage, salt, and pepper. Reduce heat to a gentle simmer over medium-low heat. Simmer until thickened to a gravy consistency, stirring occasionally, about 6 to 8 minutes.

8. Slice the sweet potato biscuits in half and serve topped with mushroom gravy.

Olives
- Mediterranean-Inspired One Pot Rice & Beans, 63

P

Parmesan cheese
- Amish-Style Chicken & Noodles, 75
- Big Veggie & Lentil Lasagna, 85
- Caramelized Shallot Pasta, 83
- Mushroom & Potato Soup, 123
- Pan-Fried Polenta with Roasted Mushrooms & Asparagus, 25
- Ricotta Gnocchi Primavera, 79
- Savory Dutch Baby, 139
- Tortellini with Cashew Pesto Sauce, 69

Parsley
- Lemony Lentil Soup, 125
- Mediterranean-Inspired One Pot Rice & Beans, 63
- Spicy Tahini Noodles, 81

Peas
- Amish-Style Chicken & Noodles, 75

Pecans
- Georgia Peach Pancakes, 133
- Warm Wild Rice Salad with Apple Cider Vinaigrette, 115

Peppers
- Big Veggie & Lentil Lasagna, 85
- Chili Cornbread Skillet, 51
- Corn Fritters, 43
- Lemony Lentil Soup, 125
- Mediterranean-Inspired One Pot Rice & Beans, 63
- Pizza Bread, 105
- Potato & Pepper Frittata, 141
- Quinoa Pizza Bake, 53
- Ricotta Gnocchi Primavera, 79
- Roasted Vegetable & Chickpea Wraps, 99
- Sheet Pan Potatoes & Peppers, 143
- Tofu & Vegetable Stir-Fry, 131

Pickles
- Fried Tofu Sandwich, 101
- Loaded Fries with Peanut Sauce, 91
- Tofu Patty Melt, 103

Pinto beans
- BBQ Jackfruit Nachos, 41
- Chili Cornbread Skillet, 51
- Grown-Up Walking Tacos, 19
- Loaded Baked Sweet Potatoes, 37

Polenta
- Pan-Fried Polenta with Roasted Mushrooms & Asparagus, 25

Potatoes
- Loaded Fries with Peanut Sauce, 91
- Mushroom & Potato Soup, 123
- Potato & Pepper Frittata, 141
- Pot Pie with Drop Biscuits, 49
- Sheet Pan Breakfast Potatoes & Peppers, 143
- Tofu Steak Dinner, 57
- Upside Down Shepherd's Pie, 31

Q

Quinoa
- Quinoa Chickpea Bowls, 17
- Quinoa Pizza Bake, 53
- Spinach & Quinoa Egg Muffins, 135

Sweet Potato Kale Salad, 113

R

Radishes
- Spring Pasta Salad, 111

Rice
- BBQ Jackfruit Nachos, 41
- Lemon Pepper Tofu Bowls, 23
- Mediterranean-Inspired One Pot Rice & Beans, 63
- Miso Butter Bean Bowls, 27
- Mushroom & Black Bean Burritos, 95
- Red Lentil Curry, 47
- Warm Wild Rice Salad, 115

Ricotta
- Ricotta Gnocchi Primavera, 79
- Savory Dutch Baby, 139

S

Shallots
- Caramelized Shallot Pasta, 83
- One Skillet Tomato Orzo, 71
- Spring Pasta Salad, 111
- Warm Wild Rice Salad with Apple Cider Vinaigrette, 115

Snap peas
- Honey Garlic Noodles, 73

Soy curls
- Amish-Style Chicken & Noodles, 75
- Pot Pie with Drop Biscuits, 49

Spinach
- Mushroom & Black Bean Burritos, 95
- Spinach & Quinoa Egg Muffins, 135
- Tortellini with Cashew Pesto Sauce, 69

Sriracha
- Green Curry Noodle Bowls, 77
- Loaded Fries with Peanut Sauce, 91
- Roasted Sweet Potato Bowls, 33

Sweet potatoes
- Loaded Baked Sweet Potatoes, 37
- Roasted Sweet Potato Bowls, 33
- Sweet Potato Biscuits & Gravy, 145
- Sweet Potato Kale Salad, 113

Swiss cheese
- Tempeh & Cabbage Reuben, 93

T

Tahini
- Spicy Tahini Noodles, 81
- Sweet Potato Kale Salad, 113

Tempeh
- Loaded Fries with Peanut Sauce, 91
- Tempeh & Cabbage Reuben, 93

Tofu
- Crispy Baked Tacos, 45
- Green Curry Noodle Bowls, 77
- Lemon Pepper Tofu Bowls, 23
- Mac and Cheese with BBQ Tofu, 35
- Not-Chicken Miso Noodle Soup, 121
- Roasted Sweet Potato Bowls, 33
- Tofu Patty Melt, 103
- Tofu Steak Dinner, 57
- Tofu & Vegetable Stir-Fry, 131

Tomatoes
- Big Veggie & Lentil Lasagna, 85
- Cherry Tomato and Corn Galette, 65
- Chopped Pizza Salad, 109
- Chili Cornbread Skillet, 51
- Corn Fritters, 43

Grits, Greens, and Beans, 29
Grown-Up Walking Tacos, 19
Lemony Lentil Soup, 125
Mediterranean-Inspired One Pot Rice & Beans, 63
Pearl Couscous Bowls, 21
One Skillet Tomato Orzo, 71
Quinoa Chickpea Bowls, 17
Red Lentil Curry, 47
Spicy Tahini Noodles, 81
Year Round Pantry Tomato Soup, 117

Tortillas and tortilla chips
- BBQ Jackfruit Nachos, 41
- Buffalo Chickpea Wraps, 89
- Crispy Baked Tacos, 45
- Grown-Up Walking Tacos, 19
- Mushroom & Black Bean Burritos, 95
- White "Chicken" Chili, 119

V

Vinegars:

Apple cider
- BBQ Jackfruit Nachos, 41
- Chili Cornbread Skillet, 51
- Loaded Baked Sweet Potatoes, 37
- Mac and Cheese with BBQ Tofu, 35
- Roasted Sweet Potato Bowls, 33
- Warm Wild Rice Salad, 115

Balsamic
- Cherry Tomato and Corn Galette, 65
- Pan-Fried Polenta with Roasted Mushrooms & Asparagus, 25
- Pearl Couscous Bowls, 21

Red wine
- Chopped Pizza Salad, 109
- Mushroom & Potato Soup, 123
- Tempeh & Cabbage Reuben, 93

Rice
- Honey Garlic Noodles, 73
- Loaded Fries with Peanut Sauce, 91
- Miso Butter Bean Bowls, 27

Sherry
- Caramelized Mushroom & Shallot Pasta, 83

W

Wine
- Mushroom & Potato Soup, 123
- Upside Down Shepherd's Pie, 31

Y

Yellow squash
- Ricotta Gnocchi Primavera, 79
- Roasted Vegetable & Chickpea Wraps, 99

Yogurt
- Georgia Peach Pancakes, 133
- Grown-Up Walking Tacos, 19

Z

Zucchini
- Big Veggie & Lentil Lasagna, 85
- Crispy Baked Tacos, 45
- Ricotta Gnocchi Primavera, 79
- Roasted Vegetable & Chickpea Wraps, 99

Acknowledgments

I have so many people to thank for their help with this cookbook. First, the daily support of my partner Trevor, who himself doesn't love cooking (it reminds him too much of work as a biochemist), but fearlessly tries all (okay, most) of the food that I make and honestly provides feedback when after the first bite I ask: "So, what do you think?" Thanks for the reminder that sometimes it's okay to scrap plans to cook and go get dinner at Hi-Lo instead.

Thank you to Molly, who is not only my trusted friend and climbing partner but who is also the one who helped me figure out how to write instructions about making sandwiches (who knew it could be so hard?), who reviewed every single recipe multiple times, who managed all the recipe testers, and who bounced ideas back and forth with me. I seriously could not have written this cookbook without you.

To my mom, who always and forever answers my calls of distress when things don't work out, and who graciously says "I told you so" when they do, thank you for your critiques and opinions on recipes and otherwise, even if most of the time I didn't want to hear them.

Thanks to so many others, in no particular order: Lynn, to whom I am so thankful for sharing her knowledge and perspective of the world and for helping to eat more than half of my leftovers; Jennie, who has responded to every text and Neomessage that I've sent since 2003; Lauren, who has informed much of my personal taste since 7th grade chemistry class; and all of the (more than 30!) recipe testers who cooked my recipes in their free time and provided incredibly valuable feedback.

Of course, thanks also to you, for buying this cookbook and visiting my website! How grateful I am to be able to do what I love every day because you trust my recipes.

And I probably shouldn't acknowledge Mr. Wilson, who spent most of the time while I was recipe testing meowing at the back kitchen door asking to be taken on his daily walk. And Bustelo and Steve, my more well-behaved cats.

THANK you!
Cassidy
(+ Mr. Wilson)

Made in United States
Troutdale, OR
02/16/2024

17742632R00090